T0277896

# THE MAYA

# THE
# MAYA
## LOST CIVILIZATIONS

MEGAN E. O'NEIL

REAKTION BOOKS

*For my teacher, Michael D. Coe (1929–2019)*

Published by Reaktion Books Ltd
Unit 32, Waterside
44–48 Wharf Road
London N1 7UX, UK

www.reaktionbooks.co.uk

First published 2022
Copyright © Megan E. O'Neil 2022

Printed and bound in India by Replika Press Pvt. Ltd

A catalogue record for this book is available from the British Library

ISBN 978 1 78914 550 2

CONTENTS

# CHRONOLOGY

| | |
|---|---|
| *c.* 1000 BCE | Creation of monumental architecture at Ceibal (Peten, Guatemala) and Aguada Fénix (Tabasco, Mexico) |
| *c.* 900 BCE | Founding of the large ancient city of Kaminaljuyu (Guatemala City, Guatemala) |
| 400–200 BCE | Painting of inscription containing the word *ajaw* (lord) at San Bartolo (Peten, Guatemala) |
| 100 BCE–100 CE | Construction of Structure E-VII-sub at Uaxactun (Peten, Guatemala) |
| *c.* 100 CE | Creation of mural paintings relating to the Maize God in a small building at San Bartolo (Peten, Guatemala). Interment of Burial 85, a royal burial, at Tikal (Peten, Guatemala) |
| 2nd century CE | Fall of Maya cities including El Mirador (Peten, Guatemala) |
| 292 | Carving of Long Count date on Stela 29 at Tikal |

| | |
|---|---|
| 378 | Arrival of Sihyaj K'ahk', a military leader affiliated with Teotihuacan, at Tikal, and subsequent installation of Yax Nuun Ahiin to the Tikal throne |
| 426 | Arrival of ruler K'inich Yax K'uk' Mo' at Copan (Honduras) |
| 445 | Dedication of Tikal Stela 31 by ruler Sihyaj Chan K'awiil, which features both Maya and Teotihuacan ancestry |
| 5th–6th centuries | Kaanul dynasty centred at Dzibanche (Quintana Roo, Mexico) |
| 562 | Defeat of Tikal by Kaanul dynasty allied with Caracol (Belize) |
| early 7th century | Reconstitution of Kaanul dynasty at Calakmul (Campeche, Mexico) |
| 615 | Accession of K'inich Janaab Pakal at Palenque (Chiapas, Mexico) |
| 683 | Death of long-reigning ruler K'inich Janaab Pakal of Palenque |
| 695 | Defeat of Kaanul dynasty, centred at Calakmul, by Tikal. Death of long-reigning Copan ruler K'ahk' Uti' Witz' K'awiil |
| 709 | Accession to throne of Shield Jaguar III, Yaxchilan (Chiapas, Mexico) |

| | |
|---|---|
| 738 | Defeat of Waxaklajuun Ubaah K'awiil, ruler of Copan, by Quirigua, under ruler K'ahk' Tiliw Chan Yopaat |
| 742 | Death of Shield Jaguar III, long-reigning ruler of Yaxchilan |
| 791 | Dedication of Structure 1 murals by ruler Yajaw Chan Muwaan, at Bonampak (Chiapas, Mexico) |
| 808 | Capture of K'inich Yat Ahk II, ruler of Piedras Negras (Peten, Guatemala), by Yaxchilan warriors |
| 9th century | Collapse of many cities in the Southern Maya Lowlands |
| 907 | Recording of last Long Count date at Uxmal (Yucatan, Mexico) |
| 909 | Recording of last Long Count date in Southern Maya Lowlands, on Monument 101 from Tonina (Chiapas, Mexico) |
| c. 1100 | Decline of Chichen Itza and founding of Mayapan (Yucatan, Mexico) |
| 15th century | Establishment of Kaqchikel and K'iche' kingdoms' capitals at Iximche' (Chimaltenango, Guatemala) and Q'umarkaj (El Quiche, Guatemala) |

| 1517–18 | Expeditions to coast of Yucatan Peninsula by Francisco Hernández de Córdoba and Juan de Grijalva |
| 1519 | Arrival of Hernán Cortés in Yucatan Peninsula, before journeying to Tenochtitlan |
| 1521 | Fall of Tenochtitlan, capital of the Mexica (Aztec) Empire |
| 1524 | Fall of Iximche' and Q'umarkaj |
| 1534 | Founding of Bishopric of Santiago de Guatemala |
| 1542 | Founding of Mérida on top of Ti'ho (Yucatan, Mexico) |
| 1558–60 | Painting of the *Xiu Family Chronicle* by Gaspar Antonio Chi |
| 1562 | Burning of Maya effigies and books at Mani (Yucatan, Mexico) |
| 16th century | Transcription of the *Popol Vuh* (Council Book) in K'iche' Maya |
| 1697 | Fall of Tayasal (Peten, Guatemala), capital of the Itza Maya kingdom |
| 1701 | Copying by Francisco Ximénez of the earliest extant version of the *Popol Vuh* |

| | |
|---|---|
| late 18th century | Commissioning of expeditions to Maya sites by the Spanish Crown |
| 1821 | Independence from Spain |
| 1825 | Founding of the Mexican National Museum in the Royal and Pontifical University of Mexico, Mexico City |
| 1827 | Passing of law in Mexico prohibiting the export of antiquities |
| 1847–1901 | Caste Wars in Yucatan Peninsula |
| 1848 | First official expedition to Tikal |
| 1866 | Initial founding of Guatemala's first National Museum, Guatemala City |
| 1871 | Opening of Museo Yucateco in Mérida |
| 1891 | Organization of project to study Copan by Harvard Peabody Museum |
| 1893 | Exhibition of casts of ancient Maya buildings at World's Columbian Exposition, Chicago |
| 1897 | Passage of Mexico's Law on Archaeological Monuments |
| 1904–10 | Dredging of the Sacred Cenote at Chichen Itza (Yucatan, Mexico) |

| | |
|---|---|
| 1910–20 | Mexican Revolution |
| 1911 | First stratigraphic excavation of a Maya building, at Holmul (Peten, Guatemala) |
| 1939 | Founding of Mexico's National Institute of Anthropology and History |
| 1946 | Establishment of Guatemala's Institute of Anthropology and History. Revelation of Bonampak Structure 1 murals |
| 1952 | Opening of the tomb of K'inich Janaab Pakal, at Palenque. Publication of Yuri Knorozov's essay demonstrating that ancient Maya writing was phonetic. Founding of Honduran Institute of Anthropology and History |
| 1955 | Founding of Department of Archaeology in Belize (then British Honduras) |
| 1956–69 | Excavations at Tikal by the University of Pennsylvania Museum of Archaeology and Anthropology |
| 1960–96 | Guatemalan Civil War |
| 1960 | Publication of Tatiana Proskouriakoff's essay demonstrating that Maya inscriptions recorded history |
| 1968 | Founding of Corpus of Maya Hieroglyphic Inscriptions |

CHRONOLOGY

| 1970 | UNESCO Convention on the Means of Prohibiting and Preventing the Illicit Import, Export and Transport of Ownership of Cultural Property |
| 1979–85 | Tikal National Project |
| 1987 | Publication of David Stuart's essay regarding evidence for the decipherment of syllables using principles of substitution |

*13*

# NOTES ON SPELLING, PRONUNCIATION AND DATES

In general, place names used in this book are the standard ones found on maps published by national governments, but accents have been dropped for names derived from Mayan and other Indigenous languages. Following accepted conventions, the adjective 'Maya' is used, except for matters related to languages, when 'Mayan' is used, unless quoting from a source that uses another form. The use of an apostrophe after vowels and consonants in Mayan words indicates a glottal stop. In the transcriptions used, the letter 'x' is pronounced like 'sh' in the English language today; 'j' is pronounced like a hard 'h'; the 'c' generally is hard; and 'ua' is pronounced 'wa', as in the American pronunciation of the word 'jaguar'. Correlations of Maya dates with the Christian calendar use Simon Martin and Joel Skidmore's Modified GMT (Goodman–Martínez–Thompson) correlation constant of 584286 (GMT + 3) and are given in the Julian calendar.

# PREFACE: A LAYERED PAST

This book is part of Reaktion's Lost Civilizations series. The series name may evoke what many people think about the ancient Maya, but it is a misnomer, for the ancient Maya were never lost. They never vanished. They were never forgotten. Even so, details of ancient Maya life have been lost. Numerous people across the centuries, from sixteenth-century European invaders to nineteenth-century explorers and contemporary archaeologists, have probed Maya sites and speculated about their origins and creators. This book explores five centuries of the history of engagement with the ancient Maya civilization, from the writings of sixteenth-century Maya scribes and Spanish conquistadors to twenty-first-century archaeological reports, museum exhibitions and Hollywood films. Addressing scientific literature, visual arts, architecture, world's fairs, New Age religions, museum exhibitions and Indigenous activism, this book aims to examine how the ancient Maya – and their buildings, ideas, objects and identities – have been perceived, portrayed and used over time in the United States, Europe, Mexico and Central America.

Although some people may ask questions such as 'Where did the ancient Maya come from, and why did they disappear?', we know that Maya civilization was an autochthonous civilization in the Americas. Furthermore, we know that although the ancient Maya experienced several major collapses of large-scale political organization in antiquity, Maya people kept reorganizing and migrating, and never disappeared. Even after sites were abandoned, whether after the second-century CE Preclassic collapse, the ninth-century collapse in the Southern Lowlands or the sixteenth-century and later Spanish conquests of Maya kingdoms, Maya people persisted, moving into the future but also looking back to the past, visiting those abandoned sites, where they would perform rituals and leave offerings in them, and even show the places to newcomers.

One theme that arises repeatedly in the history of engagements with the ancient Maya is the speculation that the people who built Maya cities had migrated from other places, such as Greece, Egypt, the legendary lost island of Atlantis or outer space. In light of today's definitive proof that ancient Maya cities were built by Maya people and resulted from independent cultural development in the Americas, many of these far-fetched migration tales seem surprising. But we must remember that many such stories were created long ago, within limited worldviews and with inadequate evidence. Indeed, there was little to no archaeological work demonstrating the development of early civilizations in the Americas until the middle of the twentieth century, and the Maya inscriptions were not deciphered until about fifty years ago, leaving much open to speculation in earlier centuries. But at the same time, many such stories were formed within a mindset of wilful myopia and misinterpretation, blindness to contrary evidence, uncritical and selective approaches, and the creation and use of falsified evidence. Questions of race are also at play, as the speculations omit or suppress the involvement of Indigenous Americans in building sophisticated civilizations, divorcing contemporary Maya people from their ancestors' legacies and connecting other world populations to those legacies instead. Moreover, there are people who continue to subscribe to such theories, despite the preponderance of evidence that discredits them.

Another major theme is the rediscovery of a 'lost' civilization that collapsed or disappeared centuries ago and awaited discovery by valiant explorers. Indeed, there has been a persistent rhetoric of personal discovery surrounding the ancient Maya. It is true that many Maya ruins were abandoned and lost to all memory, covered in soil and vegetation and forgotten over the centuries. But other places remained sites of visitation by Maya people and were maintained within social memory. Furthermore, although Spanish conquistadors and friars tried to obliterate Maya writing and religion, Maya culture, religion and languages endured, and millions of Maya people continue to speak Mayan languages and practise rites similar to those of their ancestors.

When foreign explorers entered Maya regions in the centuries after Europeans arrived in the Americas, local people often knew of the ancient cities and even revealed their locations. They were collaborators in gaining and disseminating knowledge of those places, yet the rhetoric of exploration and discovery makes it seem that it is always the outsiders who 'discover' ruins and monuments when they assign a name or publicize a place. Although this book focuses on those outsider histories, it attempts to balance them with Indigenous histories, knowledge and agency. Indeed, this book explores myriad ways of engaging with the ancient Maya by diverse groups of people, including contemporary Maya people. An enduring heritage of languages, religion and other types of knowledge has been essential to modern reconstructions of ancient knowledge systems, including ancient Maya writing. Because of the integration of this wisdom with other forms of enquiry, such as archaeology and epigraphy (the deciphering of writing), we can now read the names of Maya ancestors and the histories of their actions as written in their own words.

In the lead-up to the year 2012, which coincided with the end and beginning of a major cycle of the Maya calendar, American popular culture was awash with curiosity about – or concerns over – the concept of a Maya-predicted apocalypse. Many people thought the Maya calendar was scheduled to end, but this was not true. The Maya calendar is infinitely more flexible and interesting, involving complex mathematics and enormous cycles of time that allowed the ancient Maya to record and celebrate historical events and contextualize them within cycles spanning millions of years. Rather than being distracted by sensationalized stories such as those relating to 2012, perhaps more people will realize that the ancient Maya are a significant world civilization deserving of attention and study, because of both their major accomplishments in the past and the millions of descendants of ancient Maya kings, queens, artists, labourers and farmers that continue to live and thrive not only in their ancestral homelands but in many countries of the world today.

# ONE

# ART AND ARCHITECTURE

The civilization called the 'ancient Maya' or 'Classic-period Maya' was composed of loosely affiliated political entities that occupied many sites throughout southern Mexico and Central America for centuries. This civilization was diverse and complex, covering a large geographical region and temporal expanse, with several periods of florescence. But their world was forever transformed by the arrival in the sixteenth century of Spanish invaders, at first on the shores of the Yucatan Peninsula, in present-day Mexico. The primary subject of this book begins at that moment, considering how people have looked back at the ancient Maya civilization and endeavoured to experience, understand, frame or appropriate the culture or its artistic and architectural wonders. To help the reader appreciate these attempts at understanding, the first two chapters provide a general introduction to the ancient Maya. Nonetheless, because of the quantity and diversity of ancient Maya sites and their lengthy occupations, during which art, architecture, history and politics varied significantly, it is impossible to address here every important archaeological site or artwork, or to cover all levels of Maya society or the environmental and social conditions that enabled the ancient Maya florescence. Instead, these introductory chapters paint with broad brushstrokes a picture of the overall regions and histories, and give more detailed insight into selected artworks, places and individuals.[1]

When Spaniards arrived in the region that is today called Mexico and Central America, in the early sixteenth century, there were thriving Maya communities and kingdoms in the Yucatan Peninsula, Chiapas, Belize and Guatemala. The people we call 'Maya' were not a unified group but considered themselves as distinct families, communities or political entities. In Yucatan, the bases of political organization were the *cah* (plural *cahob*), which was a community or geographical entity, and the *chibal* (plural *chibalob*), correlating with an extended family, patronymic group or lineage. Some *chibalob* in the Yucatan Peninsula were the Cocom in Sotuta, the Pech in Campeche and the Xiu in Mani.[2] Politically separate, they were variously in alliance or conflict. Distinct kingdoms, including the K'iche' and the Kaqchikel, held sway in highland Guatemala, engaging with and competing against one another both before and after the Spanish Invasion.

Indeed, the people today called 'Maya' did not perceive a shared ethnic identity in the sixteenth century or before European arrival. But the Spaniards categorized them, along with other Indigenous Americans, as a group, as *indios* (Indians). The term 'Maya' was used in colonial Mayan-language sources but concerned references to Mayan languages. The use of the cultural category 'Maya' has developed over time, beginning in the colonial period and continuing during the nineteenth-century Caste Wars and in the context of twentieth-century ethnopolitics. Academic and popular attention to the ancient Maya has also contributed to creating this cultural category, and the pan-Maya movement of the late twentieth and twenty-first centuries reified this broader categorization.[3] Even so, there is great diversity of language and culture of Maya people across Mexico and Central America, with more than 5 million people speaking about thirty Mayan languages.[4] These diverse people speak other languages too, and live in their ancestral homelands and in diaspora in other regions of Mexico, the United States, Canada, Europe and beyond.

The ancient Maya flourished in several regions in the lowlands and highlands of southern Mexico and Central America. The Southern Maya Lowlands are in the Mexican states of Chiapas, Tabasco and southern Campeche; Guatemala's Department of Peten; Belize; and western Honduras. The Mexican states of Yucatan, Campeche and Quintana Roo, in the Yucatan Peninsula,

Maya region and select sites.

comprise the Northern Maya Lowlands. The ancient Maya flourished in the Southern Lowlands during periods called the Middle Preclassic (1000–350 BCE), Late Preclassic (350 BCE–150 CE), Protoclassic or Terminal Preclassic (150–250 CE), Early Classic (250–550 CE), Late Classic (550–850 CE) and Terminal Classic (850–1000 CE).[5] The Northern Maya Lowlands were occupied during the Preclassic and Classic periods, but following the ninth-century collapse in the Southern Lowlands, civilization especially prospered in the north in the Terminal Classic and Postclassic (1000–1521 CE) periods. There was also cultural florescence in the highlands and on the Pacific Coast of southern Guatemala and Chiapas from the Preclassic to Postclassic. Important Classic-period highland sites in Chiapas are Chinkultic and Chiapa de Corzo. In the Guatemalan highlands, the large ancient city of Kaminaljuyu was founded circa 900 BCE and grew to vast proportions; that massive city was occupied into the Postclassic and is now covered by present-day Guatemala City. Other significant sites, such as Takalik Abaj, Izapa, Ujuxte, La Blanca and La Perseverancia, thrived along the Pacific coast. In the Postclassic, the Kaqchikel and K'iche' kingdoms prospered in Guatemala's highlands, with their capitals at Iximche' and Q'umarkaj, respectively.

Scholars divide ancient Maya chronology into periods whose names – Preclassic, Classic and Postclassic – are taken from studies of European antiquity. But defining one period as 'Classic', those before it as Preclassic or Formative and those after as Postclassic implies formation before a more advanced era or decline afterwards. For the ancient Maya, those earlier and later periods were characterized by political complexity and significant cultural and artistic production, rendering those labels insufficient, and new research continues to challenge the connotations they carry. Indeed, it is abundantly clear that the Preclassic was a period of momentous cultural development and artistic innovation, with some of the largest structures ever built and some of the finest jadeite carving ever undertaken. Some scholars thus prefer to refer to centuries as opposed to relying on the broader terms for the periods. Nonetheless, the terms remain in use, especially to refer to larger expanses of time, and are used in this book.

## Ancient Maya rulership

During the Classic period in the Maya Lowlands, political entities comparable to kingdoms or city-states elsewhere in the world
shared characteristics of art, writing, religion and other aspects
of culture. But there was diversity owing to chronological and
regional variation and political distinction. These polities frequently competed against one another, and the epigraphic record
reveals numerous examples of alliances, wars and other power
dynamics. Some were able to gain control of other sites and maintain them as subsidiary allies; the subsidiary polity's ruler acceded
*u kabjiiy* (under the authority of) the more powerful entity. In
the ancient inscriptions, toponyms identify places; for example,
Lakamha' (Big Water) is the place name for the archaeological site
of Palenque, in Chiapas. But the political entity ruling that locale
was identified separately with an Emblem Glyph; for Palenque,
this was *Baak* (Bone), and Palenque's eighth-century ruler carried
the title *k'uhul baak ajaw* (sacred lord of Bone [kingdom]). It is
now known that Emblem Glyphs could be transferred to another
locale when a polity took up residence at another site; thus the
same Emblem Glyph was at times used at more than one location.[6]

Epigraphic and artistic records indicate that Maya rulers were
considered divine or semi-divine and could assume aspects of
supernatural entities such as the sun, moon and Maize God. The
*k'uhul ajaw* (sacred lord) title used for rulers derives from *k'uh*, the
word for god or deity, implying that those with this title are godlike
or filled with *k'uh* energy. The word *ajaw*, the last day name of the
ritual calendar, derives from the verb 'to shout', referring to the
importance of a leader as orator or speaker, not unlike the Mexica
*tlatoani* (speaker) title. Rulers' names and titles also included those
of deities, such as *k'inich* (radiant), an honorific of the solar deity;
K'awiil, a deity or manifestation of lightning and rulership; and
Chahk, rain and water deity. These were generally modified to refer
to aspects of those deities, such as Sihyaj Chan K'awiil (Sky-born
K'awiil) and Bajlaj Chan K'awiil (Sky-hammering K'awiil), evoking the source and effects of lightning. Such naming suggests that
rulers carried attributes of supernaturals that were forces of nature,

such as the rain, wind and sun, and could tap into those powerful aspects of the natural world.[7] Ancient depictions of rulers also suggest they were perceived to occupy the centre of the universe, at the place of the 'World Tree', signifying their supreme significance in the supernatural realm. Rulers and other elite individuals at times dressed as K'awiil, Chahk or the Maize God, and accompanying some images is the phrase *u-baah-il a'n* (it is the image in impersonation of), which is followed by the supernatural's name, intimating that the individual has become a manifestation of that deity. Music and dance appear to have allowed individuals to tap into the power of those supernatural entities. Rulers and other elite individuals also performed ceremonies of conjuring deities and ancestors, in which offerings of blood or fire helped to summon the supernatural entity.

Depictions of significant ancestors portray them with deity attributes related to cycles of rebirth. Male and female ancestors may bear solar or lunar deity attributes, respectively, anchoring them to the daily cycles of the sun and moon. Ancestors may also bear Maize God attributes that liken them to maize, which is reborn annually. Some individuals may carry attributes of several forces of nature. The Palenque ruler K'inich Janaab Pakal – today called Pakal for short – was interred in a magnificent carved limestone sarcophagus whose lid portrays his resurrection. In that image, Pakal is depicted with characteristics of K'awiil, the Maize God and the Sun God as he rises through the solar portal from the Underworld, akin to the sun at dawn, along the axis of the World Tree.[8] On the sides of the monument, his ancestors appear as fruit trees growing from the earth. Descendants publicly portrayed their links to revered ancestors through narrative texts, which connected generations by emphasizing repeated actions, or through images portraying ancestors and descendants together, either while alive or after their deaths, either symbolically present or ceremonially conjured. On both Early and Late Classic monuments, ancestors appear as supernatural entities overlooking their descendants. They also were named in textual dynastic lists, whether painted on ceramics, as on seventh-century cylinder vessels of the Kaanul (Snake) dynasty,[9] or in stone, as on the Copan Hieroglyphic Stairway.

The epigraphic record reveals many titles and hierarchies of leadership and nobility throughout the Classic period. In the Late Classic period, there was increasing growth of elite classes and ranks, particularly of rulers, subordinate governors and other roles across the Southern Lowlands, but there was a precedent for this diversification of rank in the Early Classic, too. In many polities, the principal ruler was the *k'uhul ajaw*, but beneath this office could be subordinate individuals with titles indicating their place in the hierarchy, either within the same site or affiliated polities. Several people within a site could carry the *ajaw* title, and some titles built on that word, such as *yajaw k'ahk'* (fire lord) and *yajaw te'* (tree lord). *Ajaw* could be modified to express subordination; for example, someone could be a *yajaw* (lord) of another person. A *sajal* was a provincial governor who was subject to the leader of the same polity or a larger one, one example being the leader of La Mar, a *sajal* who was subordinate to the Piedras Negras *k'uhul ajaw*.[10] Women's names and titles were generally accompanied by *ixik* (lady). There were also titles for elite youths, including *ch'ok ajaw* (sprout lord or young lord) and *chak ch'ok keleem* (great youth, strong youth), probably referring to the physical power of the young male. On the other hand, the *kaloomte'* title was superior to that of *k'uhul ajaw*. *Kaloomte'* was at times qualified by a directional phrase, as with *och k'in kaloomte'*, the west *kaloomte'*, which referred to a powerful individual from Teotihuacan, the Central Mexican metropolis to the west of the Maya region.[11] These many titles, which conveyed references to political power and interpersonal relationships, give insight into the political complexity of the ancient Maya world.

## Writing and calendars

Across diverse periods and regions, writing was essential for communication and comprised a critical art form rendered at monumental and miniature scales. The Maya writing system is a phonetic logo-syllabic system composed of signs that stand for words or syllables in a language known today as Common Mayan, an ancestral language related to Ch'orti' and Ch'olti'.[12] Words were

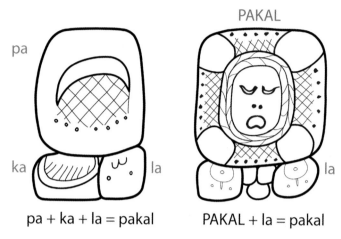

Pakal (shield), inscribed in Maya writing in two ways for the name of the Palenque ruler K'inich Janaab Pakal (Radiant Flower Shield).

written in various ways, using a principle of substitution, in which a word could be spelled with a logogram, syllables or both.[13] For example, the word *pakal* (shield) was written with three syllables, *pa + ka + la*, with the last vowel dropped, or with one sign, the logograph for shield, which could bear optional phonetic complements at the beginning or end to indicate the word's initial or final consonant. Scribes organized texts into columns and rows that are generally read from top to bottom and left to right in paired columns, but artists varied this pattern based on the available space, or for creative purposes.

Striving for creativity, scribes varied the signs used to write words and experimented with calligraphic styles. Calligraphic styles were particularized according to the tastes of individual artists, polities or regions; because of the limitations of the material or medium (for example, carved in stone or painted with a brush); or owing to a combination of these. Artists also transferred traits resulting from the intrinsic aspects of one medium to another. For example, 'whiplash calligraphy', derived from painting with a paintbrush, created undulating forms pulsing with energy, but artists also carved stone with this calligraphic style, translating features that resulted from the paintbrush into stone.[14] Moreover, scribes were honoured for their complex craft, and artists and

|   | A | B |
|---|---|---|
| 1 | Introductory Glyph (patron deity of month Yaxk'in) | 9 bak'tun (9 x 144,000 days) |
| 2 | 12 k'atun (12 x 7,200 days) | 2 tun (2 x 360 days) |
| 3 | 0 winal (0 x 20 days) | 16 k'in (16 days) |
| 4 | 5 Kib (position in 260-day tzolk'in cycle) | (Glyph G: 7th 'Lord of the Night,' in cycle of 9) |
| 5 | (Glyph F, which modifies Glyph G) | 27 huliiy (27 days since arrival of New Moon) |
| 6 | (Glyph C: 2 lunations completed in 177-day cycle of 6 lunations) | (Glyph X, which modifies Glyph C regarding lunation) |
| 7 | 29 (days in current lunation) | 14 Yaxk'in (day and month in 365-day haab cycle) |
| 8 | sihyaj (she was born) | |
| 9 | Ixik K'atun Ajaw (Lady K'atun Lord) | |
| 10 | Ixik Namaan Ajaw (Lady Lord of Namaan) | |

An Initial Series date with explanation of the Long Count components, in addition to other calendar cycles and lunar information. This text records the date 9.12.2.0.16 5 Kib 14 Yaxk'in. It correlates with 5 July 674 CE (GMT + 3 correlation and Julian calendar). It is the birth date of Ixik K'atun Ajaw. Piedras Negras, Stela 3, detail, drawing by David Stuart.

other elite personages were called *'itz'aat* (wise person). Artists were also named by their practice; for example, *aj tz'ihb (writer/ painter)* referred to those who painted with a brush or quill.[15]

The Maya developed a complex calendar system to record historical events and correlate them with solar, lunar and other celestial cycles. The Calendar Round tracked time by combining two calendar systems. The *tzolk'in* is the 260-day calendar that is composed of thirteen numbers and twenty day names. The *haab*, the 365-day solar calendar, divides into eighteen months of twenty days each plus five *wayeb* or unnamed days. These calendars move independently of each other but, when combined for a Calendar Round, come together every 52 *haab* years, when the original date repeats again. Both the *tzolk'in* and the *haab* are still used today, either alone or more rarely together, in the highlands of Chiapas and Guatemala.[16] The ancient Maya used the repetition of dates in this cycle to emphasize connections among ancestors and descendants, for example by performing a rite on the same Calendar Round date as an ancestor's action. The Long Count calendar tracked time from a zero date in 3114 BCE, a date in deep time. It counted the number of days (*k'in*) elapsed from that primordial date, but was organized into larger quantities, including the *winal* (twenty-day month), *tun* (360-day year), *k'atun* (twenty-year period) and *bak'tun* (four-hundred-year period). The Long Count allowed them to track time over longer periods, whether over the course of several generations of historical dynasts, or across millions of years, the latter used for invoking the biographies of gods in the past and future.

Many Classic-period Maya inscriptions begin with a calendrical date that may record a historic event or the day the work was dedicated, the latter as part of a dedication text. Appearing on ceramic vessels, stone monuments and buildings, among other media, dedication texts name the object, its owner and, at times, the artist.[17] For example, texts name items such as *y-uk'ib* (his/ her drinking vessel) and *u-tup* (his/her ear ornament), and are followed by the owner's name. Such texts can be short, as on many ceramic vessels, or long, as on stone monuments, where dates are correlated with several calendrical and celestial cycles. Texts may also include information about not only the person dedicating the thing, but his or her ancestors and the polity. Indeed, Maya inscriptions reveal a great deal about ancient individuals' biographies, interpersonal relations, religious practices and polity histories, as well as about the actions of deities.

## Ancient Maya architecture

Maya architects built diverse architectural forms comprising dynamic built environments that responded to natural features of their surroundings. Buildings and sites are frequently orientated to cardinal directions, acknowledging and participating in the sun's daily east–west path and other annual solar movements and presence, such as the sun's locations on the horizon during solstices and equinoxes. Builders also took advantage of or modified natural landscapes, for instance building on natural hills to create taller buildings or frame movement or vistas across the landscape. They created both volumetric structures and defined open spaces – including plazas and courtyards – that were critical places for gatherings as diverse as family congregations, diplomatic meetings and public royal performances. Clusters of buildings within a Maya city could be connected by elevated causeways, and sites could be linked by long elevated roads called *sacbe* (white road). The longest *sacbe* recorded is the 100-kilometre (62 mi.) road connecting Coba and Yaxuna in the Yucatan Peninsula.

One of the basic forms of Maya architecture comes from the common one-room Maya house, built with a perimeter wall of smoothed wattle and daub capped with an overhanging thatched roof. The smooth lower sections of many ancient stone buildings recall the common houses' bases, and the overhanging, flaring cornices recall the edge of the thatched roof. Indeed the fact that masons carved the cornices of Palenque House E, which held K'inich Janaab Pakal's throne, to make it look like thatch drives home the connection between the common and royal house.[18] 'Range structures' are one-storey buildings that often have one or more doorways leading to several rooms. Walls and pillars support the corbel vault, which is created by stacking stones closer and closer together above the cornice until the stones nearly meet, at which point a capstone closes the gap. Corbel vaults, used to construct both interior spaces and arches as city portals, create a distinct profile that modern architects later copied to make reference to the ancient Maya. Ancient Maya architects constructed buildings with corbel vaults running parallel to each other in order to create several interior rooms. Range structures may hold permanent furniture, such as benches that function as sleeping surfaces, seats and thrones. At times these buildings were placed around quadrangles to create enclosed courtyards, in some cases for royal palaces.

Another building type is the large terraced pyramid with a flattened top on which a smaller building, a superstructure, was constructed. When named in inscriptions, the pyramids were frequently identified as *witz* (mountain). Many pyramids, such as the Temple of the Inscriptions at Palenque, are funerary structures, with a ruler buried inside, at or beneath ground level, as if a planted seed, prepared for rebirth. The ancient Maya often built

Arch, Labna, Yucatan, Mexico, 600–900 CE, limestone.

Aerial view of the palace and Temple of the Inscriptions, Palenque, Chiapas, Mexico, built in 6th–8th centuries CE, limestone.

structures one on top of another over time, burying earlier structures to augment the buildings' or platforms' size and potency. The superstructure, accessed via a central stairway, functioned as a sanctuary or shrine to honour the deceased ruler or other individual. Some shrines were named *chan ch'een* (sky cave) and perceived as places where deities and ancestors dwelled.[19] The superstructure's form was often similar to that of the range structure, with one or more doorways leading to interior rooms. Stairways on pyramids and other buildings not only performed a function, but carried symbolic meaning, serving as prominent places for public performances such as processions, dances, and the humiliation and sacrifice of captives.[20]

The ancient Maya in several regions and periods, from the Preclassic to the Postclassic, also constructed ballcourts in their cities, as did many other peoples in Mesoamerica. Ballcourts are generally composed of two parallel structures with slanting benches defining a central alley for playing the ballgame, played by teams using a rubber ball. That central alley was also a symbolic locus, an opening to the underworld and a locale for the death and resurrection of deities such as the Maize God, and humans.[21] The ballgame was significant in Maya politics, and contests may have been carried out as competitions, in which losers – perhaps captives from warfare – were sacrificed after the game, their deaths symbolically feeding the earth and generating vegetation, as depicted on the Great Ballcourt bench friezes at Chichen Itza, Yucatan.

Sculptures made of modelled plaster or carved stone adorned many buildings. On Late Preclassic and Early Classic pyramid facades, artists modelled plaster into monumental faces of solar and other deities, as on Copan's Yehnal Structure and the El Zotz Temple of the Night Sun. Late Classic sculptors created dramatic facades by cutting stone into individualized pieces and arranging them in mosaics, transforming buildings into supernatural mountains or other sacred locales. In other cases, the facades were adorned with inscriptions. Many buildings were topped with a roofcomb, constructed on the building's summit, parallel to its long axis, creating a taller structure. Sculptors frequently added geometric or figural ornament or inscriptions to the roofcomb.

In the Northern Lowlands, at sites such as Uxmal and Chichen Itza, stone mosaics on buildings were at times comparable to those of southern sites or innovative in their use of stone sculpture to adorn and activate buildings. Those mosaics may comprise large zoomorphic maws around doorways, textile-like designs above cornices, or faces of animate, supernatural mountains stacked on building corners whose projecting forms interact with the sun to create dramatic effects of light and shadow. In the Early Postclassic at Chichen Itza, sculptors adorned temples with large serpents, whose bodies snake down building balustrades or whose tails hold up door lintels, activating the building with their imagined writhing forms.

Ballcourt, Copan, Honduras, *c.* 738 CE, volcanic tuff.

## Diverse artistic media

Ancient Maya artists worked in a variety of media, including enduring stone – to make small- and large-scale sculptures – as well as more perishable materials such as paper and wood. For stone-carving, sculptors used local stones – primarily limestone, sandstone and volcanic tuff, depending on the region – to create monumental sculptures such as stelae, altars and lintels. These carved images, which were often painted, portrayed rulers, their family and members of the court performing ceremonies, frequently for calendar celebrations and accession rites, or celebrating victory in warfare. Although much of their polychrome colouring has disappeared, the remains of pigments including red, green, blue and black survive on many monuments. Altars are low monuments shaped into circles, squares, rectangles or zoomorphic forms and installed in front of stelae or buildings; they may have been used as surfaces for offerings.

Serpent column at the entrance of the Temple of the Warriors, originally one of a pair supporting a lintel, Chichen Itza, Yucatan, Mexico, 800–1000 CE, limestone.

Temple I, Tikal, Peten, Guatemala, *c.* 734 CE, limestone and other materials.

Stelae are freestanding vertical monuments, taller than they are wide. They may portray a single person or several individuals in a scene, or they may have distinct individuals on all sides of the stone block, forming a pictorial narrative in three-dimensional space. Or they may be plain, with no evidence of carving or painting, suggesting that the medium of the stone stela was as important as – if not more so than – the information carved on their surfaces.[22] Stela 14 from Piedras Negras, Peten, Guatemala, portrays the ruler Yo'nal Ahk II on the first calendar ending since his accession to rulership, performing a world-renewal rite. Surrounding imagery situates him at the centre of the cosmos, and his mother stands beneath him, looking up at her son. The monument emulates his predecessors' stelae depicting the same type of scene, and his mother's prominence was part of a contemporaneous pattern of emphasizing maternal lines and marital alliances within and across Maya kingdoms.

Lintels were installed above doorways and may be carved on the front edge, visible in front of the building, or on the bottom, visible inside the doorway. On the bottom of Lintel 24 from Yaxchilan, Chiapas, Mexico, the queen Ixik K'abal Xook lets blood through her tongue, an offering to mark her husband's accession to the throne. She kneels at the feet of her husband, the powerful, long-lived ruler Itzamnaaj Bahlam III, who holds a torch. The inscriptions frame the couple as if they are in a doorway or inside a building, probably referring to the darkened interior of Structure 23, where the lintel was installed. Most existing carved lintels are in stone, but the ancient Maya carved wooden lintels, too; at Tikal, in Peten, lintels carved from sapodilla wood bear intricate carvings of rulers performing rituals on significant calendrical dates. Having survived because that hardwood resists insect damage and decay, they are among the small number of extant wooden artefacts from the Southern Lowlands.

In addition to producing relief carvings, sculptors in some regions and periods worked stone in the round. Copan sculptors carved stelae out of local volcanic tuff, which allowed them to carve three-dimensional depictions of rulers with intricate details in deep relief. The sculptors of Chichen Itza fashioned both relief

Stela 14, Piedras Negras, Peten, Guatemala, *c.* 761 CE, limestone.

carvings and volumetric sculptural forms. Some, such as the serpent columns, were integral to architecture, but others were freestanding. The chacmool sculptural type, which portrays a recumbent warrior holding a bowl, was carved with attention to the larger volumetric form and the details of the figures' regalia. Chacmools were generally placed near ruler thrones and the entrances of buildings, and thus had integral relationships with architecture, too.

Sculptors also carved and polished precious greenstones, such as jadeite and serpentine, and shells from rivers and oceans, to create earspools, necklaces, pendants, headdress elements and funerary masks. The Maya prized carved jadeite and other greenstones not only for the images and texts they presented but for the stones' rarity, preciousness, and green and blue-green colours,

Chacmool excavated by Augustus Le Plongeon, Chichen Itza, Yucatan, Mexico, 800–1000 CE, limestone.

Lintel 24, Yaxchilan, Chiapas, Mexico, *c.* 725 CE, limestone.

which evoked maize plants, water and vitality.[23] The funerary mask of the Palenque ruler K'inich Janaab Pakal, made of jadeite, shell and obsidian, created an eternally vibrant visage that transformed him into a youthful maize deity. He also wore jadeite earspools, a necklace and bracelets, and held a jadeite sphere and cube. His earspools, in the form of flowers with long pistils, evoked fragrant aromas and most likely the floral paradise of Maya ancestors.[24]

Ceramic artists created vessels for mundane and ceremonial purposes that were used in life and buried with the deceased. Ceremonial or funerary forms include vessels for holding food offerings or burning incense, rubber or other substances for deities and ancestors. Early Classic ceramic artists sculpted and painted lidded vessels into the forms of animals and deities, and made censers with the faces of solar deities. Using reed pens and brushes made of animal hair and plant fibres, artists decorated clay with slip paints coloured with mineral pigments; they then burnished them, which compacted the surface and at times produced a highly polished finish, and fired them at relatively low

Funerary mask and earflares: Máscara de Pakal (Mask of Pakal), from K'inich Janaab Pakal's tomb, Palenque, Chiapas, Mexico, c. 683 CE, jadeite, shell and obsidian.

Lidded bowl with cormorant on top of water and a turtle, from Tomb 1, Structure 5D-88 of the Lost World Group, Tikal, Peten, Guatemala, 3rd–4th century CE, ceramic.

temperatures (below 900–950°C/1,650–1,740°F).[25] Some artists painted on stucco after firing, at times using the distinctive Maya Blue, an organic-inorganic colourant invented by the Maya and made with indigo and special clays.[26]

Late Classic ceramic artists crafted cylindrical vessels whose exteriors functioned as canvases for continuous scenes of humans and supernaturals in diverse activities. Scholars have discerned several artistic styles associated with particular regions, kingdoms and artists in the Late Classic corpus. These include 'codex-style' vessels from the northern Peten and southern Campeche (in the regions of Nakbe, in Peten, and Calakmul, in Campeche),

Cylinder vessel with palace scene, likely from Peten, Guatemala, 740–800 CE, slip-painted ceramic with post-fire pigment.

whose palette of black-brown lines on a cream base slip probably emulated contemporaneous books; orange-on-cream Maize God Dancer vessels from Holmul and Naranjo, Peten; and the 'Pink Glyphs' style from Motul de San José, Peten.[27] Artists deftly rendered complex narrative scenes of humans and anthropomorphic deities. Many portray dynamic interactions of anthropomorphic and zoomorphic figures that are manifestations of forces of nature who communicate with or battle one another in supernatural narratives that correlate with terrestrial and celestial phenomena.[28] Others portray palaces with rulers, courtiers and visitors amid food and drink, providing insight into courtly behaviour. These also give insight into a lost world of Maya textiles, portraying men and women wearing garments made of woven cotton, paper, feathers and other perishable materials. When present, dedication texts may name the vessel as a *yuk'ib* (drinking vessel) for beverages including the staple food *ixim* (corn), the luxury food *kakaw* (chocolate) or the two mixed together. Painted plates were called *lak* (simply 'plate'); when depicted, plates hold corn tamales covered with sauce, perhaps containing chocolate and *chile* (chilli). Their dedication statements are revelatory regarding the societal positions of young elite men and women.[29]

In many places and periods, artists used moulds or hand-modelling to shape clay into figurines portraying animals, deities and humans dressed as warriors or performing tasks such as childcare or weaving. Hundreds of figurines, generally decorated with post-fire paint including iron-based reds and yellows and Maya Blue, were excavated from Late Classic graves on Jaina Island, but many more were looted from that island and elsewhere. Archaeologists have also excavated figurines at many other sites across the Maya world. The ceramic figurines found in a royal tomb at El Perú-Waka', in Peten, form a narrative scene related to a king's funeral and ritual resurrection, surrounded by members of the royal court.[30]

From the Preclassic to the Postclassic and beyond, the ancient Maya also practised an exquisite art of mural painting with mineral and organic pigments on interior and exterior walls of lime plaster. The Preclassic mural paintings from San Bartolo, Peten,

Jaina-style figurine of a woman weaving with a backstrap loom, Campeche, Mexico, 600–900 CE, ceramic.

painted in about 100 CE in a small building constructed behind a tall pyramid, feature mythological narratives that are painted with developed techniques and styles, indicating that they were part of a longer tradition. Furthermore, archaeologists found an earlier mural with an inscription dated 400–200 BCE that contains the word *ajaw* (lord).[31] Early Classic murals have been found in building interiors, as in Structure B-XIII at Uaxactun, Peten, which features scenes of the daily life of men and women in houses, and

Mural in Room 1, Bonampak, Chiapas, Mexico, 791 CE, plaster and pigments on wall.

an encounter of Maya and Teotihuacan warriors or diplomats. At Holmul, the La Sufricaya murals depict warriors in Teotihuacan regalia. Early Classic artists also painted the walls of royal tombs, as in the fifth-century Río Azul Tomb 12, where inscriptions identify the cardinal directions, situating the deceased at the cosmic centre.

Late Classic and Postclassic murals are diverse. Murals inside the Los Sabios structure at Xultun, Peten, depict seated men who are named as *taaj*, a type of ritual and artistic specialist, in a building where they worked and painted.[32] On the exterior of a small terraced temple at Calakmul are painted images of men and women exchanging vessels, food and other items, in what appears to be a market setting.[33] The murals in the three interior rooms of Structure 1 at Bonampak, in Chiapas, feature complex scenes related to an heir presentation, battle and victory celebration. Painters in the Northern Lowlands also adorned the interiors of buildings with images of humans and deities. Artists at Ek' Balam, in Yucatan, painted vault capstones with images of deities, and in some buildings at Chichen Itza complex narrative murals portray apparently historical and mythological figures acting within landscapes. Notably, some Postclassic Northern Lowland murals, particularly from Santa Rita Corozal, Belize, and Tulum, Quintana Roo, are painted in the so-called International Style, which was used in murals and books in the Northern Lowlands, Central Mexico and Oaxaca in the Postclassic period, indicating broader communication and artistic networks.

The Maya created books with fig-bark paper, called *huun* in Maya, made from the inner bark of several species of wild fig tree, which they covered with stucco or gesso and painted with organic and inorganic colourants. A typical form was the screenfold book, made from a long piece of paper folded accordion-style. Only four Maya books survive, the earliest being the *Maya Codex of Mexico* (formerly the *Grolier Codex*), dated to the eleventh century, and the others from the fourteenth and fifteenth centuries.[34] The contents of Postclassic books are primarily religious and astronomical. With almanacs for tracking eclipses and celestial bodies such as Venus and offering guidance for ritual practice, they would have

*Dresden Codex* 25, Yucatan, Mexico, 14th–15th century, bark paper, lime plaster and pigments.

been used for divination and ritual performance. No Classic-period Maya books survive, but we know they existed, for artists depicted books in narrative scenes on ceramic vessels, and traces of books survive in Early and Late Classic tombs.[35]

This overview of ancient Maya art and architecture – primarily from royal and other elite contexts – only begins to shed light on ancient Maya artistic production across regions and time periods. Artists, honoured members of ancient Maya society, created works that helped ancient individuals cultivate relationships with other people and with supernaturals. Furthermore, their works allow people today to appreciate the creativity and mastery of Maya artists and to catch fleeting glimpses into the lives of ancient Maya people.

# TWO
# PLACES, POLITICS AND HISTORY

Ethnohistoric, archaeological and epigraphic research reveals a rich record of ancient Maya history and politics at diverse sites across the Maya region. Studies of inscriptions, artistic and architectural styles and exchanged raw materials have reconstructed moments of interaction – whether trade, emulation, alliance or conflict – among Maya polities and other Mesoamerican civilizations. Investigations have also traced the rise, florescence and collapse of many sites and regions, as well as the recoveries, reconstitutions, migrations and other transformations after political dissolution. This chapter attempts to summarize the major periods of ancient Maya civilization, from the Preclassic to Postclassic periods, in the Southern and Northern Maya Lowlands. Because research has been extraordinarily robust, and because knowledge grows every day, this summary can function only as an incomplete sketch of ancient Maya geographical and temporal diversity and complexity, but hopefully it will provide the reader with enough information to understand basic trends, and will inspire curiosity in readers to learn more about the ancient Maya.

## The Preclassic period

Over the last half-century, knowledge about the Maya Preclassic period – which had been under-studied because its remains were often buried beneath subsequent occupation – has grown considerably. Increased knowledge has resulted from deeper excavations, improvements in techniques of excavating tunnels, and investigations in previously unexplored areas. In addition, surveys undertaken with airborne LIDAR (Light Detection and Ranging), a remote-sensing technique using lasers, have revealed new occupations from all periods. Indeed, it is now clear that thriving cities and numerous settlements were constructed during the Preclassic period in the lowlands of Mexico, Guatemala and Belize and the highlands of Guatemala and Mexico. Thrilling new discoveries are currently being made in Tabasco, Mexico, at Aguada Fénix, where people had begun to use ceramics by 1200 BCE, earlier than other Maya communities. Using airborne LIDAR survey and excavations, an international team led by Takeshi Inomata in 2019 revealed an enormous early Middle Preclassic (1000–800 BCE) artificial plateau made of clay and earth and measuring more than 1,400 m (4,600 ft) long, 399 m (1,310 ft) wide and 10–15 m (33–50 ft) high, with nine causeways radiating from the plateau to other complexes. Archaeologists identify it as the oldest and largest monumental construction in the Maya area. The site had been abandoned by 750 BCE, but people revisited it in later times.[1] Furthermore, deep excavations in the northern Peten at sites such as Nakbe and Cival, and in the Pasión region at Ceibal, have exposed Middle Preclassic architecture, art and monumental platforms from as early as 1000 BCE. Further north, excavations at Yaxuna have brought to light emergent complexity in the Middle Preclassic comparable to that in other regions.[2]

The Preclassic Maya of the lowlands interacted with and adopted features from earlier cultures and shared practices with contemporaneous groups across Mesoamerica. During this time, many Mesoamerican cultures built monumental architecture, created ceramics with figures or motifs of humans and supernaturals, or established written calendars and other record-keeping systems. These include the Olmec on the Gulf Coast (in the Mexican states of Veracruz and Tabasco) and the Pacific Coast (in Guerrero), people in Central Mexico (at sites such as Tlatilco and Las Bocas) and the Zapotecs in Oaxaca. The Olmec civilization thrived during the Early and Middle Preclassic. In the Middle Preclassic, there is evidence of active exchange between Maya sites and Olmec centres such as La Venta, Tabasco. Evidence appears both in the type of traded objects and in the manners in which they were deposited. For example, archaeologists at Ceibal found an Olmec-style jadeite head, and at both Ceibal and Cival excavations uncovered Olmec-style greenstone axes deposited in cruciform patterns as foundation offerings for plazas and buildings, similar to those at La Venta. These examples demonstrate active exchange with the Olmec civilization and a deeper chronology for the Lowland Maya.[3]

The Preclassic Lowland Maya also exchanged ideas and imagery with people of the Pacific Coast and highlands of Guatemala and Chiapas, as seen in imagery on carved stone monuments. For example, depictions of deities on stelae at Izapa, Chiapas, are comparable to Lowland Maya portrayals of deities.[4] On first-century CE stelae from Takalik Abaj (Retalhuleu Department, Guatemala), human figures face columns of text bearing Long Count dates while supernatural birds hover above. Alternatively, Kaminaljuyu Stela 11 portrays a standing human wearing a bird headdress and performing a fire ritual; that figure stands on a basal band in the form of a large zoomorphic maw, and above his head is a hovering bird. Similar templates are used later by Lowland Maya rulers performing calendrical rites and other ceremonies. These are only a few among many examples indicating that the Preclassic Lowland Maya shared ideas and forms with people across Mesoamerica.[5]

In the Late Preclassic, Lowland Maya masons constructed pyramids out of cut stone and rubble – some at an enormous scale – at sites such as El Mirador, El Tintal and Tikal in Guatemala, Calakmul in Mexico and Cerros in Belize, and there is evidence for major water-management efforts at these sites. El Mirador boasts the largest Maya pyramid ever built, La Danta.[6] Late Preclassic pyramids were adorned with monumental plaster sculptures of deities' faces or bodies. The prominence of monumental representations of deities differs from later emphases on humans portrayed in ritual paraphernalia and at the centre of the world. Nonetheless, these dramatic architectural facades appear to have been backdrops for performances of rulership. At Cerros, monumental stucco masks on Structure 5C–2nd may relate to the birth and performance of kingship.[7]

Stela 11,
Kaminaljuyu,
Guatemala,
Late Preclassic,
granite.

View of a mural of the Maize God receiving corn tamales and a flowering gourd, from a cave on on the north wall of Pinturas Sub-1, San Bartolo, Peten, Guatemala, c. 100 CE, plaster and pigments.

Mural painting at San Bartolo indicates that Maya rulers connected themselves and their rule to mythological narratives, such as that of the Maize God. On the north wall of the Las Pinturas building, the Maize God receives a bowl of corn tamales and a flowering gourd – food to support human life – from a cave entrance portrayed as a zoomorphic maw. On the west wall are other scenes from the Maize God's life cycle, including his death in water, his rebirth from a turtle shell and his crowning, which is linked to a human ruler's accession to rulership, thus situating the Preclassic ruler at the centre of the universe and showing connections with supernatural entities to validate his authority. Also painted on the west wall are four young lords letting blood from their phalli and making animal offerings in front of trees; another partially preserved scene depicts the Maize God and another tree. These depicted rituals establish the four world directions and centre; here, supernaturals perform them, but humans would have performed analogous rites, establishing ritual space by marking the cardinal directions and centre. Remarkably, the depictions of the Maya Maize God's profile face are similar to that of the Olmec rain and maize deity, suggesting the artists looked back to and adopted, yet transformed, Olmec forms and ideas.[8]

In Tikal's North Acropolis, deep excavations into layers of buildings from the Preclassic to the Late Classic revealed many tombs believed to hold the dynasty's early kings and other elite individuals. In Burial 85, from around 100 CE, were rich offerings including fine ceramics, a Spondylus (spiny oyster) shell pendant and a small greenstone maskette of a human face, with shell inlay for the eyes and teeth, that may have been attached to a mortuary bundle. Carved into its forehead is a headband with sprouting maize, the Maya royal diadem, suggesting that this is the face of a king and the tomb that of a Preclassic ruler, possibly Yax Ehb Xook. Later inscriptions identify Yax Ehb Xook as the dynastic founder who lived in the first century CE. He was not the city's first leader, since there was occupation from centuries before, but

Maskette from Burial 85, Tikal, Peten, Guatemala, c. 100 CE, greenstone and shell.

Structure E-VII-sub (northeast corner), Uaxactun, Peten, Guatemala, 100 BCE–100 CE, limestone and other materials.

some kind of shift in rulership happened during this period that was acknowledged centuries later.[9]

Notable architectural forms that developed during the Preclassic were the E-group assemblage and the terraced radial pyramid. The architectural format called the E-group assemblage, consisting of one round or square western mound in association with an elongated eastern platform, appears in Maya sites as early as the Middle Preclassic, including at Ceibal, Cival and Aguada Fénix.[10] The format is so called because it was first identified in the E Group at Uaxactun. Uaxactun Structure E-VII-sub (100 BCE–100 CE) is a radial four-sided pyramid with equal sides and stairways whose very form is a cosmogram orientated to the cardinal directions. On a platform to its east were three buildings whose placement corresponded to the position of the rising sun on the solstices and equinoxes, as seen from the E-VII-sub pyramid. The buildings thereby functioned as solar or chronographic markers.

Despite the Preclassic flourishing of art, architecture and civilization, some areas of the Maya world, including El Mirador and associated cities, collapsed in the second century CE, probably because of environmental degradation and conflict. Many sites were soon abandoned, and this collapse was as substantial as the ninth-century collapse in the Southern Lowlands. One theory proposes that the Kaanul dynasty was centred in the Preclassic period in the area of El Mirador and was dispersed after El Mirador's fall, but this is debated.[11] The period after this collapse is called the Protoclassic or Terminal Preclassic (150–250 CE), a phase primarily discerned in the ceramic record. During this period other more modest Preclassic sites such as Tikal, Uaxactun and Holmul experienced substantial growth.[12]

The beginning of the Early Classic period (250–550 CE) is marked by the first appearance of Long Count dates on stone monuments in the Southern Lowlands, specifically on Tikal Stela 29, on which a Long Count date accompanies an image of a single Maya ruler. This type of depiction appears to indicate a shift in practices related to religion and divine kingship, for there is a distinct focus on the singular ruler dressed in elaborate regalia and conducting rites such as conjuring deities through a double-headed serpent. Such images also appear on portable items such as the Leiden Plaque, made of jadeite, which probably once hung from a ruler's belt. Incised on one side is an inscription beginning with a Long Count from 320 CE, and on the other is a ruler standing on a captive and conjuring deities, wielding not only mundane but supernatural power.

In the third to sixth centuries builders in Maya cities of Peten also constructed massive architectural complexes for funerary purposes and as palaces. At Tikal, builders expanded on the North Acropolis and other areas of the city, such as the Lost World Group. In the North Acropolis, Early Classic masons constructed towering pyramids holding rulers' tombs, containing rich offerings of ceramics, stone tools and animal remains. These became places for commemoration of these personages and the dynasty.

The two inscribed sides of the Leiden Plaque, allegedly found on the Caribbean Coast of Guatemala but likely originating in Peten, 320 CE, jadeite.

Archaeologists have also found Early Classic tombs with abundant offerings at Río Azul, Holmul and El Zotz in Peten, at Altun Ha in northern Belize, and at Copan in western Honduras, among other locations.

The Late Preclassic practice of modelling and painting plaster into the form of monumental deity heads on building facades

Name of K'inich Yax K'uk' Mo' on architectural facade of the Margarita phase of Temple 10L-16, Copan, Honduras, 5th century, plaster and pigments.

continued in the Early Classic. On the exterior of the Temple of the Night Sun at El Zotz, which holds a royal tomb, archaeologists uncovered modelled polychrome stucco masks of solar deities.[13] The rendering of solar deities on a funerary structure most certainly makes reference to beliefs in male ancestors being transformed into solar deities. At Copan, deep excavations in the Acropolis revealed layers of buildings from the Early and Late Classic periods, including those inside Temple 10L–16, built over the tomb of the dynastic founder K'inich Yax K'uk' Mo', that were decorated with polychrome plaster adornment with references to the founder as a solar deity. The mid-fifth-century Yehnal phase features solar deity heads, the Margarita phase spells out the name of K'inich Yax K'uk' Mo' in an enormous glyph featuring intertwined birds, and the Rosalila structure's plaster decoration transforms the building into a supernatural mountain and makes reference to the ancestor as a supernatural solar and avian entity, all painted in brilliant polychrome.[14] Plaster adornment elsewhere uses other metaphors for the continuing vitality of ancestors. For example, a building dating from about 590 CE at Holmul bears astounding polychrome stucco decoration in which the ruler Tzahb Chan Yopaat Mahcha' is seated in the cleft of a supernatural mountain, a metaphor for rebirth.[15]

The archaeological record indicates that during the Early Classic period and even earlier, several Maya cities in Peten, Chiapas, Yucatan Peninsula, Belize and Honduras interacted with the great city of Teotihuacan in Central Mexico. Trade is evidenced in several media, including ceramics, lithics, architecture and murals. For example, Maya and Teotihuacan ceramics have been found in both regions; green obsidian from the Central Mexican Pachuca source has been found in Maya cities; and obsidian from the Chayal source in Guatemala appears at Teotihuacan. In addition, the distinctive *talud-tablero* architectural form – a type of architectural profile prominent at Teotihuacan – was used at Tikal, Copan, Dzibanche, Becan and Oxkintok, among other Maya sites, and artists painted Maya-style murals in several architectural complexes at Teotihuacan.[16] Moreover, epigraphic research reveals that there was a significant change in the Maya cities of Peten in the late fourth century with the arrival in 378 CE of Sihyaj K'ahk', apparently a military leader affiliated with Teotihuacan, whose presence is recorded in El Perú-Waka', Naachtun, Tikal and Uaxactun, among other sites. At Tikal, the arrival appears to have constituted a violent takeover, resulting in the death of the king and the installation of a new ruler, the usurper Yax Nuun Ahiin.[17]

Following were innovations in sculpture, ceramics and architecture emulating Teotihuacan sources that created hybrid works. These include the stucco-painted tripod cylinder vessels from Tikal Burials 10 and 48, and ones from Río Azul and Copan that take the shape of the tripod cylinder, characteristic of Teotihuacan, and are adorned with polychrome stucco with designs in both Teotihuacan and Maya styles.[18] Tikal Stela 31, dated 445 CE and created for the ruler Sihyaj Chan K'awiil, Yax Nuun Ahiin's son,

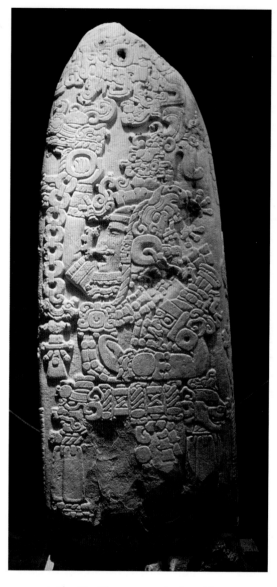

Stela 31 (front), Tikal,
Peten, Guatemala,
*c.* 445 CE, limestone.

recounts the Teotihuacan arrival and incorporates these events into a narrative of his ancestry, both Maya and Teotihuacan-affiliated. There also is substantial evidence for exchange with Teotihuacan at Kaminaljuyu and on the Pacific Coast in Guatemala, particularly in the Department of Escuintla, and in Chiapas, at Los Horcones, where artists created hybrid art and architectural forms.

Teotihuacan incursion into these regions most probably related to acquiring luxury resources such as feathers, shells and chocolate.[19]

Early Classic Copan art and architecture also feature extensive use of Teotihuacan imagery and styles. Inscriptions state that the ruler K'inich Yax K'uk' Mo' arrived at Copan in the early fifth century, and although images depict him dressed as a Teotihuacan warrior, he appears to have come from Peten.[20] Indeed, the connections with Teotihuacan ideology may have passed to Copan from Tikal or another site in Peten. His tomb, found in Temple 10L–16's Hunal phase, and another from the Margarita phase, possibly his wife's tomb, contained imported goods from Teotihuacan, Peten and Kaminaljuyu, and Teotihuacan-style objects made locally.[21] One extraordinary vessel from the Margarita tomb is a stucco-painted tripod cylinder vessel with images of an animate Teotihuacan-style building with bird wings and human hands;

Painted Cylinder Tripod vessel from Margarita tomb, Structure 16, Copan, Honduras, 5th century CE, ceramic, stucco and pigments.

a Teotihuacan-style goggled face fills the doorway. This may depict the burial structure of K'inich Yax K'uk' Mo', for the building phases portrayed the ancestor as a supernatural solar avian deity. The Teotihuacan legacy was long-lived in Maya cities, for at Copan, Tikal, Piedras Negras and other Maya sites, Late Classic rulers made retrospective references to Teotihuacan, connecting themselves to that once powerful city and to their ancestors who engaged with it.[22]

Another crucial Early Classic development is the growth of the Kaanul (Snake) dynasty, which was centred at Dzibanche, Quintana Roo, as early as the fifth century. *Talud-tablero* architecture and Teotihuacan-style stucco decoration appear at Dzibanche, particularly on the Cormorantes pyramid, a funerary structure.[23] In the early seventh century the Kaanul dynasty – or a splinter group of that dynasty – left Dzibanche and reconstituted at Calakmul, Campeche, where it grew into an especially powerful force.[24]

## Late Classic in the Southern Lowlands

In the Late Classic period (550–850 CE), many cities prospered across the Southern Maya Lowlands, and as new power dynamics emerged, these polities developed distinct styles of architecture, stone sculpture and other artistic media. In Chiapas were Palenque, on the edge of the Tabasco plain; Tonina, built where the lowlands give way to the highlands; and Yaxchilan, Piedras Negras and Bonampak, near the Usumacinta River or its tributaries. In Peten and southern Campeche, major cities included Tikal and Calakmul, significant rivals that entangled other polities in their long-term conflicts. In the southeast are Caracol, nestled in the Maya Mountains of southwestern Belize, and Copan and Quirigua, on the southeastern periphery of the Maya region near the Motagua Valley source of jadeite. Epigraphy and archaeology have together revealed abundant information about the complex histories and politics of these and other Southern Maya Lowland polities, which produced astonishing works of art and architecture.

The long-lived K'inich Janaab Pakal ruled Palenque for nearly seventy years, from 615 to 683, a time of great prosperity for the Baak kingdom. His throne, found in Palace House E, was ornamented with carved limestone and modelled plaster. The carved stone back, shaped as a pillow, depicts Pakal's mother handing him the headdress of rulership, acknowledging the prominence of the maternal line. After Pakal's death, House E was maintained as a memorial to him. Adjacent to the palace, builders constructed the Temple of the Inscriptions as his funerary pyramid, built partially on a natural hill. The sanctuary at the top of the pyramid contains large carved panels with inscriptions recounting events in the polity's history, including ritual activities that Pakal and his predecessors performed, emphasizing the importance of ritual practice and continuity across generations.

Pakal's lengthy reign left an indelible mark on the city, and his descendants repeatedly linked themselves to him. Indeed, finely carved panels from later generations show Pakal participating in rituals with his descendants, even decades after his death. His son K'inich Kan Bahlam also took advantage of the hilly topography to construct three pyramidal structures for the Cross Group. The inscriptions on carved panels set in the shrines of these three buildings call part of the shrine a *pib naah* (pit oven house), a name for a sweat bath, but they are symbolic ones, where the kingdom's patron deities were born.[25]

Palenque architects used the corbel vault common to Maya architecture, but they experimented in various ways to create larger and more open interior spaces. They constructed some corbel vaults parallel to each other, which allowed them to build taller interior spaces, and they constructed crossing vaults, building some vaults perpendicular to each other, resulting in wider and taller interior spaces at their intersection. Architects also rounded some of the vaults' upper profiles, which created more interior space and provided aesthetic variation. Painted plaster decoration in the palace and other buildings commemorated rites performed by rulers and court members.[26]

South of Palenque was Tonina, built on a steep hillside. The Acropolis buildings were constructed on terraces cut into

Sculpture of a captive, Tonina, Chiapas, Mexico, 600–800 CE, sandstone.

the hillside, commanding dramatic views and visible to those approaching from far away. Sculptors shaped the local sandstone into nearly three-dimensional human forms, whether for stelae depicting standing rulers with tall headdresses or ballcourt sculptures portraying kneeling captives with their hands tied behind their backs. One unusual Tonina monument from 711 CE depicts the Palenque ruler K'inich K'an Joy Chitam II – another son of Pakal – as a humiliated, bound captive seized by Tonina, certainly in revenge for Palenque's capture of Tonina Ruler 2. Although captives were often sacrificed in the captor's city, K'inich K'an Joy Chitam II appears to have been released, for the epigraphic record indicates that his kingship was later restored.[27] Tonina Monument 101 bears the last Long Count date on a Maya monument from the Southern Lowlands, dedicated in 909, after other cities stopped erecting monuments during the collapse of the region.[28]

Powerful kingdoms also flourished in the Late Classic in the Usumacinta River Valley, which forms the contemporary border between Chiapas and Peten. Especially prominent during the seventh and eighth centuries are images of powerful queens, wives and mothers, and inscriptions narrating marriage alliances that were crucial to inter-polity diplomacy. Also frequent are artworks relating to warfare and military alliances. At Yaxchilan, buildings were constructed on terraces moulded from the natural topography rising from the Usumacinta River, and adorned with plaster and cut-stone mosaic decoration. In many doorways are finely carved limestone lintels commemorating rites performed by the ruling class. Several lintels feature wives and mothers executing rites relating to the births of key individuals, or to rulers' accessions. In front of the buildings were carved stelae portraying rulers performing rituals such as scattering *pom* (copal) incense or dominating humiliated captives. But inscriptions also refer to difficulties in dynastic politics. Bird Jaguar IV, successor to the long-reigning Itzamnaaj Bahlam III, did not accede to power until ten years after his father's death, probably because there was a ruler in between, who was erased from publicly displayed history. Bird Jaguar IV's numerous monuments display his right to rule by portraying his father and mother in scenes that allegedly took place years before.

These retrospective monuments created a public history for his reign, apparently to smooth over ruptures and demonstrate his legitimacy to rule the kingdom.[29]

An allied site was Bonampak, which was built on a hillside in the Selva Lacandona near a tributary of the Usumacinta River. Bonampak's eighth-century ruler Yajaw Chan Muwaan, who acceded under the authority of Yaxchilan's Itzamnaaj Bahlam III, is renowned for artworks commissioned during his reign. His especially tall stelae highlight distinct but overlapping aspects of Maya kingship and politics. Stela 1 depicts the king standing above a supernatural mountain from which the Maize God emerges, equating the ruler and the Maize God, whereas Stela 2 depicts him with his mother and his wife, a Yaxchilan princess, emphasizing maternal lines and marriage alliances, and Stela 3 portrays him as a victorious warrior. The murals he commissioned in Structure 1 similarly address several aspects of religion and politics, depicting royal ceremonies, heir designation, battles and captive display, and victory celebration. But the displayed power was short-lived, for the polity collapsed soon thereafter.[30]

At Piedras Negras, about 40 km (25 mi.) from Yaxchilan, funerary pyramids and palace structures were built into the rolling topography on the Guatemala side of the Usumacinta River. Architects took advantage of that topography to create taller pyramids and the multi-level Late Classic palace, whose buildings were used for administration, sleeping, crafts and diplomatic visits. The predominant type of stone sculpture was the freestanding stela depicting the ruler performing a calendrical rite or outfitted for war. On stelae and panels, sculptors strove to release the portrayed bodies – or at least heads – from the stone to create more three-dimensional forms, a challenging endeavour given the characteristics of the local bedded limestone. Yaxchilan and Piedras Negras participated in periods of alternating alliance and conflict from the sixth to the ninth century, and increasing warfare between these two polities contributed to their downfall. The last record of such conflict was Yaxchilan's seizure of the Piedras Negras ruler K'inich Yat Ahk II in 808 CE; after this, the political structures at both cities fell apart, and the sites were largely abandoned.[31]

In Peten in the beginning of the Late Classic, Tikal continued to grow, but its fortunes soon changed because of threats by the Kaanul dynasty, centred at Dzibanche and later Calakmul. Tikal had expanded and prospered after the fourth-century takeover by Teotihuacan, and in the sixth century it allied with other sites, including Naranjo and Caracol. But Caracol later allied with the Kaanul dynasty and turned against Tikal and Naranjo. For instance, the Kaanul dynasty attacked Naranjo in 546, and the Kaanul dynasty in alliance with Caracol defeated Tikal in 562; for more than a century after this, no monuments were erected at Tikal. In the meantime, in 629, Bajlaj Chan K'awiil acceded to rulership at Dos Pilas, in the Petexbatun region of Peten to the southwest of Tikal, perhaps seeded by his father, a Tikal ruler. Dos Pilas in turn added sites to its dominion through force and diplomacy. However, by 648 Dos Pilas was under Kaanul dominion, and it later turned on Tikal. But the story did not end there, for subsequently there were other battles and reversals of fortune; for instance, Tikal reclaimed Dos Pilas, and the Kaanul dynasty claimed it again, in a series of dynamic power struggles.[32]

The Kaanul dynasty expanded considerably in the Late Classic, especially under the rule of Yuknoom Ch'een II. The dynasty had established itself at Calakmul at least by 631, apparently taking over a site occupied by another dynasty that used a Bat emblem glyph.[33] The Kaanul dynasty expanded on the architectural foundations at Calakmul, constructing massive buildings and erecting many stone monuments. Kaanul also allied with several sites, such as El Perú-Waka' and La Corona (whose ancient name was Sak Nikte'), in Peten, and Caracol to the east, in Belize. One strategy was to send Kaanul princesses to smaller polities for marriage alliances with local men, which bound the smaller allies to the more powerful dynasty. Monuments record these marriages and visits from Kaanul rulers. Monuments at La Corona reveal that the Kaanul dynasty sent at least three princesses to marry Sak Nikte' rulers, and they used such alliances with subsidiary sites to counter Tikal's power and control a jadeite trading route from Calakmul south towards the Motagua Valley.[34] The Kaanul dynasty also sent princesses to El Perú-Waka' to marry local rulers; one was Ixik K'abel, whose monuments and rich tomb reveal that she came to hold significant political and military power.[35]

Despite the sixth-century defeat of Tikal by the Kaanul dynasty and its allies, Tikal recovered and returned to counter Calakmul in 695 CE, and subsequently defeated several Kaanul allies. During the seventh- and eighth-century reign of Jasaw Chan K'awiil, the polity was invigorated, again erecting monuments and large pyramids, and that continued under the reigns of his successors. The roofcombs of these rulers' ever larger pyramids soar above the jungle canopy, and their shrines have carved wooden lintels. Tikal Temple I, Jasaw Chan K'awiil's funerary pyramid, rises on one side of the Great Plaza, opposite Temple II (probably his wife's funerary pyramid) and next to the tombs of the dynasty's Early Classic kings. Jasaw Chan K'awiil connected Tikal's renewed vigour to his ancestors' power from centuries before by re-erecting older stelae in the Great Plaza, burying Stela 31 in Structure 33 before building a new, larger version, and linking his victories to earlier moments in Tikal's history, some involving Teotihuacan.[36] Lintel 3, installed in the Temple I shrine, celebrates his victory over the Kaanul dynasty on a date in 695 CE that coincides with the 260-year or 13-*k'atun* anniversary of the death of Jatz'oom Kuy, also known in contemporary scholarship as 'Spearthrower Owl', probably a Teotihuacan ruler.[37] The lintel thus acknowledges that memory as part of renewing the Mutul polity after the lengthy period of defeat and decline.

Dos Pilas also recovered after the seventh-century wars, defeating Tikal and allying with Aguateca, which became its twin capital. In 735 CE they celebrated the capture of a Ceibal ruler on two stelae, one at Dos Pilas and the other at Aguateca, on which the Dos Pilas–Aguateca ruler, wearing Teotihuacan-style regalia, dominates the humiliated Ceibal king.[38] Increased warfare in this region in the eighth century weakened power structures and created additional problems that ultimately led to the abandonment of Dos Pilas and Aguateca. Yet Ceibal resurged in the ninth century, producing stelae with images in a hybrid style with elements of Maya, Central Mexican and Gulf Coast traditions, perhaps because of new alliances. But by 900 CE Ceibal, along with much of the Southern Lowlands, had fallen as well.[39]

At Copan, Late Classic rulers, including the long-lived and esteemed K'ahk' Uti' Witz' K'awiil (also known as Ruler 12) and his successor, Waxaklajuun Ubaah K'awiil, built atop their predecessors' structures and tombs in the Acropolis and dedicated many stelae and altars on the Great Plaza. The stelae depicted the rulers in various ritual guises and achieved remarkable three-dimensionality in those renderings, allowing the rulers, dressed in intricate regalia and surrounded by deities, to come alive in the plaza. After his death in 695 CE, K'ahk' Uti' Witz' K'awiil was buried in a new, larger version (called the Esmeralda phase) of Temple 10L–26, where Waxaklajuun Ubaah K'awiil created a hieroglyphic stairway that recounted four centuries of the polity's history, highlighting ancestors and their victories up to 710 CE.[40] But his own reign would be tragically cut short when he was assassinated by Quirigua, a dependent state.

Quirigua, on the Motagua River, is renowned for its carved sandstone monuments dating from the fifth, eighth and early ninth centuries CE. Its ruler K'ahk' Tiliw Chan Yopaat acceded to the throne under the authority of Copan's Waxaklajuun Ubaah K'awiil in 724 CE, but in 738 CE Quirigua defeated and sacrificed their overlord from Copan.[41] Quirigua subsequently dedicated several stelae honouring their ruler K'ahk' Tiliw Chan Yopaat on the Great Plaza's north end. These emulate the Copan stelae but exceed them in their impressive heights; they are the tallest of all Classic-period Maya monuments. Also notable are the innovative zoomorphic altars portraying rulers being reborn out of the mouths of great turtles and other supernatural reptiles.

Copan later recovered, and continued to expand on the Acropolis foundations and link the polity to its earlier, glorious past. On Temple 10L–26, K'ahk' Yipyaj Chan K'awiil (Ruler 15) reconstituted and extended the Hieroglyphic Stairway, recounting the history of the kingdom up to 755 CE, moving beyond the dark period of its crippling defeat and Waxaklajuun Ubaah K'awiil's assassination.[42] Sculptures of the kingdom's ancestors dressed as warriors in Teotihuacan-style regalia sit on these steps, dominating captives and emphasizing the victories of the kingdom's long-term history. K'ahk' Yipyaj Chan K'awiil's successor, Yax Pasaj

Altar Q, Copan, Honduras, 776 CE, volcanic tuff.

Chan Yopaat, also drew on the power of the past with Altar Q, installed in 776 CE in front of the last version of Temple 10L–16, the place where dynasty founder K'inich Yax K'uk' Mo' was buried. On the sides of the altar are images of the dynasty's sixteen rulers, arranged such that Yax Pasaj faces the dynastic founder, K'inich Yax K'uk' Mo', who is dressed in Teotihuacan regalia. On the top, an inscription links Yax Pasaj's actions to Yax K'uk' Mo's arrival at Copan in the fifth century. In both image and text, Yax Pasaj's rule is authorized by the ancestral connection. Teotihuacan iconography is pronounced on this and other eighth-century creations; indeed, the recall of the dynasty's past is intertwined with that of Teotihuacan, which had long since fallen but whose memory was maintained at Copan and other prominent locales across the Maya lowlands.

Despite their comeback, Copan and other polities in the Southern Lowlands, including Piedras Negras and El Perú-Waka', collapsed in the ninth and tenth centuries, when the ruling classes abandoned their cities. This disruption resulted from combined stressors including environmental degradation, drought and warfare. But there was variability across the Southern Lowlands, for some sites were abandoned, some devastatingly burned and others reconfigured.[43] Yet even when sites were abandoned, some people stayed and continued to engage with the older architecture and sculpture, as at El Perú-Waka', where people moved or broke several Late Classic stelae or gave offerings to them.[44] People from southern cities also retreated into smaller groups in the area and moved to other regions, including the Northern Lowlands.

## The Northern Lowlands in the Late Classic and Early Postclassic periods

Chichen Itza, one of the most visited sites of the Maya world today, is known for its florescence after the collapse in the Southern Lowlands, but it and many other Northern Lowland sites were already well-established cities. For instance, Oxkintok was occupied from the Preclassic to the Postclassic, and had a substantial Early Classic settlement.[45] Furthermore, it is clear that the Northern and Southern Lowland sites developed in communication with one another, and there are similarities in the architecture and sculpture in both regions. For example, limestone stelae at Uxmal and Ek' Balam bear carved images of a single ruler accompanied by inscriptions, similar to those in the south, and builders at Uxmal constructed range structures set in a quadrangle next to a large pyramid, similar to the layout of Palenque. But Northern Lowland masons and sculptors also created new forms, such as round buildings and carved architectural jambs portraying many figures performing rites, as at Uxmal and Edzna, respectively.

Two major Late Classic architectural styles from the Northern Lowlands are the Chenes and Río Bec architectural styles, which overlapped in some sites in Yucatan and Campeche. Both architectural styles – as well as Puuc-style architecture – share features with Southern Lowland buildings, including the use of the corbel vault, the construction of low-lying one-storey buildings, and the emphasis on facades with smoothed surfaces below the cornice and adornment above it. But they created new aesthetic traditions in their use of complex stone mosaic sculpture. Chenes-style one-storey buildings feature prominent adornment around the central portal that covers the entire height of the facade; in particular,

Structure II, Chicanna, Campeche, Mexico, 700–900 CE, limestone.

mosaics forming large zoomorphic maws around the doorways turn the buildings into supernatural, animate mountains exuding breath and vitality. Río Bec-style architecture, found primarily in Campeche, also features zoomorphic portals leading to the interior rooms of one-storey buildings, but unique characteristics are large towers that appear to be tall pyramids. These are in fact false pyramids; although they have central stairways and superstructures with zoomorphic portals, they can neither be climbed nor entered. The image of the impressive pyramid – as opposed to its practicality – was key.

Some features of Chenes-style architecture appear in Puuc-style architecture, a predominant Late Classic style at Uxmal and other sites in the Puuc region of Yucatan. Nonetheless, there is more diversity in Puuc architecture, which makes use of both tall truncated pyramids and low-lying one-storey structures with several portals leading to interior rooms to create dynamic architectural complexes. The lower parts of the facades have a veneer of smooth limestone blocks, and above the cornices are cut-stone mosaics creating designs of textiles, writhing serpents, miniature houses and more. Puuc architecture continued to use the corbel vault as a structural element, but this type of vault was also used as an aesthetic feature on facades (as on Uxmal's Palace of the Governor, where the vault narrows sharply to accentuate its upward rise), or as arched entrances in city walls (as seen at Labna). Another notable feature of Puuc architecture is the stacking of range structures on terraces of pyramid-like architectural forms, as at Sayil and Ek' Balam.

The walled city of Ek' Balam, a major urban centre, was occupied from the Middle Preclassic to the sixteenth century, but flourished particularly in the Late and Terminal Classic periods. Five *sacbeob* radiate from the centre towards elite architectural complexes outside the walls.[46] Inscriptions relate information about the reigns of Ukit Kan Le'k Tok' and his successor in the late eighth and ninth centuries. On one side of the large main plaza is the six-tiered Acropolis, with various buildings on its terraces. On the fourth level, archaeologists uncovered a stunning zoomorphic portal of modelled plaster on the facade of a building containing the tomb of Ukit Kan Le'k Tok'. In a way that is similar to Chenes-style portal sculptures, the creature's eyes and nose are above the doorway, and its large mouth surrounds the doorway, with a prominent row of projecting teeth on the ground. The facade was carefully buried in antiquity, leading to its excellent preservation.[47]

At Chichen Itza, designers constructed buildings in styles similar to those of Uxmal and the Southern Lowlands, and ones in dialogue with Central Mexican traditions from Tula (in the state of Hidalgo) and the fallen city of Teotihuacan. This eclectic assemblage of architectural and sculptural styles shaped a cosmopolitan city whose eclecticism may have related both to its role as a pilgrimage centre and to a larger Mesoamerican trend of incorporating art and architectural styles from distinct regions, also seen at Cacaxtla and Xochicalco in Central Mexico, which grew after Teotihuacan's sixth-century demise. One of Chichen Itza's commanding buildings is the Castillo, a radial temple – a form seen

Palace of the Governor, Uxmal, Yucatan, Mexico, 900–920 CE, limestone.

earlier in the Maya region, including at Uaxactun. In addition, the area of the site Sylvanus Griswold Morley called 'Old Chichén' has Puuc-style buildings and lintels with carved Maya inscriptions. On the other hand, the Temple of the Warriors, a truncated pyramid with rows of piers featuring warriors, is similar to Temple B from Tula. The chacmool form is also seen in both cities, and in Chichen Itza relief carvings warriors wear regalia similar to that seen at Tula.

The similarities in the art and architecture of Chichen Itza and Tula have inspired many theories as to the mechanisms of exchange, with some arguing for the conquest of Chichen Itza by Toltec warriors from Tula or the abandonment of the site by the Maya and replacement by the Toltecs. Others propose that

the city's eclectic artistic and architectural styles result from the city's cosmopolitan nature. Notably, the appearance of several styles at Chichen Itza, along with sixteenth-century ethnohistoric references to the *tolteca* at Tollan – whom the Mexica (Aztec) extolled as their predecessors in civilization, writing and art – and to Topiltzin Quetzalcoatl's journeys from Tollan, contributed to nineteenth- and twentieth-century speculations about not only migrations within Mesoamerica but the diffusion of culture from Europe to the Americas (discussed in later chapters), in which the Toltecs play a starring role as the progenitors of civilization across Mesoamerica.[48]

The Chichen Itza Great Ballcourt is the largest ballcourt in Mesoamerica, and may have functioned as a ritual space instead of an actual field for playing the ballgame. Benches on the sides of the main alley depict a victorious player holding a decapitated

Castillo, with Temple of the Warriors colonnade in background, Chichen Itza, Yucatan, Mexico, 800–1000 CE.

head. Adjacent is a kneeling, decapitated figure from whose neck emerge streams of blood transforming into snakes and flowering squash plants, indicating a connection between ballgame sacrifices and plant regeneration. Other carvings at the Great Ballcourt depict Maize God narratives, another association between the ballgame and agricultural vitality. Chacmools at Chichen Itza may also relate to sacrifice and agricultural regeneration, for their distinctive form recalls Southern Lowland portrayals of Maize Gods and captives.[49]

As a cosmopolitan pilgrimage city, Chichen Itza was a locus for the exchange of materials from distant lands, including turquoise from northern Mexico or the American Southwest and gold from lower Central America. People deposited objects made from these materials inside buildings; for example, mosaic discs made of

Detail of the digital reconstruction of a relief from the bench of Great Ballcourt, Chichen Itza, Yucatan, Mexico, 800–1100 CE, by the cultural heritage group INSIGHT.

turquoise and shell were offered in an early version of the Castillo, and penitents tossed copper bells, gold discs with embossed narrative scenes, and many other offerings into the Sacred Cenote during Chichen Itza's florescence and after its decline in about 1100. Objects made of turquoise and gold have also been found at other Postclassic Northern Lowland sites, such as Santa Rita Corozal, Belize.

## The Postclassic across the Maya world

Artists and architects were continuing to build fantastic architecture in centres in the Yucatan Peninsula at the time of the arrival in the sixteenth century of Spanish conquistadors. At Mayapan, a major Postclassic capital, archaeologists have found evidence of activity as early as the eleventh century, including at a small shrine contemporaneous with Chichen Itza. But Mayapan thrived in the twelfth century and later, after the fall of Chichen Itza, and drew on that city's legacy by emulating its architecture, although the Mayapan buildings were much smaller. Mayapan fell in the fifteenth century after a period of intense conflict, as evidenced by burned buildings and mass graves.[50] Information about Mayapan has survived through both its material remains and references in sixteenth-century documents.

In the Postclassic, the number of settlements along the coasts increased, reflecting a greater dependence on maritime resources and long-distance trade.[51] Tulum, a walled city on the east coast of the Yucatan Peninsula in Quintana Roo, overlooking the Caribbean Sea, was populated when Europeans arrived. Surviving in several of the buildings are mural paintings in the Postclassic International Style, also seen in murals at Santa Rita Corozal, indicating connections across Mesoamerica. Ceramic artists at Tulum and Mayapan created distinctive censers with images of deities such as Chahk or the aged God N that were painted post-fire in brilliant colours such as Maya Blue.[52]

There were also substantial Postclassic settlements in Peten that are known through archaeology and sixteenth- and seventeenth-century documents. Tayasal, on a peninsula in Lake Peten Itza, was occupied from the Preclassic to the Postclassic. It was ruled by the Itza Maya, who said they had come from Chichen Itza. Nojpeten, on the island now called Flores, was their capital when the Spaniards arrived in 1525. Resisting Spanish dominion for more than a century and a half, the Itza maintained autonomy until they submitted to the colonial authorities in 1697.[53]

Postclassic kingdoms also established capitals with monumental architecture in the highlands of Guatemala. When Spaniards arrived in this region in 1524, Iximche' was the capital of the Kaqchikel kingdom, and Q'umarkaj was the capital of the K'iche' kingdom. Both were fortified sites with terraced pyramids arranged around plazas, a large palace complex and several ball-courts.[54] Some buildings were decorated with polychrome murals. Archaeologists have found gold artefacts at these Postclassic sites, indicating long-distance trade analogous to that in Yucatan.

The diversity and complexity of the ancient Maya world seen in the archaeological record align with what is recorded in sixteenth-century documents. This reminds us that even though we may ascribe an overall identity to the ancient Maya, the archaeological and ethnohistoric records make it clear that the larger category of 'Maya' is made up of many smaller groups whose affiliations and identities were and are dynamic and contingent, as with many groups of people around the world. For brevity's sake this chapter has necessarily omitted a great deal of information, not only about the rulers and elite societies on which this account has focused, but about other levels of Maya society, including commoners and farmers, whose labour tending the soil was the inspiration for foundational stories relating to maize and other foods that were crucial to ancient Maya religion and political authority. The fact that this book does not address their lives does not mean they were trivial. Indeed, their labour and agricultural innovations formed the bedrock of these societies.

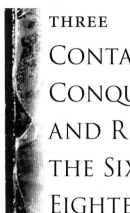

THREE

# Contact and
# Conquest, Resistance
# and Resilience, in
# the Sixteenth to
# Eighteenth Centuries

lthough the Maya never disappeared, many details of
ancient Maya society were lost to the historical record.
Much information was intentionally destroyed in the
sixteenth century by Spanish colonial authorities, who burned
books, dismantled buildings, and tortured and executed Maya
people. Other information was lost when the holders of that
knowledge died, for countless Indigenous people in the Americas
succumbed to illnesses brought by Europeans. But even before
Spaniards wreaked havoc in the Maya world, information was
lost as polities rose and fell, or as environmental or anthropo-
genic stressors rendered sites or regions uninhabitable and people
configured themselves in new groups and places.

The attempts to recover information about the ancient Maya
comprise a long journey, at times circuitous and rife with misun-
derstanding, that continues today. Nonetheless, the work of many
people, both Maya and non-Maya, has added to our collective
knowledge and changed the way people today see and understand the ancient Maya. The remainder of this book traces these
many engagements, including those seeking knowledge about the
ancient Maya and those appropriating their legacy, for better or for
worse. This exploration begins with accounts of contact between
Maya people and Europeans in the early modern world, encompassing encounter, conquest, evangelization and oppression, and

will examine Maya narratives about their own histories and texts by European or Euro-American authors pondering the origins of the Indigenous people of the Americas. We begin with Gaspar Antonio Chi, a multilingual Maya scribe who lived in the sixteenth century.

## Gaspar Antonio Chi

The 'Xiu Family Tree' and the 'Landa alphabet' are sixteenth-century documents that were wholly or partially made by Gaspar Antonio Chi, the son of noble Maya families in Yucatan. Both documents draw on Maya and European traditions. Chi was born in Mani, Yucatan, during a period of intense conflict, as Spanish conquistadors waged war in their quest to conquer Maya communities. His parents were nobles from different *chibalob* (lineages), the Xiu and Chi. During Chi's childhood his father, a Xiu noble, was murdered in a conflict with the Cocom, a rival lineage that opposed the Spanish, with whom the Xiu had allied.[1] Chi was later educated by Franciscan friars in Mani. His mother tongue was Yucatec Maya, he learned Nahuatl, Spanish and Latin and he served as scribe, notary, interpreter and organist. For some time he worked for the friars, including Diego de Landa, who is known both for recording information about Maya culture and for destroying Maya cultural heritage. In later years Chi left the Franciscans and worked as a civil servant and provincial governor.[2] He was like other young Indigenous men throughout the Americas after the Conquest who functioned as linguistic and cultural interpreters in the new realm, straddling worlds and forging new identities during a time of immense change.

In the 'Xiu Family Tree' (1558–60), Chi presented a bicultural identity engaging with Indigenous Mesoamerican and European forms, produced because the Xiu – in common with other Indigenous families – needed to advocate for their property and rights in the face of loss and trauma. This genealogical tree, which is part of the Xiu Chronicles, a collection of documents used as proof of nobility, records members of the Xiu lineage from the fourteenth to the sixteenth centuries. The primary image is derived

Gaspar Antonio Chi, 'Xiu Family Tree', from the 'Xiu Chronicles', Yucatan, Mexico, 1558–60, European paper and pigments.

from the European Tree of Jesse, a form used to show Jesus' family heritage emerging from the body of Jesse of Bethlehem. In the Xiu image, the tree grows out of the body of Tutul Xiu, and the names of Xiu men and women line the branches. But the image also draws on Maya and Nahua forms, leading the art historian Constance Cortez to call it a bilingual and bivisual hybrid document. Cortez demonstrates that parts of the image are Mesoamerican forms related to the claiming of primordial ancestry. The hill, cave and offering at the bottom of the page are frequent in ancient Maya and Central Mexican imagery, and the large genealogical tree evokes the Maya World Tree; finally, four smaller trees form a quincunx pattern and microcosm of the universe.[3]

The Maya 'alphabet' – actually a collection of syllables – resulted from a meeting between Chi and Landa as part of efforts to compile information about Maya culture and religion for what would later be known as the *Relación de las Cosas de Yucatán* (Narrative of the Things of Yucatan). Although Landa is credited as the author and the date given as 1566, the *Relación* appears to be a collection of manuscripts written by him and others, including Chi, and compiled in the late seventeenth or eighteenth century.[4] Documents in this compilation – and others in the Americas – were made to collect information about Indigenous society and religion to aid in evangelizing and in extirpating Indigenous religions. They are thus biased, but remain an essential source

Maya syllables recorded by Gaspar Antonio Chi in the 16th-century *Relación de las Cosas de Yucatán* (Narrative of the Things of Yucatan), whose compilation is attributed to Diego de Landa, p. 45r, European paper and ink.

of information about Maya culture. As part of one interview, Landa asked Chi to help him explain Maya writing by drawing characters that Landa expected would comprise an alphabet. Chi drew the characters for each sound Landa enunciated in Spanish, but there was some conflict, for Chi wrote two or more signs for each of Landa's letters. Indeed, because Maya writing was based on syllables, while trying to spell *ha'* (water), Landa's request for the Spanish letter 'h' ('a-che') required two characters, and the repeated *ha* yet one more, which confused Landa and resulted in frustration, such that the next phrase Chi volunteered to write was *ma in k'ati'* (I do not wish).[5] Although the friar misunderstood and thus misrepresented Maya writing, this document would be crucial for the decipherment of Maya writing in the twentieth century.

In creating both the 'Xiu Family Tree' and the 'Landa alphabet', Chi served as a bridge between Maya and Spanish cultures, and the documents shed light on the sixteenth century as a period of vast change and power imbalance. They also offer windows into Maya writing, culture and religion, and thus are relevant to the themes of this chapter. For instance, how did Maya people envision themselves as individual families and communities, and how were they perceived by the Spaniards who invaded Maya lands? What were the events and tenor of the sixteenth-century encounters between Maya people and Spaniards? Finally, how do documents provide insight into sixteenth-century life and serve as sources for understanding Maya people in later and earlier centuries?

## Documents

Our earliest records of interaction between Maya and European people come from early sixteenth-century Spanish documents and are thus one-sided. Spanish sources include conquistadors' *probanza de mérito* (proof of merit) documents, such as *Historia verdadera de la conquista de la Nueva España* (True History of the Conquest of New Spain) by Bernal Díaz del Castillo, a soldier in Hernán Cortés's army. Such narratives were sent to the Spanish Crown as evidence of work in conquering lands, and as petitions for rewards. This genre emphasized the promotion and exaggeration of the individual's activities.[6] Furthermore, Díaz del Castillo's text and others like it responded to criticism from Bartolomé de Las Casas, a Dominican friar who dedicated himself to defending Indigenous people from atrocities committed by conquistadors, priests and lay landowners and reporting the injustices to the Spanish Crown. Despite their biases, Díaz del Castillo's *Historia* and other sixteenth-century documents remain essential sources for understanding this period.

The perspectives of Maya people on these encounters survive in later documents, written in Spanish and Mayan languages in the Roman alphabet. They include court and land-claim records, primordial titles and petitions to colonial authorities claiming mistreatment by Spanish priests. Some include references to the past, narrating Conquest events or other encounters with Spaniards because of the impact on Indigenous peoples' rights or lands. Primordial titles such as the Chontal account from Acalan-Tixchel, the K'iche' *Popol Vuh* (Council Book) and the Title of Calkini were designed for community self-promotion, to request benefits from the Spanish Crown. The historian Matthew Restall asserts that Yucatec Maya documents containing accounts of the Conquest emphasize continuity and thereby demonstrate survival; further, some communities' primordial titles highlight their role as conquerors and petition for rewards.[7] In contrast, the Books of Chilam Balam of communities such as Mani and Chumayel were written for Maya audiences.

## Encounters and battles

The earliest narrations of encounters between Spaniards and Maya people are recorded in Spanish sources. The first known encounter was in 1502, recorded by Hernando Colón, son of Cristóbal Colón (Christopher Columbus). According to this account, during his fourth voyage to the Americas Columbus sighted a large canoe laden with goods, which his men seized.[8] This is one of few accounts of the large seaworthy canoes and distant journeys that the Maya and other Indigenous people used in complex trading networks.

Díaz del Castillo, who travelled with various conquistadors including Cortés, recorded attempts to enter Maya territory in the Yucatan Peninsula. During an expedition from Cuba led by Francisco Hernández de Córdoba in 1517, the sailors sighted land and a large town. Ten large canoes subsequently approached them, and more than thirty men boarded the Spaniards' ship. On a later day, locals brought the Spaniards to shore, but then warriors attacked the Spaniards. The Spaniards escaped and took two prisoners, whom they named Julian and Melchior, who later assisted them in communicating with Maya people whenever the Spaniards made landfall. In another episode, the Spaniards landed on the Campeche coast looking for fresh water. Local people approached and led them to their town, where the Spaniards saw temples on whose walls 'were figured the bodies of many great serpents'. But the locals asked the Spaniards to leave, and threatened them; the Spaniards retreated to their ships.[9] The Spaniards tried again to make landfall, but each time the Maya drove them away, leading the expedition to return to Cuba.

The Spanish explorers continued to try to make headway, however. In 1518 another expedition, under Juan de Grijalva, arrived on the island of Cozumel, but the locals had taken flight. The Spaniards travelled on, later landing on the Campeche coast, where they fought and ultimately took possession of Champoton. This was one of their first victories, and it emboldened them to continue exploring and invading. However, when the Spaniards arrived at the Grijalva River, the local people encouraged them to seek the land of the Colua or Culhua, in Mexico, who possessed gold.[10] That strategy seemed to work to redirect explorers from Maya lands, for when Cortés mounted his expedition of 1519 he spent little time in the Yucatan Peninsula, lured instead by tales of the wealthy Aztec or Mexica Empire.[11] To reach Central Mexico, he travelled by water to the Veracruz coast and then moved inland, towards the imperial capital of Tenochtitlan.

But before that journey, while he was in the Yucatan Peninsula and the Gulf Coast of Tabasco, individual Spanish or Maya people voluntarily or involuntarily joined Cortés's company and played significant roles as linguistic or cultural translators in later encounters between Spaniards and Indigenous Americans. For example, Julian and Melchior helped the Spanish to communicate in Yucatan. Another was Gerónimo de Aguilar, a Franciscan friar who in 1511 had been shipwrecked and captured by Maya people, who taught him Yucatec Maya. After Cortés's men rescued Aguilar, he too served as a translator between the Maya and Spanish, although Gonzalo Guerrero, another shipwrecked Spaniard, refused rescue, remaining with his Maya wife and children.[12] Another noteworthy individual was Malintzin Tenepal, also known as Doña Marina or, later, as Malinche. Díaz del Castillo relates that she was born in Veracruz to a Nahuatl-speaking family, but in girlhood she was sold into slavery among Chontal Maya traders, who taught her their language.[13] The traders gave her and other women to Cortés and his men. As a speaker of Nahuatl, Chontal Maya and later Spanish, Marina would help Cortés immensely in his communication. Indeed, she and Aguilar translated between Maya and Spanish and helped Cortés communicate with the Mexica, who spoke Nahuatl.

From 1519 to 1521 the Spanish expedition under Cortés repeatedly and ruthlessly attacked the Mexica and, aided by Tlaxcalans who had been enemies of the Mexica, ultimately defeated their empire. The Spaniards subsequently moved south towards Guatemala, and on the way passed through various Maya territories. Cortés's expedition, with more than two hundred Spanish soldiers and cavalry and 3,000 Nahua auxiliaries, headed south to the Chontal-speaking province of Akalan. They arrived near Lake Peten Itza in 1525, when Cortés visited the Itza capital of Nojpeten and met the principal ruler, Ajaw Kan Ek'. They visited the Chontal province, too, and met their leader, Pax Bolon Acha.[14]

Meanwhile, expeditions led by men who had been in Cortés's army focused on reaching other regions and kingdoms. In 1524 an expedition under Luis Marín conquered Chiapas, and subsequently the Spaniards took Maya people into slavery and demanded crippling tribute. Those conditions, in tandem with overwhelming epidemics, devastated Maya populations of Chiapas, reducing them by two-thirds.[15] Also in 1524, Spanish forces under Pedro de Alvarado, accompanied by Native auxiliaries from Central Mexico, arrived in the Guatemalan highlands, where they encountered the Kaqchikel and K'iche' kingdoms. In the same year the capitals of those kingdoms, Iximche' and Q'umarkaj, fell to the Spaniards, although the Kaqchikel and K'iche' continued to resist conquest.[16]

In 1527 Spanish forces under Francisco de Montejo returned to the Yucatan Peninsula and waged war. Yucatan had changed since the expeditions of the previous decade. For one, smallpox had ravaged the population.[17] The eighteenth-century *Book of Chilam Balam of Chumayel* retrospectively recounts the sixteenth-century trauma, referring to the time before the foreigners' arrival:

> There was then no sickness; they had then no aching bones; they had then no high fever; they had then no smallpox; they had then no burning chest; they had then no abdominal pains; they had then no consumption; they had then no headache. At that time the course of humanity was orderly. The foreigners made it otherwise when they arrived here.[18]

There was also economic disruption caused by the breakdown of trade routes because of conquests elsewhere in Mesoamerica. These factors weakened Maya communities, and the Spaniards exacerbated interregional conflict.[19]

Spanish forces exploited this vulnerability and advanced across the peninsula. Montejo established a settlement at Xelha, in Quintana Roo, but it was plagued by disease, hunger and death. Even so, the settlement ultimately survived. They established camps in Campeche from which they conducted expeditions in the north and centre of the peninsula from 1529 to 1534.[20] Montejo's son Francisco de Montejo the Younger used the ruins of Chichen Itza as a base in 1532, naming the town Ciudad Real (Royal City); the Cupul Maya initially allowed the occupation, but later forced the Spanish to abandon the settlement.[21] Montejo's expedition, plagued by lack of water and having found no gold, left Yucatan in 1534, but they returned in 1540. In that period, drought, famine and war between some *chibalob* created further devastation among the Maya of Yucatan. The Spanish exploited this instability, allying with the Xiu against the Cocom, and within a year they conquered provinces in the west and north of the peninsula, forcing many Maya people to flee to other regions, such as Peten.[22] In 1542 the Spanish founded the city of Mérida on top of the Maya settlement of Ti'ho, and although there were continued battles and resistance, particularly from the Cocom, the Spanish alliance with the Xiu helped them to endure.[23] Following was the conversion of Ti'ho into a Spanish colonial city, involving both political and physical transformation.

Indeed, with these conquests, Spaniards frequently destroyed towns and tortured or otherwise unjustly treated Indigenous people throughout Central America. The Dominican friar Bartolomé de Las Casas recounted the atrocities Spaniards committed against Indigenous people, writing in *A Short Account of the Destruction of the Indies* of 1542,

> I therefore concluded that it would constitute a criminal neglect of my duty to remain silent about the enormous loss of life as well as the infinite number of human souls despatched to Hell in the course of such 'conquests', and so resolved to publish an account of a few such outrages ... in order to make that account the more accessible to Your Highness.[24]

Las Casas laid the blame on greed, accusing Christians of having murdered on a vast scale in order to 'line their pockets with gold'. He accused Spaniards such as Pedro de Alvarado of looting and burning Maya towns as part of a scorched-earth policy, and of killing the inhabitants in large numbers. He specifies that the chief of Utatlan (the Nahuatl name for Q'umarkaj) greeted Alvarado in peace, receiving him 'with all due ceremony', but Alvarado responded by demanding gold and directing the Kaqchikel chiefs to be burned alive, which caused others to flee their towns. Of Yucatan, Las Casas wrote, 'There is no way the written word can convey the full horror of the atrocities committed throughout this region ... The wretched Spaniards actively pursued the locals, both men and women alike, using wild dogs to track them and hunt them down.'[25]

Despite such stark criticism, the atrocities continued, plaguing Maya people across Mexico and Central America with resettlement, forced labour, slavery, land expropriation and other forms of oppression. This brutality and many epidemics devastated populations and destroyed communities. Maya texts document these miseries. For example, the *Chilam Balam of Tizimin* laments events in the *k'atun* 11 Ahau, stating, 'How we wept when they came!' It also describes what ensued after the arrival of the Spanish, in the *k'atun* 9 Ahau:

> It was also the start of the hanging, and there began too the epidemic of stones under the arms, white lumps. They brought their diseases and their ropes with them to those districts, to all over the community, coming to infants and younger brothers with their forceful demands, their forced tribute.[26]

### Religious oppression and the destruction of Maya cultural forms

Also pernicious was long-term oppression by men in Christian religious orders, who arrived within a few years of each region's conquest to implement evangelization. The Franciscans and Dominicans arrived in Mexico City in 1524 and 1526 respectively, after the fall of Tenochtitlan (capital of the Aztec Empire), and the same pattern followed in Maya regions. The Bishopric of Santiago de Guatemala was founded in 1534, and the Dominicans arrived soon afterwards. Franciscans arrived in Yucatan beginning in 1545, and established missions in Mérida and elsewhere. The friars used books, painted murals and plays to teach Catholic doctrine. They also taught Maya elites Latin letters and worked with scribes to determine how to write Mayan languages in those letters. But their evangelization efforts seriously harmed Maya people, writing and religion. Colonial religious authorities arrested, punished and tortured people who had books or deity effigies or were suspected of practising traditional religions.[27] They seized and destroyed those items because they perceived them as loci for idolatry that would inspire Maya people to practise traditional rites and worship their gods. In the auto-da-fé in Mani in 1562, Landa ordered the burning of more than twenty books and thousands of deity effigies.

But this was one of many extirpation campaigns in colonial New Spain, and there are many accounts of seized codices in Yucatan from 1589 to 1625.[28] Friars also punished scribes for writing in the Maya script because they feared scribes used it to hide traditional practices from the clergy.

But they did not destroy all the books, and some were transported to Europe. Three of the four pre-Hispanic Maya books that survive today presumably left Mexico in the sixteenth century. They were either seized and sent to religious authorities as evidence of idolatry or given to Spanish kings or other authorities as tribute, gifts or curiosities. The historian John Chuchiak IV makes a strong case that the *Madrid Codex* was seized in 1607 during an extirpation campaign and given to the Spanish Crown.[29] In the eighteenth and nineteenth centuries the three Maya books that are now in Europe turned up in private and royal collections and libraries. The *Dresden Codex* was in a private collection in Vienna by 1739 and was purchased by the Royal Library in Dresden. The *Paris Codex* was found in the Bibliothèque Nationale in Paris in the nineteenth century.[30] The *Madrid Codex* came to light in Europe in the 1860s as two separate documents, the *Codex Troano* and the *Codex Cortesianus*, the latter of which Madrid's Museum of Archaeology purchased in 1872 or 1875, and the linguist Léon de Rosny determined in the early 1880s that they were from the same codex. The Museum of Archaeology acquired the *Codex Troano* fragment in 1888, after which the combined documents were renamed the *Madrid Codex*; this codex is now under the care of the Museo de América in Madrid.[31]

Friars in Yucatan and elsewhere expressed admiration for the grandeur of pre-Hispanic Maya buildings, at the same time as they partially or completely destroyed them. Landa wrote:

If the number, grandeur and beauty of its buildings were to count toward the attainment of renown and reputation in the same way as gold, silver and riches have done for other parts of the Indies, Yucatan would have become as famous as Peru and New Spain have become, so many, in so many places, and so well built of stone are they, it is a marvel.[32]

de aora, y muy de mayores cuerpos; y fuerças y aun vee se esto
mas aqui en Yzamal que en otra parte en los bultos de media talla
que digo estan oy en dia de argamasa en los bestiones que son
de hombres creçidos; y los estremos de los braços y piernas del hom
bre cuyas eran las ceniças del cantaro que hallamos en el edi
ficio que estauan a marauilla por quemar, y muy gruessos.
Vee se tambien en las escaleras de los edificios, que son mas de
dos buenos palmos de alto, y esto aqui solo en Yzamal y en Merida.
Ay aqui en Yzamal un edificio entre los otros de tanta altura y her
mosura que espanta, el qual se vera en esta figura y en esta
razon della. Tiene                                    XX gradas de a mas
de dos buenos pal                                     mos de alto, y aun
ç so cadavno                                          y ternan mas
de cien pies                                          de largo. son estas
gradas de                                             muy grandes
piedras labra                                         das, aunque co
el mucho                                              tiempo, y estar
al agua                                               estan ya feas
y mal tratadas.                                       Tiene despues labra
do en torno como                                     se nala esta raya re
donde labrado de                                      canteria una muy
fuerte pared                                          a la qual como esta
do y medio en                                         alto sale una cesa
de hermosas piedras todo a la redonda y desde ellas se
torna despues a seguir la obra hasta ygualar con el altu
ra de la plaça que se haçe despues de la primera escalera
Despues de la qual plaça se haçe otra escalera como la
primera aunque no tan larga ni de tantos escalones siguien
do se siempre la obra de la pared redonda ob la redonda
Encima destos escalones se haçe otra buena plazeta, y en
ella algo pegado a la pared esta hecho un cerro bien alto con
su escalera al medio dia, donde donde caen las escaleras
grandes y encima esta una hermosa capilla de cante
ria bien labrada. Yo subi en lo alto desta capilla, y como
Yucatan es tierra llana se vee desde ella tierra quanto pue
de la vista alcançar a marauilla, y se vee la mar. Estos
edificios de Yzamal eran por todos XI o XII aunq es este el
mayor, y estan muy cerca unos de otros. No ay memo
ria de los fundadores, y parecen auer sido los primeros.
Estan VIII leguas de la mar en muy hermoso sitio, y bue
na tierra, y comarca de gente por lo qual nos hizieron
los

En el dibujo: capilla · escalera · descanço o plaça · Plaça muy grande, y hermosa · Escaleras muy agras de subir

Drawing of Maya structure at Izamal, from *Relación de las Cosas de Yucatán*
(Narrative of the Things of Yucatan), whose compilation is attributed to Diego
de Landa, p. 46v, European paper and ink.

Convent built on a Prehispanic platform, Izamal, Yucatan, Mexico, 16th century, limestone and other materials.

However, he ordered their partial or complete destruction and the addition of new structures dedicated to Catholicism on top. For example, he said that in 1549 'we had the Indians build a house for St Anthony' on the largest structure at Izamal.[33] By destroying some Maya buildings and constructing Christian ones on top of others, the Spaniards transformed Maya cities such as Ti'ho and Itzmal into the colonial settlements Mérida and Izamal, respectively. This was particularly effective for Spanish purposes in Maya sites of significant ritual or ceremonial importance, such as Izamal, which had been a Maya pilgrimage site, for in building atop those locales, the Spanish attempted to physically and symbolically appropriate their perceived potency.

The Spanish thus took advantage of the sizes of the Maya platforms and buildings to create more impressive Catholic structures and to draw on the religious power vested in those locales. The art historian Amara Solari, discussing these actions as the 'selective appropriation of space' and the transformation of Native places into Christian ones, relates them to the history of Christian conversion, particularly in the British Isles in the sixth and seventh centuries, when Pope Gregory I 'called for the intentional recycling of non-Christian sacred architecture' that could be purified or transformed into Christian places through ceremony.[34] Yet the reuse of buildings or stones may also have been of help to Maya people in continuing to practise their beliefs or connect to their past, as Jesper Nielsen argues of the stones reused in Catholic buildings, characterized as *spolia*, in early colonial Yucatan. Significant examples are two carved stones with the Maya sign for *k'ahk'* (fire) that were embedded into the architecture of Izamal's colonial convent and church, one on the central axis of the atrium's western entrance. Other pre-Hispanic Maya stones reused in early colonial architecture in Yucatan have been found in Mérida, Piste, Pixila and Dzibilchaltun (where a sixteenth-century chapel was constructed in the plaza of an ancient Maya site).[35]

In contrast to populated Maya cities that were transformed in the early colonial period, other Maya cities had fallen long before the Spanish arrival, and some sixteenth-century expeditions visited those abandoned sites. In 1532 Spaniards briefly used Chichen Itza as a base, and other expeditions visited Copan and Uxmal, in 1576 and 1588 respectively.[36]

## Questioning origins

The incursion into the Americas stimulated extensive questioning in Europe of the history of the world and its people. These activities continued for centuries, with such questions as who were the Maya and other Indigenous people of the Americas, and who built the abandoned cities? Before Columbus's arrival in the Americas, Europe had not known about these populated continents, and some European writers expressed their perplexity as to how the people of the Americas fitted into the Bible's narrations of the origins and migrations of humans, who were all alleged to be descendants of Adam and Eve beginning in the Garden of Eden.[37] Thus began a search for the cultural and geographical origins of the Maya and other Indigenous peoples of the Americas.

Sixteenth-century Spanish historians tried to determine whether there was contact with the Americas before Columbus's arrival, and if the people of the Americas had migrated there earlier from Europe or elsewhere. Some proposed that European navigators had landed on uninhabited islands in the Atlantic

Ocean, and others asserted that people from Europe, Egypt or elsewhere had migrated to the Americas. Another conjecture was that the Americas were populated by people from the alleged lost continent of Atlantis, an island in the Atlantic Ocean about which Plato had written as a fictional or allegorical story. For instance, in a book published in 1535, Gonzalo Fernández de Oviedo, royal chronicler of the Indies, proposed that Carthaginian merchants had travelled to the Americas before Columbus. He drew on a text that he said was by Aristotle, although the historian Jaime Gómez de Caso Zuriaga notes that this is a pseudo-Aristotelian text. Fernández de Oviedo recounted that Carthaginian merchants sailed west and found an island in the Atlantic Ocean, which he said was in the Indies, that was inhabited by wild animals but without people. The Carthaginians began to populate the island, but their senate ordered them to withdraw and not return to the island. Las Casas discussed a similar story, but proposed instead that the Phoenicians were the ones who arrived in the Americas.[38] The implications were that the people in the Americas were descended from these migrant populations. Granted, there were contemporaneous Europeans who questioned these and other narratives. The Italian friar and philosopher Giordano Bruno, for example, was burned at the stake in 1600 for challenging Catholic doctrines, including doubting whether all humans came from the Garden of Eden and proposing instead that humans had existed before Adam.[39]

Accompanying such speculation was the question of who built the cities and buildings across the Maya region. Landa, comparing the clothing represented on the sculptures to clothes that contemporary people wore, thought they were local: 'To say that other nations compelled these people to such building, is not the answer, because of the evidences that they were built by the Indians themselves.'[40] But writers in subsequent centuries doubted, dismissed and even denigrated the connection between Maya people and those cities, associating the ruins with Atlantis, the Lost Tribes of Israel and other cultural diffusion narratives that disconnected ancient cities from contemporary Indigenous people in the Americas. For example, in his *Origen de los Indios de el Nuevo*

*Mundo, e Indias Occidentales* (Origin of the Indians of the New World, and West Indies) of 1607, the Dominican Fray Gregorio García repeated the idea that Carthaginian merchants travelled to the Americas, and proposed that the ancient buildings in Chiapas were Carthaginian works. He also reviewed the speculation that Indigenous people of the Americas derived from the Lost Tribes of Israel.[41] Francisco Núñez de la Vega, a Creole priest assigned to Chiapas and Soconusco, also connected Indigenous Americans to the Lost Tribes of Israel. He discussed a legendary figure called Votan, a descendant of Noah and supposedly the first man to divide up land in the Indies.[42] These various notions have continued for centuries in different forms, although today it is clear that ancient Maya cities were built by ancestors of contemporary Maya people.

## Maya resistance and resilience in the face of conquest and oppression

In response to Spanish atrocities and oppression against Maya communities, Maya people resisted colonial authorities in many ways. Some revolted, for example by burning Catholic churches, as at Lamanai (in Belize) sometime before 1641.[43] Across Mexico and Central America, many people fled Spanish invaders and colonial authorities and established independent communities or retreated to the forests or mountains. But other significant ways to resist authority were to maintain continuity and practise traditions, for example by retaining books and deity effigies, making new ones and following traditional calendars. When faced with the seizure of books and other sacred objects, Maya people hid them and obscured their religious content, although it is clear that the colonial authorities knew about those strategies, for numerous court cases accused individuals of such practices.[44]

Maya people also disguised religious content by writing in Latin letters. The books of Chilam Balam, written in Yucatec Maya in Latin letters on European paper, allowed scribes to preserve Indigenous knowledge while hiding it from colonial authorities. Several scribes made these handwritten books in the colonial

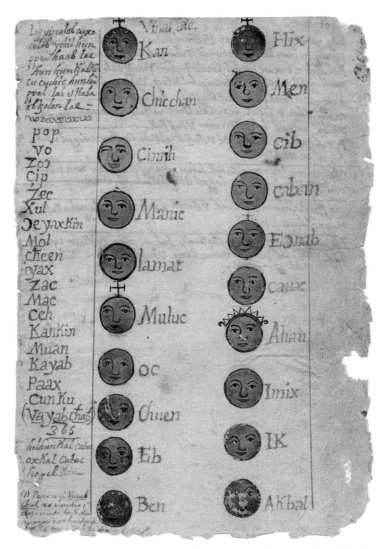

*Chilam Balam of Ixil*, p. 20r, with Maya calendar names, 18th century. List of *haab* month names on left, and list of *tzolk'in* day names with images on right. The day *ahau* (lord) is marked with a crown.

period and the nineteenth century, copying both from Maya codices written in logo-syllabic script, and from other Chilam Balam books. Scribes added Christian material, metaphors and riddles to obscure their religious content.[45] For example, as Laura Caso Barrera and Mario M. Aliphat Fernández explain, a passage in the eighteenth-century *Chilam Balam of Ixil* concerns the deity Ah Zac Cimi as the personification of a disease born on the date *ox ahau* (3 *ahau*). But instead of saying *ox ahau*, the text says *oxtul ahau*, meaning 'three kings', and names 'Melchior, Gaspar and Balthazar', the three wise men, using a Christian allusion to cloak the Maya reference.[46] Such books constitute a crucial example of the resilience of Maya people in protecting knowledge and situating themselves in a changing world.

But Maya scribes in colonial Yucatan wrote in Maya inscriptions, too, practising what Chuchiak describes as 'graphic pluralism', through which scribes resisted colonial authority and created new identities within new political and social systems. Chuchiak describes the *chilan* (prophet) Couoh, who in the 1560s wrote in both Maya logo-syllabic writing and the Latin alphabet. Chilan Couoh preached the superiority of Maya writing and urged Maya people to take up arms against the Spanish.[47] Nonetheless, the efforts to suppress Maya writing led to its tragic extinction in the colonial period.

Maya people also worked to maintain their rights to ancestral lands and to establish authority to rule themselves. Many documents were produced to display rights and prove the legitimacy of families or communities. For example, the Xiu Chronicles (including the 'Xiu Family Tree') were compiled as proof of family origins and rights. Also in the sixteenth century, communities created maps for land claims such as the 'Mani Land Treaty', which Gaspar Antonio Chi made in 1557 to demonstrate the historic territory of the Mani province.[48] Other significant documents come from the K'iche' and Kaqchikel kingdoms in highland Guatemala. The K'iche' Maya *Popol Vuh* and the *Kaqchikel Chronicles*, for example, record these kingdoms' histories, partially to help communities situate themselves within the colonial system. The *Popol Vuh* was recorded in the sixteenth century, although the earliest extant version is a copy made in 1701 by Francisco Ximénez. It narrates the history of the K'iche' people from the creation of the world to the present day, recounting both the actions of the Hero Twins, who battle the Lords of Death and ultimately are reborn as celestial bodies, and K'iche' genealogies over many generations.

Contemporary leaders are presented as analogous to the cosmic heroes.[49] The narratives derive from centuries of tradition, but their recording in that moment relates to their condition in a changing society, in order to establish authority and rights in the present.

Maya communities and kingdoms also continued to resist conquest and remained independent. The Itza, who occupied the forests around Lake Peten Itza, remained autonomous until 1697, with its capital at Nojpeten. This region was far from the principal areas of colonial settlement, but colonial authorities pursued various strategies to destroy and disperse this kingdom and other communities. For example, Martín de Ursúa y Arizmendi, later governor of Yucatan, proposed to the Spanish Crown in 1692 a plan for a north–south road connecting Mérida to Guatemala, to conquer the Itza Maya.[50] The Itza submitted to colonial forces in 1697 but continued to fight for their autonomy. Nonetheless, epidemics and continuing violence, oppression and reconquest by colonial authorities reduced their population and strength. The Itza were the last of the Native autonomous kingdoms that had ruled in the Americas for thousands of years. Thus David Stuart characterizes their defeat poignantly 'as a momentous and transformative episode in human history'.[51]

The many encounters between Maya people and Europeans in the sixteenth and seventeenth centuries include stories of violence, conquest and oppression, as well as resistance and cultural survival. During this period conquistadors, viceregal authorities and representatives of the Catholic Church carried out sustained attempts to conquer Maya polities and stamp out Maya religion and culture, by means including killing and torturing people and destroying architecture and other forms of material culture. At the same time, there were limited efforts to record information about the Maya and other Indigenous people in the Americas, but this often related to authorities trying to document resources and people in their dominion in order to capitalize on their economic or tribute systems or to aid in extirpating what they perceived as idolatrous behaviour. Despite these motivations and the inherent bias of the documents, some of the material they contain has been crucial in reconstructing aspects of pre-Hispanic Maya society.

At the same time, in this period Maya people from various political entities or language groups strove to record information about themselves and their ancestors. They did so for many reasons, for instance as part of court cases, land-claim records, primordial titles and petitions. Such records may include recent family and land-use documents, or may stretch far back in time to recount groups' distant origins, as is the case of the K'iche' Maya *Popol Vuh*. Although at times created under duress, as part of a conflict with a colonial power or another Indigenous group, these documents endure as key resources for Maya people today to learn about the past and understand what their ancestors experienced during these centuries.

Although the Itza Maya kingdom fell in 1697, Maya people in subsequent centuries in different regions have continued to strive for autonomy. This has taken place through both revolts and revitalization movements, including uprisings in Chiapas in 1712 and 1867, in highland Guatemala in 1820, and in the Yucatan Peninsula in 1761. Maya communities in the Yucatan Peninsula also waged war for more than five decades (1847–1901) during the Caste Wars to regain or maintain cultural and political autonomy, pushing back against cultural and economic colonization. The Caste Wars consumed the Yucatan Peninsula, and even after much of the area was returned to state control, resisting communities in the eastern and southern parts of the peninsula retained independence until the beginning of the twentieth century.[52] Although deeply affected by oppression, poverty and violence over the last five centuries, Maya communities have remained resilient and maintained connections to their traditions in myriad ways, by preserving language and culture, advocating for bilingual teaching in schools, producing dictionaries to record and disseminate Mayan languages, continuing craft-making and engaging with their history in new contexts.

# FOUR

# EXPLORATION, DOCUMENTATION AND THE SEARCH FOR ORIGINS IN THE EIGHTEENTH AND NINETEENTH CENTURIES

O ver the course of the eighteenth and nineteenth centuries, there was burgeoning interest on the part of government officials, independent explorers, scholars and others to learn about the ancient Maya and other pre-Hispanic cultures. Before independence from Spain, expeditions were generally carried out under the direction of the Spanish imperial government, but after Independence in 1821, more people outside the Spanish Empire began to visit ancient Maya cities. Explorers travelling with artists documented Maya sites, some experimenting with drawing and photographic techniques to seek objective or clearer records of buildings, sculptures and carved images and inscriptions. These images were included in reports to government entities or published in journals and books, which also featured descriptions of the sites and, at times, of the people who lived near them. Some expeditions collected artefacts that were either taken to Europe or the United States or kept in local private, university or viceregal collections. In the late nineteenth century government-sponsored expeditions sought to collect artefacts more systematically; these were shown in international expositions in which the displays were often tied – either explicitly or implicitly – to notions of imperialism and cultural hegemony.

Nineteenth-century rhetoric emphasized explorers' discoveries of ancient Maya sites, but Maya people already knew about, lived near and made offerings in these places. For example, Lacandon Maya people went to, performed rites in and left incense burners (*u lakil k'uh*, god's plate) and other ceramics at several sites, including Yaxchilan, Piedras Negras, Budsilha and Bonampak.[1] Furthermore, the Lacandon Maya spoke about the ruins as potent spaces, calling centres such as Palenque and Yaxchilan 'the dwelling-places of the gods'.[2] Maya people in many regions also guided explorers and artists to sites, but the names of Maya leaders or guides were often not recorded, with credit going to those who published information in national or international media. For many years, the record of the first official expedition to Tikal, in 1848, was credited to Peten commissioner and future governor Modesto Méndez. But scholarship has revealed that Peten governor Ambrosio Tut, an Indigenous man, played a key role in that expedition, for his grandfather had told him about the place. In the account of the expedition, Méndez reported that Lacandon Maya people lived near Tikal, and subsequent archaeological excavations have confirmed this.[3] Indeed, Tikal was known to Maya people in the region before that first official expedition.

Despite the fact that invading Spaniards had encountered Maya people in vibrant political capitals, and despite clear connections of many Maya groups to the ruins, nineteenth-century writers continued to speculate about who had built these ancient cities, conjecturing – as in earlier centuries – that invading or otherwise migrating populations from Europe, the legendary island of Atlantis or elsewhere had constructed them. But their methods of argumentation were problematic, and their use of evidence selective. Other writers asserted that the builders of these cities were the ancestors of contemporary Maya people living in the regions; the latter assertions ultimately prevailed, although the diffusionism notions have been remarkably enduring.

### Colonial-period explorations and collecting

In late colonial New Spain, writers and politicians in the Creole elite promoted the use of the Indigenous past to develop an identity for the Americas that was distinct from Europe. This constituted a shift from beliefs that ancient buildings should be dismantled to those encouraging the exploration, documentation and protection of ancient sites and monuments. In Guatemala, the seventeenth-century historian Francisco Antonio de Fuentes y Guzmán encouraged learning about ancient sites such as Copan, Zaculeu and Kaminaljuyu as part of crafting Guatemala's history.[4] In Mexico, the Jesuit scholar Francisco Xavier Clavijero was instrumental in elevating perceptions of the pre-Hispanic past (primarily of Central Mexico) and advocating for its equivalence with European Classical cultures.[5] He pleaded for protecting antiquities and forming a museum, stating in 1780, 'I pray my fellow countrymen to guard what little is left of the military architecture of the Mexica, so many fine antiquities having already been allowed to perish.'[6] The Royal and Pontifical University of Mexico assumed the mantle, taking into its care the Aztec Coatlicue sculpture and the Calendar Stone, which were uncovered while repaving Mexico City's Zócalo in 1790 (although the Coatlicue sculpture was soon reburied beneath a university corridor amid fears it was inspiring idolatry). Other Aztec sculptures found in the 1820s and '30s were accepted into the university's collections, too.[7]

Even with the primary focus on the Aztec history and monuments, there was burgeoning interest in the Maya region. In the late eighteenth century viceregal governments and the Spanish Crown commissioned explorations of Maya sites, often by pairs of explorers and artists, generally from New Spain or the Spanish Empire. Several went to Palenque, first during the reign of Charles III (1759–88). News of Palenque had come from two priests, Antonio de Solis and Ramón Ordoñez, who informed José Estechería, of the royal court in Guatemala, about the ruins. Estechería commissioned expeditions, but the first were insufficient. For example, in 1784 José Antonio Calderón, from Santo Domingo de Palenque, produced four drawings of Palenque, but he was not a trained artist; his rough sketches are out of proportion and do not capture details.[8] In 1785 Estechería commissioned the Guatemalan royal architect Antonio Bernasconi to investigate the site, but that report was sketchy and brief. In 1786 Estechería appointed the military captain Antonio del Río and artist Ricardo

José Antonio Calderón, panel from Palenque, *Descripción del terreno y población antigua nuevamente descubierta en las inmediaciones del pueblo de Palenque* (Description of the Land and Ancient People Newly Discovered in the Vicinity of the Town of Palenque; 1784).

Almendáriz to go to Palenque, and these drawings were more detailed. Their report, first submitted in 1787, was published in English in 1822, along with plates prepared by the eccentric artist Jean-Frédéric Maximilien de Waldeck, who would later visit Palenque to make his own drawings.[9] The differences between Calderón's illustrations of 1784, with their hesitant lines, simple outlining of forms and invented motifs, and those of Almendáriz are dramatic, for Almendáriz used shading to indicate the three-dimensionality of the relief sculptures, and tried to capture proportions and details of images and inscriptions. Distribution of the del Río report from 1822 was limited, but did expose people beyond the Spanish Empire to Palenque.

Ricardo Almendáriz, panel from Palenque Palace, in *Coleccion de estampas* (1787).

Del Río also took antiquities from Palenque, sending one support from K'inich Janaab Pakal's stone throne and a stucco head to the Royal Collection of Natural History in Madrid. He claimed that removing and possessing monuments would give credit to the Spanish Empire, writing: 'how greatly the glory of the Spanish arms would be exalted, and what credit would accrue to the national refinement, so superior to the notions of the Indians, in becoming possessed of these truly interesting and valuable remnants of the remotest antiquity.'[10] Such rhetoric of possession and superiority marked subsequent expeditions and collecting enterprises. The removed pieces are now in Madrid's Museo de América, but other pieces of Pakal's throne remain at Palenque.[11] The dismantling and dispersal of a coherent sculptural assemblage form a pattern that would continue for centuries in the collecting of ancient Maya art, whether sculptural assemblages or ceramic sets.

In 1788 the new king of Spain, Charles IV, commissioned Guillermo Dupaix, who had been a captain of dragoons in the Spanish military, to survey New Spain's antiquities, this time spanning the large area from Mexico City to Palenque. Between 1805 and 1808 Dupaix travelled with José Luciano Castañeda, a professor of drawing and architecture in Mexico City, whose illustrations followed contemporary standards of academic drawing. Their report was published decades later, after Independence, first in London in 1831 by the eccentric Irish bibliophile Edward King, Lord Kingsborough, and in Paris in 1834.[12] The introduction to the Paris publication explicitly compares the journey to French expeditions under Napoleon in Egypt.[13] Indeed, as the art historian R. Tripp Evans observes, the Dupaix expedition – like Napoleon's efforts – was 'intended to amplify the conquering nation's cultural hegemony'.[14] But since the report was published after Independence, the intended glory for Spain was inevitably diminished.

The publications by del Río and Dupaix drew on several genres and both aspired to technical accuracy and promoted fanciful speculation. As Evans notes, their format was modelled on the French *encyclopédie*, pairing technical illustrations and scholarly commentary. But the texts varied widely, some aiming for description alone, others offering some conjecture, and yet others recounting grand narratives of transoceanic diffusion.[15] For example, del Río speculated that visiting or invading Romans or another culture had influenced the ruins:

> It might be inferred that this people had had some analogy to, and intercourse with the Romans, from a similarity in the choice of situation as well as a subterranean stone aqueduct of great solidity and durability, which passes under the largest building. I do not take upon myself to assert that these conquerors did actually land in this country; but, there is reasonable ground for hazarding a conjecture that some inhabitants of that polished nation did visit these regions; and that, from such intercourse, the natives might have imbibed, during their stay, an idea of the arts, as a reward for their hospitality.[16]

His suggestions echoed those from previous centuries of transatlantic contact and colonization of the Maya region, but he tempered them with speculative language. However, in an essay published in the same volume, Paul Félix Cabrera, an Italian living in Guatemala, recounted stories about Egypt, the Lost Tribes of Israel and the diffusion of culture from the Old World to the Americas. Drawing on the early eighteenth-century writings of Francisco Núñez de la Vega, Cabrera argued for 'maritime communication between the two continents in the very remotest ages of antiquity', and for the legendary Votan as the 'first populator of the new world'. He also claimed that del Río's Palenque illustrations included images of Votan and the Egyptian god Osiris.[17]

Others endorsed similar or even more outrageous speculation. In a history of Guatemala in 1808, Domingo Juarros y Montúfar argued that there were strong similarities between the writing and images of Palenque and Egypt, and concluded that Palenque and other sites were an Egyptian colony.[18] Lord Kingsborough, who is known for his compilations of pre-Hispanic and sixteenth-century documents, asserted that the Maya were ancient Hebrews who had colonized America.[19] The Church of Jesus Christ of Latter-Day Saints (Mormon) religion also drew from and contributed to such narratives. Joseph Smith claimed he had angelic visions in 1823 and received inscribed golden plates, which he translated, telling stories of a small group of Israelites who came to the Americas, settled among established Indigenous cultures and built cities and earthworks. Smith also spoke of Jesus' alleged appearance and establishment of Christianity in the Americas. This is one of many cases of nineteenth-century Americans claiming a personal connection to ancient American cities and appropriating the ancient Maya legacy from contemporary Indigenous people.[20]

The publication in 1834 of Dupaix's expedition includes several essays deliberating about who built the ancient cities, weighing both transatlantic speculations and possibilities for autochthonous development. Dupaix wrote that those who built Palenque may have immigrated from Atlantis, whether voluntarily, accidentally or by force, and although he also considered evidence that the works were indigenous to the region, he wrote that he firmly believed that the people who lived in New Palenque were not the descendants of those who had built the monuments.[21] The Castañeda illustrations seem to reinforce this idea, for they include images of local people wearing little clothing and carrying bows and arrows, suggesting a lack of civilization, in contrast to the refined architectural forms. Nonetheless, this may be one of the first depictions of a modern Maya person in an ancient Maya archaeological site.[22]

Other essays accompanying the Dupaix report argued more strongly for diffusion from the Old World, and for connecting the Maya ruins to Egypt.[23] The French antiquarian Alexandre Lenoir deliberated whether Maya cities and monuments derived from the Old World or from their own genius. He compared the Maya cities and monuments to ones in Egypt and 'Asiatic nations', and viewed certain symbols from Palenque through an Egyptian lens, for instance interpreting the Maya *ik'* (wind) symbol as an Egyptian 'Tau'. Furthermore, he concluded that the people of the Americas must have been in contact with people from Asia, but did not state definitively that the resemblances were the result of this contact, ending his essay by saying, 'we cannot know if the arts at Palenque were the result of these communications, or if they were a native product of the country'.[24] In another essay, David Bailie Warden reviewed several possible migrations to the Americas, discussing

Guillermo Dupaix, 'Tower at Palenque', in *Antiquités mexicaines* (1834), plate 15.

the options of Atlantis, Phoenicians, Carthaginians, Israelites, Africans and Polynesians, and making reference to Núñez de la Vega and Cabrera's proposals that the people in Chiapas were descendants of Votan.[25] He did not say which option he deemed to be correct. Although their language is tempered by speculation, the fact that these essays accompanied the Dupaix report allowed those ideas to endure.

In the late colonial period, one expedition was conducted by individuals from outside the Spanish Empire. The Prussian geographer and naturalist Alexander von Humboldt travelled in the Americas from 1799 to 1804 with the botanist Aimé Bonpland, arriving in Mexico in 1803. In Mexico City, he requested that the Coatlicue be disinterred so that he could draw it, but it was reburied thereafter.[26] Humboldt published the drawings in *Vues des Cordillères, et monumens des peuples indigènes de l'Amérique* (Views of the Cordilleras, and Monuments of the Indigenous Peoples of America) of 1810, which covered the two men's travels in Mexico and Central and South America. They did not visit the Maya region, but unknowingly published two Maya works in that tome, including a Palenque panel (one of Almendáriz's illustrations), identified as a Mexican relief found in Oaxaca, and five pages of the *Dresden Codex*. The *Dresden Codex* pages were not categorized as distinct from the other pre-Hispanic Mexican manuscripts, although, notably, Humboldt did not use the word 'Mexican' in the caption to *Dresden Codex* images. Given how little people knew about the characteristics of Maya art at the time, not recognizing either as Maya was understandable.[27] In contrast to the essays from contemporaneous authors advocating for the diffusion of cultures, Humboldt ascribed the ancient cultures of the Americas to Indigenous autochthonous development.[28]

## Exploration, archaeology and national museums after Independence

Independence from Spain in 1821 created opportunities for additional explorers and artists –from both inside and outside the Spanish Empire – to enter the Maya region. Many had read the del Río and Dupaix reports. Some went to document cultural remains, either as a nationalistic endeavour after Independence or to explore another world civilization. Others journeyed to exploit forest resources such as mahogany and rubber, and encountered Maya ruins. Explorers often photographed or made casts of sculptures from these sites or collected items for display in international exhibitions or museums. Furthermore, archaeology and museum development became part of nationalist projects in the new Mexican and Central American republics, which began to collect and display pre-Hispanic art as part of their building of post-colonial identity.

As in the late colonial period, insurgent generals, politicians and writers endeavoured to use Mexico's pre-Hispanic past in creating a national narrative both during and after the War of Independence. The revolutionary general and Catholic priest José María Morelos portrayed an independent Mexico as a continuation of Aztec history. The historian Carlos María Bustamante, who wrote speeches for Morelos and others, drew on the Aztec past in envisioning an independent Mexico, using the Nahuatl name 'Anahuac' to refer to the region, and invoking Moteuczoma, the *tlatoani* who was ruling when the Spaniards arrived. After Independence, writers and politicians looked for visual symbols from Central Mexico's pre-Hispanic past to create a new narrative and identity for the Mexican nation, and Bustamante's writings became important resources in that endeavour.[29] In 1825, during the First Mexican Republic, the Mexican National Museum was founded in the Royal and Pontifical University of Mexico. At this time, the museum held pre- and post-Conquest monuments, documents and other items related to Mexican history, natural history and geology. Furthermore, in 1827 Mexico passed a law prohibiting the export of antiquities, to try to keep them inside the country.[30]

After Independence, research into the pre-Hispanic past and museum-building became part of Guatemala's formation of identity as well. As the anthropologist Oswaldo Chinchilla Mazariegos recounts, José Cecilio del Valle, president of the Sociedad Económica, wanted to raise Guatemala's profile by promoting connections with the K'iche' and Kaqchikel kingdoms, thereby emulating Mexican Creole patriots who connected themselves with the Aztec Empire. Del Valle encouraged research into the pre-Hispanic past and claimed 'the pre-conquest Indians as the exemplary "fathers" of the modern Guatemalan state, who set models for the appropriate conduct of government and society'. Indeed, the connections between contemporary Maya people and those who had built Iximche' and Q'umarkaj were unavoidable, for these were the documented capitals of the Kaqchikel and K'iche' kingdoms. The government under chief of state José Felipe Mariano Gálvez called for the creation of a national museum and commissioned explorations of Copan, Iximche' and Q'umarkaj as part of a plan formed in 1834 to write Guatemala's history. But Gálvez was ousted from power, and the museum did not open.[31]

Despite this appreciation of the ancient sites and the acknowledgement of their links to contemporary Maya people, there was extensive oppression and exploitation of contemporary Indigenous people. As Chinchilla Mazariegos reveals, 'Guatemalan Creoles appropriated the pre-Hispanic past with little consideration for the country's contemporary Indian population,' and del Valle 'regarded the majority Indian population as a hindrance to the country's progress, to be regenerated through political liberty, education, and racial mixture'.[32] Moreover, the period of Gálvez's rule was a time of harsh land expropriation and labour drafts for contemporary Maya people.[33] Indeed, Indigenous communities were often harmed by activities carried out in the name of economic progress. For instance, nineteenth-century colonization and exploitation of resources such as land for cattle, farming, new settlements and timber resulted in the destruction of rainforests and the expropriation of Indigenous community lands.[34]

Independence from Spain opened the Maya region to foreign, independent explorers and artists. Jean-Frédéric Maximilien de Waldeck, who had prepared the prints for the del Río report, visited Palenque and Uxmal in 1832–4, partially funded by Lord Kingsborough, and published his drawings in France.[35] Trained as a Neoclassical painter, Waldeck was a talented artist with the ability to render sculptural forms beautifully on the two-dimensional page. In pursuing support for his trip to Palenque, he claimed that the renderings by Castañeda and del Río were poor, and that with his skill and instruments, he would be able to provide better ones.[36] However, despite their technical skill and apparent exactitude, the Palenque drawings are embellished with motifs supporting Waldeck's narratives of transoceanic diffusion, particularly from Asia.[37] For example, he wrote about Asian architectural styles and elephants in the architectural adornment at Palenque, and in one unpublished illustration changed an avian form from the Palenque Palace into an elephant. Later authors based their interpretations on Waldeck's inventions. Indeed, nearly a century later, in 1924, Grafton Elliot Smith stated that the presence of elephants, among other features, demonstrated 'that there was no longer any room for doubt as to the reality of the diffusion across the Pacific of the essential elements out of which the Pre-Columbian civilization of America had been built up'.[38] Smith made this assertion in the face of substantial opposition by contemporaneous scholars of the ancient Maya and other civilizations in Mexico and Central America.

Some of those who visited and documented Maya archaeological sites in post-Independence Central America seem to have had

Jean-Frédéric Maximilien de Waldeck, detail from Palenque Palace ('elephant' at Palenque), paper, ink, pencil and wash.

little respect for the contemporary Maya people in the regions. Juan Galindo, a native of Dublin who lived in Central America, went to Palenque in 1831 and Copan in 1834, and published reports about those visits in Europe and the United States.[39] His letter of 1831 in the *London Literary Gazette* about Palenque reached a new audience – 'the literary world' – for news about Palenque. In it, he recounts his desire to 'rescue ancient America from a charge of barbarism', and connects the builders of ancient Palenque to local people, writing that 'Every thing bears testimony that these surprising people were not physically dissimilar from the present Indians.'[40] However, in his Copan report of 1834, Galindo speculated about cultural diffusion, arguing that civilization originated in Central America and moved westwards to Asia, Persia and Egypt, and that similarities among ancient cultures result from these migrations.[41] But he saw a second wave of civilization in Central America, after the first was wiped out by the Toltecs moving southwards from Central Mexico and spreading civilization into Central America. He thought Copan was a 'colony of Tultecos' whose 'king held dominion over the country extending to the eastward from that of the Mayas or Yucatan, and reaching from the Bay of Honduras nearly to the Pacific.'[42] This narrative of Toltec migrations was based partially on interpretations of Central Mexican ethnohistoric accounts regarding the journey of Topiltzin Quetzalcoatl from Tollan, even though they should be understood in the context of Mexica or Aztec explanations of their own history and early colonial politics.[43] Needless to say, that narrative took agency away from the local, contemporary Maya people regarding the cities the ancient Maya had built.

Moreover, both reports disparaged contemporary Maya people. In 1831 Galindo referred to the 'wild Maya Indians' in Peten and Chiapas, and in 1834 he wrote, 'the Indian race is in the last centuries of its existence, and must soon disappear from the earth.'[44] He thus contrasted the presumed civilized nature of the ancients with the alleged barbarity of contemporary people. This conclusion is troubling, since, as governor of Peten, he had control over their fate. Furthermore, his writing precedes others emphasizing similar distinctions in order to justify taking monuments from places such as Palenque and Copan.

At the end of the decade, the American writer John Lloyd Stephens and the British artist Frederick Catherwood, who had already worked together to record monuments in Egypt, visited Central American and Mexican archaeological sites and created illustrations for what became wildly popular books.[45] They also had a political motivation, for Stephens had a diplomatic appointment from the United States to determine the seat of power for the Central American Federation and establish relations with this government.[46] Although that mission failed, Stephens and Catherwood made a lasting contribution to Maya studies, for their books contain rich descriptions that convey adventure, wonder and intrigue, popularizing Maya sites among countless people.

Stephens made at least two essential points that established his importance in the historiography of the ancient Maya. First, he proposed that the Maya inscriptions contained historical content: 'One thing I believe: its history is graven on its monuments. No Champollion has yet brought to them the energies of his inquiring mind. Who shall read them?'[47] Referring to Jean-François Champollion's decipherment of the Rosetta stone, his predictions that the Maya inscriptions could be read and that they recorded history were correct. But it would be more than a century before Tatiana Proskouriakoff proved that the inscriptions narrate history. Second, Stephens proposed that the ancient cities were connected to Maya people living in the region and thus were indigenous to Mexico and Central America:

> we have a conclusion far more interesting and wonderful than that of connecting the builders of these cities with the Egyptians or any other people. It is the spectacle of a people skilled in architecture, sculpture, and drawing, and, beyond doubt, other more perishable arts, and possessing the cultivation and refinement attendant upon these, not derived from the Old World, but originating and growing up here, without models or masters, having a distinct, separate, independent existence; like the plants and fruits of the soil, indigenous.[48]

Catherwood's illustrations were essential contributions that walked the line between objective academic illustrations and romantic images for entertainment. Stephens emphasized that Catherwood's techniques presented the architecture accurately: 'Mr Catherwood made the outline of all the drawings with the camera lucida, and divided his paper into sections, so as to preserve the utmost accuracy of proportion. The engravings were made with the same regard to truth.'[49] But several scholars have noted that Catherwood's illustrations are made with an attention to romantic aesthetics and narrative. Merideth Paxton argues that Catherwood's training with the painter J.M.W. Turner at the Royal Academy in London and his study of Giovanni Battista Piranesi's drawings of classical ruins 'influenced his general interest in combining didactic content and aesthetic concerns.'[50] Furthermore, the art historian Khristaan Villela contextualizes them within Catherwood's larger oeuvre, which included artistic productions for theatres and operas and large-scale panoramas recreating foreign or ancient locales, and argues that Catherwood's Maya illustrations were also created for entertainment.[51]

A close look at Catherwood's illustration of a building in the Palenque Palace reveals both his attention to accuracy and the framing for aesthetic pleasure. In contrast to Waldeck's

Frederick Catherwood, Casa III (now known as House A), Palenque, Chiapas, Mexico, colour lithograph from *Views of Ancient Monuments in Central America, Chiapas and Yucatan* (1844).

misrepresentation of Palenque sculpture, Catherwood portrays House A of the Northeast Court in such detail that it is instantly recognizable. Yet it is also a romantic image, showing the building partially overgrown with vegetation, some trees just cut, allowing sunbeams to illuminate the structure. The Native people stand at ease inside the building and relax in front of it, probably for the visual pleasure of the image.

Some of the rhetoric in Stephens's writings supported the removal of Maya monuments for u.s. museums. For example, Stephens commented on Maya sites being abandoned or neglected. He wrote about Copan, 'The city was desolate. No remnant of this race hangs round the ruins . . . It lay before us like a shattered bark in the midst of the ocean, her masts gone, her name effaced, her crew perished, and none to tell whence she came.'[52] Engaging in such rhetoric of neglect or abandonment was perhaps part of the romanticizing of places and exploration, but it also contributed to his attempts to legitimize the purchase of sites and the removal of antiquities for a proposed museum in New York (although it was never built). Stephens purchased Copan for fifty dollars with the intention to

> remove the monuments of a by-gone people from the desolate region in which they were buried, set them up in the 'great commercial emporium,' and found an institution to be the nucleus of a great national museum of American antiquities! . . . I resolved that ours they should be; with visions of glory and indistinct fancies of receiving the thanks of the corporation flitting before my eyes, I drew my blanket around me, and fell asleep.[53]

Stephens also imported antiquities from Yucatan and displayed them in a panorama building in New York City with the 'Panorama of Jerusalem', which was based on Catherwood's drawings. In 1842 that building burned down, destroying most of the artefacts, but some pieces were saved and later donated to the American Museum of Natural History in New York.[54] Stephens had also requested that the right panel of the Palenque Tablet of the Cross be removed. In 1842 Charles Russell, American consul in Isla del Carmen, Campeche, accomplished this, arranging for the panel to be shipped to New York and then Washington, DC, where it entered the National Institute for the Promotion of Science and later the Smithsonian Institution. Nonetheless, in 1908 the panel was returned to Mexico's National Museum.[55]

Stephens's books inspired other museums to attempt to acquire Maya sculptures and add to collections already encompassing the ancient Mediterranean, Egypt and Near East, through which they displayed the world and what they perceived as the cultural primacy of the West and modernity. Robert Aguirre has revealed that the participants in a secret British government plot, over the course of fourteen years starting in 1851, tried without success to obtain Maya sculptures for the British Museum in London. In letters from the foreign secretary Lord Palmerston to his chargé d'affaires in Guatemala, Palmerston identified Copan sculptures published by Stephens as potential acquisitions.[56] One letter quoted Stephens's emphasis on sites overgrown with vegetation, and his claim that locals did not appreciate the ruins, as justification for taking the sculptures. Yet Palmerston knew that revealing the plot might doom it, for he stresses the need for secrecy, stating, 'You will be careful therefore that in making any inquiries in pursuance of this instruction you don't lead the people of the country to attach any *imaginary value* to things which they consider at present as *having no value at all*.'[57]

However, claiming that those countries did not care about their antiquities was misleading, for the new nations were trying to build museum collections and protect archaeological sites by passing laws prohibiting their spoliation. For example, in 1827, before Stephens arranged to remove the Palenque panel, Mexico forbade the export of antiquities without approval. In 1845, soon after Stephens purchased Copan and years before the British government investigated taking sculptures, the Honduran government passed a declaration to protect Copan.[58] More legislation followed, yet foreigners continued to remove Maya artefacts.

Nineteenth-century collectors in Mexico also amassed Maya artefacts. The brothers Leandro and José María Camacho, both

Spanish priests, lived in San Francisco de Campeche and collected natural-history specimens and pre-Hispanic artefacts, including Maya figurines from Jaina Island tombs, which they displayed in their own museum. The Campeche writer and newspaper publisher Justo Sierra O'Reilly hoped those collections would join the museum he was trying to establish to support independence efforts, but neither the dream of independence nor that of the museum was fulfilled. The items were ultimately dispersed to other museums, including the National Museum in Mexico City, the Museo Yucateco in Mérida and the Trocadéro Ethnography Museum in Paris.[59] Florentino Gimeno Echevarría, a Spanish merchant living in Campeche, collected thousands of Maya artefacts in the second half of the nineteenth century. He created a private museum and made a detailed catalogue specifying where the pieces were found. He recorded figurines from many locations, including 'Jaina, Bacú, Ysla de Piedra, Uaymil, Tinum, Tekax, Champotón, Ta-chán, Pich, Nilchí, San Felipe, Jonuta, Palizada, Tabasco' and Palenque,[60] thus recognizing the diversity of the figurines' sources in a way that the twentieth-century art market did not. He attempted to sell his collection to museums in the United States, France and Spain, but finally agreed on a price with the Royal Museum for Ethnology (later the Ethnological Museum) in Berlin. Museums in Sweden and the United States ultimately acquired some of the pieces through exchanges with the Berlin museum.

The Frenchman Claude-Joseph-Désiré Charnay, best known for his innovative field photography and sculptural casts, also built a collection during his journeys to Maya and Zapotec sites in Chiapas, Yucatan and Oaxaca. In his expedition of 1858, he used a collodion or wet-plate camera that required substantial equipment and a quick succession of steps, including preparing and processing large glass plates in a darkroom (or tent); although cumbersome in the field, it was an improvement on the daguerreotype technique, both in quality of image and in the ability to print directly from negatives. These were published in Charnay's *Cités et ruines américaines* (American Cities and Ruins) of 1863. In the early 1880s Charnay used dry-plate technology, which required less equipment, and a printing process that allowed mass reproduction while maintaining fidelity to the original.[61] These innovations allowed his photographs to be distributed more widely. But his collections, destined for export to France, ultimately inspired vociferous debate in Mexico's congress regarding the export of artefacts.

*Cités et ruines américaines* contained several texts and included claims for transoceanic connections and diffusion. In his short preface, Charnay was non-committal, mentioning that Maya cities and monuments resemble those of other cultures but leaving open the question of influence, asking, 'Must we conclude that these resemblances are the result of the exclusive action of ancient civilizations and renounce the hypothesis of an original American race? The history and origin of these people offer only a vast field of hypotheses.'[62] However, in the same publication, the architect Eugène-Emmanuel Viollet-le-Duc argued polemically that Aryans built the Maya cities. He named the Toltecs culture bearers, but they were Aryan Toltecs, thus shifting agency to a mythical group of white people who traversed the world spreading advanced civilization, their ethnicity matching that of the majority of the United States at the time.[63] Charnay clarified his own views in subsequent books, and in 1880 he asserted that the Toltecs were responsible for archaeological sites throughout North and Central America.[64] However, the anthropologist Daniel Brinton argued in 1887 that Charnay and others were misreading Central Mexican documents, and that the stories of the Toltecs verged on myth or legend, exaggerated by the Mexica in order to elevate their own status.[65] Nonetheless, the Toltecs hold their place, even today.

Speculations about Atlantis also persisted. The French cleric and historian Charles-Étienne Brasseur de Bourbourg pursued Mesoamerican civilizations by travelling in Mexico and Central America and studying Kingsborough's volumes of pre-Hispanic and sixteenth-century documents, among other publications. He found both the *Popol Vuh* and the compilation of documents now known as Landa's *Relación*, publishing them in 1861 and 1864 respectively.[66] Like Kingsborough and others, he argued for transoceanic contact, but, contrary to them, he saw the origins of civilization in the Maya world and its subsequent diffusion to Egypt and Europe, countering understandings of civilization deriving from the Old World. Later in his career, he promoted diffusion from Atlantis, a mythic continent first imagined by Plato.[67] Brasseur built such arguments by claiming similarities among cultures in the Mediterranean, Mesoamerica and Asia, and by comparing stories of devastating floods, arguing, for example, that the flood portrayed in the *Troano Codex* – part of the *Madrid Codex* – depicted a real flood and was evidence that the Maya and others had experienced the flooding of Atlantis.[68] However, the images on page 32a of the *Madrid Codex* and page 74 (54) of the *Dresden Codex* refer to a flood in mythological time and do not constitute a historic reference to Atlantis.[69]

The American historian Hubert Howe Bancroft challenged Brasseur in his lifetime,[70] but other writers, including Augustus Le Plongeon, a French-American photographer and writer, celebrated

Alice Le Plongeon, Augustus Le Plongeon with Maya men and chacmool, Chichen Itza, Yucatan, Mexico, *c.* 1875, photograph.

and pursued his ideas while publishing about ancient Maya sites. Augustus and his British wife, Alice Dixon Le Plongeon, photographed Maya sites in Mexico and conducted excavations at Chichen Itza. Augustus, an infamous self-promoter, experimented with and advanced field photography in Yucatan. He also created romantic images of himself with the chacmool that he uncovered in 1875 in the Platform of the Eagles and Jaguars.[71] He publicized this discovery widely; he and other authors published about it in Mexico and Europe, and the Trocadéro Museum displayed a cast of it. (It was the cast in the Trocadéro that the British sculptor Henry Moore used as inspiration for his *Reclining Figure* of 1929; the piece drew on and transformed the chacmool form, which became a recurring sculptural form throughout his career.[72]) But ownership of the chacmool was soon contested, as Le Plongeon and both regional and federal governments claimed it.

The Le Plongeons spread their predecessors' transoceanic diffusion speculations and developed new ones, using alleged pictorial, architectural and linguistic evidence to argue for similarities that they claimed indicated transoceanic connections, including triangular arches in the architecture of the Maya, Chaldea, Egypt and Greece.[73] Augustus also argued for similarities in Egyptian and Maya writing, comparing them in tables that juxtaposed 'Maya Hieratic Alphabet according to mural inscriptions' with the 'Egyptian Hieratic Alphabet', but the alleged Maya letters do not correspond to Maya writing.[74] He massaged these supposed similarities into a story about the origins of world civilizations, arguing that Maya colonists spread civilization by journeying to other places, including Egypt. He thus claimed primacy for the Maya as the origin of advanced civilization, concluding that the writing, as well as 'cosmogonical conceptions, so widely spread, originated with the Mayas, and were communicated by them to all the other nations among which we find their name'.[75] The assertion of primacy of the Maya in world civilizations was personally relevant to him, for he and Alice maintained that they were reincarnated Maya royalty, Queen Moo and her husband, Prince Coh – or Chac Mool – thus promoting the ancient Maya for their own self-aggrandizement.[76]

Augustus Le Plongeon also argued that the Maya and Egyptians participated in Freemasonry, and that Central America was its birthplace.[77] He wrote:

> I will endeavor to show you that the ancient sacred mysteries, the origin of Free Masonry consequently, date back from a period far more remote than the most sanguine students of its history ever imagined. I will try to trace their origin, step by step, to this continent which we inhabit, – to America – from where Maya colonists transported their ancient religions and ceremonies, not only to the banks of the Nile, but to those of the Euphrates, and the shores of the Indian Ocean, not less than 11,500 years ago.[78]

Le Plongeon of course shared Freemasonry with many Mexican men, for it had been common in Mexican political circles for decades, both during the War of Independence and after, when the Freemason lodges were important political forces.[79]

The scholarly community responded to the Le Plongeons with both indifference and resistance, and some publishers rejected their manuscripts, but the couple also gained many disciples. Regarding *Sacred Mysteries*, Augustus acknowledged that 'two of the most prominent firms in New York have positively refused to publish[,] believing it to be a bad speculation.'[80] Even so, his legacy in more popular literature and pseudo-science is vast, influencing William Scott-Elliot's, Lewis Spence's and James Churchward's later books about lost continents. In *The Story of Atlantis* (1896), the theosophist Scott-Elliot quoted Augustus Le Plongeon, repeating the claim that 'One-third of this tongue (the Maya) is pure Greek,' although this is untrue.[81] He also drew on earlier diffusion conjecture, extolling the 'Toltec race' that 'ruled the whole continent of Atlantis for thousands of years in great material power and glory', and asserting that 'hundreds of thousands of years later we find one of their remote family races ruling magnificently in Mexico and Peru.' But new were his claims that 'astral clairvoyance' could be used to study history, that Atlantean peoples possessed 'psychic attributes', and that 'the most advanced had undergone the necessary training in the occult schools' (another evocation of Freemasonry).[82] Speculation about transoceanic diffusion has been disproved time and again, but it endures in some circles.

## Archaeology, exploration and national museums

The second half of the nineteenth century brought increased activity in museums and exploration in Mexico and Guatemala, but progress came in fits and starts as governments and ideologies changed repeatedly. Benito Juárez, a Zapotec lawyer from Oaxaca, was Mexico's first Indigenous president, serving before and after the French Intervention. He supported Mexico's National Museum during his presidency by increasing its budget, and his regime advanced the professionalization of archaeology by prohibiting excavations without a permit.[83] His first term was cut short when he was forced into exile by French forces and the Austrian Archduke Maximilian, of the house of Habsburg, was installed as emperor of Mexico for the Second Mexican Empire (1864–7), although Juárez returned to power after the expulsion of the French.

During the French occupation, the French Scientific Commission organized expeditions to document more of Mexico's natural and cultural resources, including archaeology, botany and other sciences, emulating expeditions to Egypt under Napoleon. In 1866 the national museum collections were moved to the old mint on Calle Moneda and renamed the Public Museum of Natural History, Archaeology and History.[84] The occupying regime also planned to participate in the 1867 Exposition Universelle in Paris, with a pavilion designed to look like a pre-Hispanic temple and holding objects collected by the commission. The amateur archaeologist Léon Méhédin designed the fair building, using drawings, photos and casts of the Feathered Serpent temple from Xochicalco, Morelos, as inspiration.[85] The base of the building copied the Xochicalco temple, but Méhédin's superstructure added elements from Maya and Aztec cultures, including Chichen Itza-style serpent columns and copies of the Aztec Calendar Stone and Coatlicue sculpture. But, because of discord between Méhédin and the Scientific Commission, the pavilion did not exhibit the zoological, mineralogical, geological and botanical samples and casts of ancient sculptures that the commission had compiled. Instead, Méhédin displayed photographs and casts that he had acquired in Mexico and Egypt.[86] The display thus changed from an embodiment of empire to the presentation of one explorer's interests. Still, the pavilion, which was set amid other fair buildings that emulated structures from Egypt, China, Rome and elsewhere, allowed Parisians to visit the world, conjuring both travel and France's colonial history. Yet Maximilian's execution in June 1867 must have cast a pall over the pavilion.

In Yucatan, endeavours to honour and preserve ancient Maya materials accompanied efforts to establish regional identity and support independence movements. As the historian Arturo Taracena Arriola has discussed, in the 1840s Sierra O'Reilly promoted the establishment of a museum in Campeche to aid in the search for historical memory and the formation of regional identity by emphasizing Yucatan's ancient Maya heritage and colonial transformation.[87] These ideas were disseminated in newspaper articles, particularly in the journal *Museo Yucateco*, founded by Sierra O'Reilly, about the glories of the Maya past, including Chichen Itza and Uxmal architecture. Also expressed was the desire to create a museum and preserve Maya objects, citing existing collections in Mérida and Campeche, and arguing for the state to protect them and prevent foreigners from removing items. However, accompanying this praise for the ancient Maya was bias against contemporary Maya people, and some people explained their perception of the contrast between ancient and contemporary Maya with yet more diffusion speculation. For one, the Austrian Emanuel von Friedrichsthal, who was the first to take daguerreotypes at Uxmal and Chichen Itza, wrote in 1841 that Palenque was built by people appearing to be Caucasian in race who, coming from the north, had enslaved the people who were already there, from whom the contemporary Maya people descended. As elsewhere, such stories dissociated contemporary Maya people from the legacy of their ancestors, and connected them with other populations. Regardless, neither the museum nor independence was achieved following the outbreak in 1847 of the Caste Wars, in which many Maya people rose up against the oppressive powers that had been enslaving and harming them.[88]

In the 1860s leading citizens in Yucatan renewed efforts to create a museum and protect Maya ruins. As Lynneth Lowe and Adam Sellen recount, Crescencio Carrillo y Ancona, a Catholic priest who wrote about the importance of studying the archaeology of the Yucatan Peninsula, proposed creating a museum in Mérida in 1861. He later communicated with Emperor Maximilian and his wife, Carlota, about the protection of ruins in Yucatan, leading in 1866 to an imperial decree establishing the Museo Yucateco in Mérida. However, the Second Empire fell, Maximilian was executed and the French were expelled; no museum materialized. But, after the French fled Mexico, Carrillo y Ancona persisted and in 1871 opened the Museo Yucateco, whose mission was to value, conserve and protect the natural, historic and archaeological patrimony. It was founded partially with his collection, which included a Maya censer from Cozumel that he had received from Augustus and Alice Le Plongeon. He also asked for donations to the collections, and began to collect natural-history specimens and Maya artefacts.[89]

In Central Mexico during Porfirio Díaz's reign (1877–80, 1884–1911), learned nationalists promoted the pre-Hispanic past in Mexico's national museum and beyond. In these years the museum was reorganized, and there were efforts to research, publish and display pre-Hispanic monuments. They worked on cataloguing the collection, and in 1877 commenced publication of the *Anales del Museo Mexicano*, which produced in-depth publications of pre-Hispanic monuments. In 1887 the Gallery of Monoliths was opened, where they displayed impressive, large stone monuments.[90] Inspired by congressional debates, particularly those regarding Charnay's collections, the central government also took steps to stem foreign collecting. In 1885 the General Inspectorate of Archaeological Monuments of the Republic was established (the predecessor of the National Institute of Anthropology and History), headed by the archaeologist Leopoldo Batres. Furthermore, Mexico enacted stricter laws relating to archaeological sites, including the 1897 Law on Archaeological

María I. Vidal, Gallery of Monoliths, Museo Nacional, Mexico City, *c.* 1925, photograph. Note Chichen Itza chacmool in right foreground, amid many Aztec and Teotihuacan stone sculptures.

Monuments, which stated that such monuments were the property of the nation, challenging the contemporaneous trend towards the privatization of land.[91]

During the Porfiriato, the National Museum also acquired important pieces, including Maya monuments, from other parts of Mexico. One major acquisition was the chacmool from Chichen Itza that Augustus Le Plongeon had excavated, but not before a colourful and contested journey. Le Plongeon had hoped to send it to the Centennial International Exposition in Philadelphia (scheduled for 1876), but the then Mexican president, Sebastián Lerdo de Tejada, prevented its export. Angry that Mexico was trying to take the sculpture from him, Le Plongeon transferred it to Piste in an attempt to hide it. In 1875 officials of the Museo Yucateco ordered its retrieval – by an armed military force in case of resistance. The chacmool was conveyed to Mérida with much pomp and circumstance, carried in an open carriage and accompanied by a parade with a military band. Despite this triumphal celebration, or perhaps because of it, the chacmool was soon transferred to Mexico's

National Museum, for the new (and brief) governor of Yucatan, Agustín del Río, pressurized by Mexico City, sent it as a gift to Díaz, who had just become president after overthrowing Lerdo de Tejada. Juan Peón Contreras, second director of the Museo Yucateco, was none too pleased, calling the transfer a *despojo* (dispossession).[92] Both he and Le Plongeon mourned the loss of the sculpture. The Mexican National Museum's appropriation of the chacmool brought the Maya into the national spotlight, although the Aztecs remained the primary focus, both in the National Museum and in the national narrative.[93]

The National Museum also acquired the sanctuary tablet from the Palenque Temple of the Cross, but this happened in several steps because the tablet's three panels experienced distinct trajectories. The Smithsonian in Washington, DC, possessed the right panel, removed from Palenque at Stephens's request in 1842, but the central and left panels remained at the site. As the historian Christina Bueno recounts, the National Museum retrieved the central panel in 1884, first to make a plaster copy for the International Exposition in New Orleans. Decades later, in 1908, the United States repatriated the right panel, inspiring Batres to retrieve the left one in an expedition in 1909. After having been

Agustín Víctor Casasola, Porfirio Díaz in front of the reunited Temple of the Cross sanctuary tablet at the Museo Nacional, Mexico City, *c*. 1910, photograph.

separated for almost seventy years, the three parts were reunited in the National Museum, just in time for the centennial of the Mexican Revolution in 1910. Displaying pieces from several cultures of Mexico in the Gallery of Monoliths presented both a synthesis of the nation and its political centralization, emphasizing its power over diverse regions.[94]

Mexico also capitalized on its pre-Hispanic past when presenting itself on the world stage. For the 1889 Exposition Universelle in Paris, the Mexican government sponsored a pavilion designed by the Mexican architect Antonio Anza and the archaeologist Antonio Peñafiel, who were working for Díaz and the 'wizards of progress'. The exterior of the 'Aztec Palace', at the base of the Eiffel Tower, partially emulated the Xochicalco temple (and the pavilion from the 1867 fair), but the pre-Hispanic references were more eclectic, peppered with Teotihuacan, Aztec, Zapotec and Toltec motifs from Central Mexico and Oaxaca, Díaz's homeland. Classicized relief sculptures of Aztec emperors punctuated the exterior, providing an image of the Mexican republic arising from Indigenous rulers. The interior was modern, with iron staircases, glass skylights and marble ornaments;[95] it contained archaeology, anthropology and natural history exhibits, and emphasized Mexico's engagement with science. According to the historian Mauricio Tenorio-Trillo, the organizers promoted the pre-Hispanic past as civilized and heroic, and acknowledged Mexico's economic and natural resources, cosmopolitanism and modernity as part of a strategy to attract foreign investors and European immigrants.[96] But this emphasis on the heroism of the pre-Hispanic past contrasted with the fair's presentation of contemporary Indigenous people, for the fair inaugurated 'ethnographic villages', where Native people from around the world performed daily routines while visitors watched, thus establishing difference between them and their observers.[97] Tenorio-Trillo argues that the juxtaposition of Mexico's Indigenous past with exemplars of modern industry and science presented contemporary Indigenous people as backward and classified within an anthropological frame.[98]

For Mexico's participation in the Historic-American Exhibition in Madrid in 1892, which celebrated the fourth centenary of

Columbus's arrival in the Americas, the organizing committee (called the Junta Colombina de México) intentionally included objects from several pre-Hispanic cultures in Mexico. The *junta*, which included the Mexican archaeologist and poet Alfredo Chavero, the Museo Nacional director Francisco del Paso y Troncoso and the historian Joaquín García Icazbalceta, displayed antiquities, casts of monuments, photographs of archaeological sites and copies of codices. They organized collecting expeditions across the nation, producing – they claimed – a synopsis of Mexican cultures, including Nahua, Zapotec, Mixtec and Maya.[99] Among the objects displayed were the middle panel of the Palenque Tablet of the Cross and the 'Relieves de Chiapas' (Chiapas Reliefs) from the National Museum, but the latter were in fact forgeries whose images were collages of Maya, Aztec and Mixtec designs or altogether fanciful invention. The committee fell prey to the forgeries in part because, at the time, few people knew much about the conventions of ancient Maya art – the flip side of Humboldt not recognizing authentic Maya pieces. Forgeries notwithstanding, displaying the works in an exposition that presented various cultures from across Mexico symbolized Mexican national power.

In the same years, Guatemala also pursued continued explorations of archaeological sites and the creation of a national museum. As Chinchilla Mazariegos describes, the Guatemalan politician Manuel García Elgueta unskilfully excavated sites in the western highlands in the 1880s and '90s. He collected from Chalchitan objects that were shown at the 1893 World's Columbian Exposition in Chicago, but they did not return to Guatemala, going instead to overseas collections including the California Academy of Sciences in San Francisco. The perception of sites such as Iximche' in the western highlands as ancestral places for contemporary Maya people was more apparent, for they were occupied when Spaniards arrived, but García Elgueta and others believed the Maya had been reduced by the conquest. In his work in archaeology and language study, García Elgueta endeavoured to learn more about and valorize the Maya past to inspire contemporary Maya people.[100] Guatemala also responded to foreign museums' removal of monuments by issuing laws in 1893 'that entrusted the protection of archaeological remains to the government'.[101] The National Museum, which encompassed history, ethnography, archaeology, zoology and mineralogy, opened in 1866 but closed in 1881, reopening in 1898. As in other regions, the story of the museum is not one of steady growth.

At the end of the century other explorers travelled in the Southern Maya Lowlands to document ancient Maya sites, producing essential documentation that aided decipherment and iconographic study. Beginning in 1881, Alfred Percival Maudslay, a British diplomat and photographer, explored Copan, Quirigua, Tikal and Yaxchilan, documenting sites through maps and plans, dry-plate photography and plaster and paper moulds. He sent these to London, where the artist and illustrator Annie Hunter and her sisters used them to make drawings for the magnificent

Adela Breton, copy of polychrome mural from the west wall of the Upper Temple of the Jaguars at Chichen Itza, Yucatan, Mexico, *c.* 1907, paper and watercolour.

volumes of the *Biologia Centrali-Americana*.[102] His photographs were also displayed in late nineteenth-century exhibitions. In addition, Maudslay shipped sculptures from Yaxchilan (which he called Menché Tinamit, before the Austrian explorer Teobert Maler renamed it) to the British Museum, with permission from the Guatemalan authorities.[103] Maudslay also recruited the British artist Adela Breton to be an archaeological illustrator at Maya sites, including Chichen Itza, where she assisted in checking drawings and making copies of murals and reliefs in the Great Ballcourt buildings.[104] Breton strove to render images with correct proportion and colours, and her illustrations are the only surviving record of some deteriorated paintings. Maler, who first went to Mexico with Maximilian's army, travelled across Mexico and Central America visiting and documenting Maya sites, where he undertook dry-plate photography and innovated in the use of artificial lighting.[105] That lighting gives the photographs depth and brings out the detail in complex surfaces, especially those of the intricately carved stelae from Piedras Negras. His high-quality photographs and accompanying descriptions of sculptures, buildings and site layouts, published by Harvard's Peabody Museum, became indispensable sources for later scholarship.[106]

Concurrent with these efforts was significant progress in deciphering Maya calendrical inscriptions and imagery, for which Maudslay's photographs and drawings, the surviving Maya codices and Landa's *Relación* (after its publication in 1864) were critical resources. By 1832 Constantine Samuel Rafinesque-Smaltz had connected the Palenque inscriptions to those in the *Dresden Codex*, worked out the values of the number system's bars and dots, and suggested that contemporary Mayan languages were crucial to deciphering the inscriptions. In the late 1880s Ernst Förstemann of the Royal Library in Dresden used the *Dresden Codex* to figure out basics of the Maya calendar, including the days and months, vigesimal counting, the Long Count and the 260-day *tzolk'in* calendar. The American archaeologist and journalist Joseph Goodman followed by identifying head-variants for numbers and proposing a correlation with the Christian calendar.[107] In 1892 the ethnologist Cyrus Thomas used Landa's *Relación* to propose that Maya writing was phonetic, but Eduard Seler, a prominent German anthropologist (although not a Mayanist), criticized this theory, probably encouraged by the explorer Philipp Valentini, who in 1880 had claimed that Landa's alphabet was a fabrication. Although Thomas was on the right path, he crumpled in the face of that criticism, ultimately denying the phoneticism and setting back decipherment for half a century.[108] Paul Schellhas, a German lawyer and scholar, studied the representations of deities in the Dresden, Madrid and Paris codices, meticulously separating them by visual characteristics into deities named by letters of the alphabet, for example Gods A, B, C, and so on.[109] His method was comparable to that of Seler, who studied Central Mexican and Oaxacan sources, and was fundamental to future iconographic studies, especially those of the contemporary anthropologist Karl Taube, who has updated and surpassed those earlier studies.

During the eighteenth and nineteenth centuries, distant travellers visited Maya sites, making them known far beyond the Maya people who lived near them, and publicizing them in literary gazettes, popular books and academic treatises. Furthermore, researchers made great strides in understanding the ancient Maya civilization and disseminating materials for study. The governments of the newly independent Mexican and Central American nations supported some studies and worked to preserve sites and antiquities, but they competed with explorers seeking material for foreign museums. At the same time that their ancestral monuments gained international fame, Maya people suffered oppression and exploitation, and persistent transoceanic origin speculations continued to divorce them from their ancestral legacy. Even so, the proposal that the contemporary Maya were connected to ancient cities became more self-evident by the end of the century. Indeed, advances in decipherment became essential building blocks for twentieth-century discoveries that established an indisputable connection between the ancient sites and contemporary Maya people.

# FIVE

# REDISCOVERING MAYA HISTORIES IN THE TWENTIETH AND TWENTY-FIRST CENTURIES

Nineteenth-century exploration in the Maya region paved the way for the development of more in-depth research into ancient Maya iconography, epigraphy and archaeology in the twentieth century, nourished by the new disciplines of anthropology and linguistics. These breakthroughs were soon paired with discoveries of tombs with associated inscriptions, which by the end of the twentieth century had inspired research revealing the physical, historical and political histories of Maya kings and queens. Indeed, after more than one hundred years of distracting, irrelevant and ill-formed interpretations, scholars acknowledged that the ancient Maya recorded history and engaged in politics and warfare, on a par with other world civilizations. Yet, at the same time, some archaeologists began to critique the primary emphasis on elite buildings and site centres, and broadened or shifted their approach to consider various levels of Maya society.

Archaeologists also worked with ethnohistorians and ethnographers to integrate archaeological and epigraphic evidence with sources about Maya culture from later periods, in order to connect past and present and to shed light on the past. Conceiving of the Maya across time demonstrated long-term Maya cultural patterns (while also recognizing change), leaving behind the diffusionist narratives that looked to other parts of the world to explain the ancient Maya. Also transformative has been an increase in archaeologists from Latin American countries who have initiated new projects. In addition, communities near archaeological sites have become more involved in archaeology and collaborations for sustainable tourism and other economic opportunities. Furthermore, online publications have augmented the dissemination of knowledge, allowing the increased democratization and internationalization of Maya studies, previously the domain primarily of elite institutions.

## Early twentieth-century archaeology in the Maya world

At the beginning of the twentieth century, some archaeological methods and techniques, as practised in the Maya area, still belonged in the realm of the amateur, but there was a shift in the first half of the century towards scientific archaeology and professional excavation and documentation. Furthermore, the elaboration of anthropological theories shaped more research projects, and institutions in both Mexico and the United States, including Mexico's National Institute of Anthropology and History (INAH) after its foundation in 1939, supported integrating archaeology with ethnology and linguistics. Indeed, Mexico focused more attention on archaeology and anthropology after the Revolution as part of a larger national project that placed increased value on the pre-Hispanic past. Archaeologists working in Mexico in the first half of the twentieth century included Mexicans and foreigners, at times in collaboration. North American universities and other institutions generally conducted projects in Honduras and Guatemala, and British and U.S. archaeologists carried out the few projects in Belize (then British Honduras).

One goal of several projects was to collect material for museums, including artefacts and moulds of sculptures, continuing the efforts of the previous generation of explorers. In 1891 the Harvard Peabody Museum mounted a project to study Copan. The team convinced Alfred Maudslay to return for more documentation, and he urged them to study the Hieroglyphic Stairway, the longest extant Maya inscription. The stairway's lowest fifteen steps were in situ, but the remainder had become dislodged and were in disarray. The researchers cleaned, photographed and made moulds of

Honduran government representative Don Carlos Madrid stands next to a sculpted ruler from the Hieroglyphic Stairway, Copan, Honduras, c. 1900.

the blocks, but because they did not have a good understanding of the inscriptions, many blocks ended up out of order. Nevertheless, these detailed photographs and moulds proved invaluable in later years for understanding Maya writing and sculptors' styles.[1]

Other contemporaneous projects left behind gouged buildings and exposed monuments. Between 1896 and 1936 Thomas Gann, an Irish medical doctor stationed in British Honduras, excavated at Santa Rita, Nohmul, Wild Cane Cay and elsewhere, and collected objects that he sold and donated to the British Museum. Gann made some important discoveries, such as the Postclassic murals at Santa Rita, but his excavations – some of which used dynamite to blast holes in mounds – did not align with updated archaeological techniques and were at times destructive.[2]

The archaeologist Edward Herbert Thompson, although inspired by stories of Atlantis and more, performed solid work with Maudslay and others, and assisted in creating the famed architectural casts for the 1893 World's Columbian Exposition in Chicago. At Chichen Itza, he was inspired by Landa's recently rediscovered manuscript to search the Sacred Cenote, a natural sinkhole filled with water that was an important offering locale during Chichen Itza's florescence and later. Landa had written: 'They also threw in many other offerings of precious stones and things they valued greatly; so if there were gold in this country, this well would have received most of it, so devout were the Indians in this.'[3] Supported by his patron Charles Pickering Bowditch through the Peabody Museum, Thompson secured a machine to dredge the cenote from 1904 to 1910, finding artefacts in great numbers, without recording the deposition layers. He defied the Mexican government by removing those artefacts from Mexico without permission, sending troves of materials to Cambridge stashed in the suitcases of visitors and colleagues, including Alfred Tozzer of Harvard University, who travelled with cenote jades sewn into his waistcoat.[4]

Harvard archaeologists also participated in the International School of American Archaeology and Ethnology in Mexico City. The school was founded in 1910 as an international collaboration of scholars from Mexico, Prussia and the United States. The directorship rotated among the countries and institutions and included Eduard Seler, Franz Boas, Jorge Engerrand and Manuel Gamio. Boas stated that it was essential for the institution to be in Mexico, to incorporate living peoples, to publish and retain collections in Mexico and to support Mexican students and send them abroad for study. Despite its initial success, the institution was suspended in 1914 because of the Mexican Revolution, and was not revived.[5] Today one might wish to see such international collaboration

– especially when juxtaposed with a rogue operator like Edward Thompson – as a sign of things to come, but it made little impact at the time.

One director of the International School was Tozzer, an anthropologist, linguist and archaeologist from Harvard University, who offered new ideas and methods for archaeology in the Americas. Tozzer studied Mayan languages and applied himself to comparing the colonial and contemporary Maya, especially in his tomes on the Lacandon Maya and Landa's *Relación*. He also worked as an archaeologist in Yucatan and Peten, and promoted the integration of ethnology, archaeology and linguistics.[6] As a professor at Harvard he taught Alfred Kidder, Sylvanus Griswold Morley and others who further developed archaeological methodologies grounded in anthropology for the Maya area. Raymond Merwin, another of Tozzer's graduate students, performed the first stratigraphic excavation of a Maya building, at Holmul in 1911.[7] In Building B Group 2, Merwin opened burials ranging from the Preclassic to the Late or Terminal Classic, revealing an extraordinary array of ceramics in careful stratigraphy. He died before finishing the report, but it was finished by another Harvard student, George Vaillant, and yielded a lasting model for the study of Maya archaeological ceramics.[8]

One Mexican anthropologist who was crucial to the International School was Gamio, who had studied with Boas at Columbia University and researched at Teotihuacan in the 1910s and subsequently at Chichen Itza and Kaminaljuyu. Gamio framed his research within anthropological theory and envisioned his work as part of revolutionary changes in Mexico, with the ideal of valorizing Mexico's Indigenous past and present and instituting constitutional reform to improve the conditions of contemporary Indigenous people.[9]

## Iconography and aesthetics

The publication of Maudslay's and Teobert Maler's photographs and drawings of Maya monuments made additional materials available for the study of Maya inscriptions and imagery in the early twentieth century. Herbert Spinden, in his dissertation at

Harvard in 1909 (also under Tozzer's direction) and his *A Study of Maya Art: Its Subject Matter and Historical Development* (1913), was the first to focus on Maya imagery across media, including codices and monuments. In the latter – a wide-ranging study – and later publications, Spinden addressed religious content, identifying Maya gods and symbols, and historical material, suggesting that Maya sculptures portrayed human rulers accompanied by inscriptions comprising 'memorials of conquest'.[10] He was right; but without confirmation from the still-undeciphered inscriptions, those interpretations were dismissed.[11] Nonetheless, Spinden's legacy still advanced iconographic and art-historical studies.

The English art critic Roger Fry, working solely from photographs and materials in the British Museum, concentrated on form and aesthetics in evaluating ancient Maya sculpture. In 1918, in an essay on American archaeology, Fry encouraged looking at ancient American objects 'seriously as works of art' of aesthetic interest.[12] His approach aligns with a trend towards the aestheticization of pre-Columbian art promoted by collectors, curators and modern artists in the first decades of the twentieth century.[13] Fry also expounded his perception of the superiority of Maya art and civilization, particularly over the Aztecs, comparing this difference to that between Greek and Roman art, perceiving Greek art to be of higher aesthetic value than Roman art.[14] Such comparisons resonated with nineteenth-century writings comparing Maya and Greek art and claiming the Maya and Greeks shared a common origin in Atlantis.

Morley, an explorer, archaeologist and epigrapher whose work had a profound effect on Maya studies, popularized such aesthetic judgement and comparison of the Maya and Greeks. Morley was an unapologetic Maya booster, seeing in the seeming realism of Maya art, and the complexity of Maya writing, a tradition that could be likened to that of fifth-century BCE Greeks. Defeated in his attempts to crack Maya writing, he turned to the aesthetic qualities of Maya art and the intricacies of Maya writing and calendars. He compared Maya sculptors to the famed Greek sculptors Phidias and Praxiteles, called the Maya a 'highly gifted people, not inaptly called "the Greeks of the New World"', and wrote that they had 'the only system of writing in the New World worthy of comparison' with Old World writing systems.[15] Nonetheless, Morley rejected speculation that the Maya descended from the Israelites, Egyptians or another Old World civilization. Calling the Maya '100% American', he stated definitively that 'Maya culture owes nothing to Old World inspiration.'[16]

Morley also continued in the vein of Maudslay's and Maler's endeavours at documentation, but he was especially interested in probing chronology and the calendar. In *Inscriptions at Copan* (1920) and *Inscriptions of Peten* (1937–8), he compiled and deciphered numerous calendrical inscriptions that were crucial to understanding chronologies, often failing even to make note of additional texts. Morley assumed that the rest of the inscriptions also dealt with the passage of time, a conclusion that fostered the idea that the Maya were a peaceful theocracy focused solely on tracking time. Although early in his career, in 1915, he believed that the Maya inscriptions were fundamentally historical, after continuing decipherment recognized only calendrical and astronomical texts he wrote in 1922 that, as far as had been deciphered, there is 'little or no historical matter in Maya writings'.[17] Such commentary aligned with that of Eric Thompson, who worked at Chichen Itza under Morley and later for the Chicago Natural History Museum, the Carnegie Institution of Washington and the British Museum. In 1932 Thompson wrote, 'I feel convinced that no civil events were recorded [on Maya stelae]', and for decades he maintained that the singular purpose of Maya sculptures was to track time, part of a culture of peaceful calendar priests focused on predicting astronomical phenomena.[18] Morley's stance was less dogmatic, for although he saw no evidence for the recording of history on monumental stone sculptures, he thought that the Maya must have recorded history in other media such as books, which did not survive from the Classic period. The power of these respected, institutionally supported scholars strongly influenced Maya studies for decades, limiting the interpretation of historical content in ancient Maya inscriptions or imagery.[19]

## Institutional Period

Morley also played a fundamental role in what archaeologists call the 'Institutional Period' of 1925–60 (or 1925–70), in which major North American institutions sponsored large, multi-year archaeological projects in the Maya area. In this period, countries in the Maya region also established or reorganized institutions for protecting and administering their archaeological, ethnological and historical resources: Mexico in 1939, Guatemala in 1946, Honduras in 1952 and Belize (then British Honduras) in 1955.[20] There were also shifts towards more systematic studies, mapping and stratigraphic excavations using new techniques and grounding in anthropology and the continuing integration of linguistics and ethnology. However, the archaeologists Jason Yaeger and Greg Borgstede observe that 'contemporary Maya people remained largely excluded from most components of archaeological practice, save as labour during fieldwork or as objects of analogical reasoning in interpretations of archaeological data.'[21]

From 1926 to 1930 the British Museum sponsored excavations by trained archaeologists in Southern Belize, but one purpose was to recover artefacts for the museum, a practice that came under criticism. Indeed, the British Museum was possibly one of the unnamed institutions to which Kidder referred when in 1932 he decried museums conducting excavations to obtain material, calling them 'collecting agencies rather than scientific laboratories' and accusing them of looting and destruction.[22]

The most influential u.s. institution for archaeology and anthropology was the Carnegie Institution of Washington, particularly the Division of Historical Research. Kidder was chairman of the Division from 1930 to 1950, and Morley was one of its most prolific researchers. The Carnegie funded large projects across the Maya region, notably at Chichen Itza, Tulum and Mayapan in Mexico, and at Uaxactun and Kaminaljuyu in Guatemala, and supported Morley's research documenting inscriptions. Also critical, in addition to the projects' integration of archaeology, linguistics, ethnology and ethnohistory, was the emphasis on stratigraphy and typological analysis to probe chronology and compare findings across the Maya region.[23]

Two archaeological teams – a Carnegie project led by Morley and a Mexican government project led by José Reygadas Vértiz and later Eduardo Martínez Cantón – worked alongside one another at Chichen Itza in the 1920s and '30s. Morley's project focused on the excavation and reconstruction of major buildings, principally the Temple of the Warriors, the Caracol and the Mercado, in an attempt to discern how Chichen Itza differed from Maya cities in the Southern Lowlands. The Mexican team focused primarily on the cleaning, consolidation and reconstruction of the Castillo, Great Ballcourt and other structures on the Great Terrace. Gamio played a critical role in the Mexican project and recruited the archaeologist and artist Miguel Ángel Fernández, who took careful measurements and made drawings in preparation for architectural consolidation and reconstruction, particularly of the Ballcourt.[24]

Both teams carried out reconstructions of buildings to support tourism, but for different reasons. The art historian James Oles observes that the socialist government in Yucatan in the early 1920s imagined that reconstructing architecture could build pride for local Maya people, and that the resulting tourism would economically benefit Yucatan more broadly. In contrast, the ethnographer Quetzil Castañeda writes that the Carnegie reconstructions were designed to encourage tourism, with the hope that this would help archaeology by arousing public interest.[25] The result was ancient Maya buildings that were completely rebuilt in the twentieth century, framing the way we understand those buildings today and reducing opportunities for later research on them.

While working at Chichen Itza, Morley met rebel Maya leaders who held considerable power in the region after the Caste Wars. The anthropologist Paul Sullivan describes the visit in December 1935 of a delegation of Maya officers. Preceded by a letter from Pedro Pascual Barrera (Patron of the Cross of Xcacal Guardia, one of the venerated talking crosses) that announced their imminent arrival, the Maya delegation walked around Chichen Itza with Carnegie archaeologists. Their recorded comments shed light on the Maya leaders' assessment of the significance of the place. For example, they perceived the acoustical effects of the reconstructed Great Ballcourt, which produces echoes when one speaks or shouts, as evidence of the continued presence of the souls of the old inhabitants, their ancestors, with whom they were communicating. They also spoke about the ruins in relation to their continued fight for autonomy, stating that the site's great feathered serpents, sculpted in stone, would rise up and create war if they did not defend their people from foreign encroachment.[26] This belief in the power and animacy of the sculptures and in the site's connection to their own goals of cultural and political autonomy is crucial to understanding their perceptions of this ancient city.

Hermann Beyer of the Carnegie team studied the Chichen Itza inscriptions, making the first systematic study of a single site's inscriptions, compared to a focus only on calendrical inscriptions. Using structural analysis, he noticed repetitions of series of signs, including one pattern that appeared at Chichen Itza and neighbouring sites. Although Beyer was not able to explain it, he had a hunch that these were historical. However, Beyer's life took a dramatic turn when he returned to Germany to serve in Hitler's army; he died while a u.s. prisoner of war in Oklahoma in 1942.[27] Later scholars would demonstrate that through his structural analysis he had found the name of a historical Maya ruler.

Contemporaneous with the Chichen Itza research, the Carnegie launched a project at Uaxactun, at the time a very remote location, from 1924 to 1937. The Carnegie announced the discovery of the site in 1916, naming it Uaxactun – *Uaxac* = 8; *tun* = stone or year – because they found a stela with a Cycle 8 Long Count date, and as a pun on Washington, the home city of their institution.[28] Notable work was done on architecture, showing the development from Preclassic houses to Early and Late Classic monumental structures, and in the chronological study of ceramics; both types of research offered essential comparisons for other sites. However, the research team's removal of later architectural phases to reveal earlier ones destroyed many buildings, including those in the A-V complex, an approach that would not be allowed today. The prevalence of Harvard graduates in the Uaxactun project influenced Maya archaeology in the long term, because the archaeologists were trained in similar ways and believed they were correct in their strategy.[29] But other people participated in these projects too.

In 1937 the Guatemalan artist Antonio Tejeda, part of the Carnegie team, made a copy of the mural in Structure B-XIII that became an essential record of that critical painting, which was destroyed after its excavation. Tejeda later worked for the Carnegie in Mexico to make copies of the Bonampak murals after their discovery in 1946.

Other important research took place in highland Guatemala and contributed to revising understanding of Mesoamerican chronologies. Most archaeology in Guatemala at this time was done by archaeologists from the United States,[30] but Gamio conducted stratigraphic excavations in the Finca Miraflores sector of Kaminaljuyu in 1925 because he wanted to compare Guatemala's Archaic and Preclassic periods with Formative materials in the Valley of Mexico. This international approach to research was essential in noticing larger patterns of migration and cross-cultural exchange. Kidder and Oliver Ricketson excavated at Kaminaljuyu in the subsequent decade, studying Preclassic and Early Classic monumental architecture. They uncovered tombs holding Teotihuacan-style vessels, leading them to recognize Early Classic connections with Teotihuacan. The international approach of both projects allowed them to reconceive Mesoamerican chronology, the study of which was then limited (before the use of radiocarbon dating). Gamio was able to conclude that Teotihuacan was older than had previously been thought, and the Kaminaljuyu research proved that the Early Classic Maya and Teotihuacan were contemporaneous, resulting in the conclusion that the historical Toltecs could not have built Teotihuacan. This opened the door for support of proposals relating to Tula, Hidalgo, having been the centre of the legendary Toltecs lauded by the Mexica.[31]

Both Mexican and U.S. institutions also conducted surveys and excavation of Postclassic sites in the Yucatan Peninsula, in both Quintana Roo – where exploration had been restricted in earlier decades because of political unrest – and Yucatan. Under the direction of César Lizardi Ramos, the Mexican Scientific Expedition explored Postclassic sites in Quintana Roo in the 1930s, surveying the architecture of coastal sites and conducting excavations and architectural restoration in Tulum, now a popular tourist site because of its proximity to Cancun.[32] Archaeologists of the

Carnegie and the Middle American Research Institute at Tulane University also focused on the Northern Lowlands. A significant aspect of those studies was their integration of ethnohistory and archaeology; notably, they also expanded archaeological knowledge of areas beyond Chichen Itza and other oft-studied places.[33]

North American universities also sponsored large excavation projects in Guatemala and Belize during this period. The University of Pennsylvania Museum of Archaeology and Anthropology (now called the Penn Museum) organized projects at Piedras Negras in the 1930s; at Caracol in the 1950s; and at Tikal in the 1950s and '60s. The Piedras Negras project encompassed mapping, the documentation of sculptures and architecture, and excavations in large buildings that held tombs. The museum's later work at Caracol focused on investigating the site's stone sculptures and publishing photographs and drawings of them, a significant resource for studying their images and inscriptions. The museum also removed sculptures from Piedras Negras and Caracol for display in the Penn Museum and Guatemala's National Museum. Most of the Piedras Negras monuments sent to Philadelphia were later returned to Guatemala, but some Piedras Negras and Caracol sculptures remain in the Penn Museum.

## Overturning theories of the 'peaceful Maya'

In the mid-twentieth century two especially thrilling revelations from Chiapas contributed to changing understanding of the ancient Maya. One was the exposure of the Bonampak murals in the Selva Lacandona. In 1946 Chan Bor, a Lacandon leader, led the Americans John Bourne and Carlos Frey to a small site. When Chan Bor brought the American archaeologist Giles Healey to the same place later that year, they followed a deer and encountered the astonishing polychrome painted murals in a small building on a terraced hillside. Tejeda made sketches of the murals in 1946, and later both Tejeda and the Mexican artist Agustín Villagra created full-scale copies, which allowed them to be disseminated in full colour. (The Guatemalan-Mexican painter Rina Lazo Wasem, who had worked with Diego Rivera, also made copies in 1966, and they remain on view in a reproduction of Structure 1 at Mexico's National Museum of Anthropology. In 2001 Heather Hurst and Leonard Ashby created yet another copy, informed by new research.[34]) Although the historical details of the murals' eighth-century dedication by the Bonampak ruler Yajaw Chan Muwaan were not known at the time, the vivid battle and captive presentation defied notions of the peaceful Maya, as Villagra argued in his book of 1949.[35]

Beginning in 1949, Alberto Ruz Lhuillier led an INAH project at the Palenque Temple of the Inscriptions, with riveting results. His team lifted a stone from the floor of the back room of the sanctuary, revealing a 23-metre-long (75 ft) stairway descending into the depths of the pyramid, ending about 1.8 m (6 ft) below the level of the plaza. It took the team four seasons to clear the rubble-filled stairway, and in 1952 they reached a chamber with a monumental carved sarcophagus. The body inside was covered with jadeite ornaments and a mosaic funerary mask.[36] This was the tomb of the seventh-century ruler K'inich Janaab Pakal, whose name and historical identity would be revealed two decades later. The exposure of an apparently royal tomb in a large pyramid was another critical piece of evidence indicating that many Classic Maya buildings functioned as funerary temples for honoured rulers. These conclusions led the archaeologist Michael Coe to hypothesize that 'authority may have been vested not in a priestly class, but in a line of hereditary rulers who perpetuated themselves in the same manner as the Egyptian kings.'[37] Within a few years, new decipherments had rendered this proposal indisputable.

## Expanding scope and questions

Soon after these revelations, however, significant demands in Maya archaeology arose to expand the nature of research itself. Archaeologists wished to move beyond the elite sector of society to address broader questions and problems. Gordon Willey of Harvard was a major innovator in such transformations, particularly with the excavation of house mounds at Barton Ramie, Belize, in 1953–6, and the Belize Valley Survey, which studied settlement patterns and sought to understand non-elite parts of Maya sites and their larger configurations.[38]

Other projects combined the study of elite monumental architecture with settlement surveys, as did that carried out by the University of Pennsylvania Museum's Tikal Project, which studied the city in various ways from 1956 to 1969. The team explored the expanse of the city, producing a settlement survey and an extensive map of the site and surrounding areas, exploring residential groups away from the centre, and researching reservoirs and other environmental topics. They also analysed major stone sculptures and probed layers of monumental architecture in the Acropolis and elsewhere. There they found major tombs, which allowed the reconstruction of the long-term material history of the site that could subsequently be connected to historical figures from the inscriptions. The long-term plan to create publications addressing several areas of the city included detailed publication of the findings.[39] There were also challenges with the North Acropolis tunnel excavations, for the Tikal Project decided to dismantle the eighth-century phase of Structure 33 (5D–33–1st), leaving only the smaller Early Classic temple (5D–33–2nd) visible; they deposited the material from the removed layer in the large excavation trench that the project had opened in the North Acropolis. These acts were criticized in their day for destroying the archaeological record and this important building.[40]

## Maya art, writing and history

The second half of the twentieth century heralded critical breakthroughs in Maya art, writing and history. In 1952 the Russian linguist Yuri Knorozov published a groundbreaking paper demonstrating that ancient Maya writing was phonetic and syllabic. Working in a library in Russia, Knorozov used a facsimile of the *Dresden Codex* and the syllabary documented by Gaspar Antonio Chi and Diego de Landa to crack the Maya script.[41] Eric Thompson criticized Knorozov's methodology, almost silencing it, but other scholars, notably Michael Coe, lauded his work, and Coe's wife, Sophie, translated the Russian scholarship, allowing it to be disseminated more widely. Knorozov's publication, although not free of errors, was transformative, and inspired other scholars to research phoneticism in Maya writing.

Other progress in decipherment used structural analysis to find patterns in Maya inscriptions. Heinrich Berlin was born in Germany but fled to Mexico in 1935, later entering the National Autonomous University of Mexico (UNAM) to study anthropology. He worked as an archaeologist with Guatemala's Institute of Anthropology and History (IDAEH) and the Carnegie, researching Maya archaeology at Palenque and Tikal.[42] But his most lasting contribution was to epigraphy, particularly his study of 1958 identifying 'Emblem Glyphs', titles connected to Maya polities or kingdoms. Although he could not determine whether they referred to individuals, states, places or tutelary deities, his detection of the pattern furthered research into the historical content of Maya inscriptions. Berlin recognized the import of his discovery, writing that 'the emblems appear to promise to break the wall of the non-calendrical glyphs and open, at the least, investigations into the geographic arrangement' of the ancient Maya world.[43]

Tatiana Proskouriakoff, an artist and architect who was born in Russia but spent most of her life in Pennsylvania, used structural analysis to make fundamental contributions to decipherment after making significant strides in studies of Maya architecture and sculpture. She carried out architectural drafting at Copan, Chichen Itza and Uaxactun for the Carnegie, and in 1946 published *An Album of Maya Architecture*, which contained exquisite renderings of buildings and bird's-eye views of sites, based on gathered data but with some creative licence to present the cities as they may once have appeared. These illustrations are sparsely populated with figures, visually reifying contemporaneous understandings (now invalidated) that Maya sites were vacant ceremonial centres. In 1950 Proskouriakoff published *A Study of Classic Maya Sculpture*, the first to trace regional and temporal styles of Maya carved stone sculpture. Later, she published groundbreaking essays on Maya inscriptions. In a detailed article on Piedras Negras in 1960, she analysed the inscriptions in tandem with the images and placement of the sculptures, and hypothesized that they narrated

Tatiana Proskouriakoff, painting of Structure K-5 1st, Piedras Negras, Peten, Guatemala, *c.* 1950, paper and watercolour.

significant events in the lives of historical individuals, particularly of seven 'rulers' in a 'dynastic succession'.[44] This essay definitively disproved earlier arguments that the inscriptions addressed only calendars, deities or stargazing priests. Instead, the Maya inscriptions recorded history. This breakthrough had an immediate and profound impact on Maya studies, encouraging the investigation of historical details and political relationships, and inspiring archaeologists to connect material findings with the historical record, such that the individuals found in tombs could be connected to the biographies of rulers, their families and members of the court. After Proskouriakoff's work, there was no turning back.

Another thrilling breakthrough combined Knorozov's phonetic method with Proskouriakoff's understanding of the historical content of Maya inscriptions. In a paper of 1962 the American epigrapher David Kelley turned to signs in Chichen Itza inscriptions that Hermann Beyer had identified as a repeating series. Using the Chi and Landa syllabary, he deciphered the signs phonetically, reading Kakupacal, which correlated with a name in documents from the colonial period.[45] Kakupacal was the first personal name of a Maya ruler to be read from an ancient inscription in centuries, an astonishing moment in Maya studies. This pronouncement cemented beyond doubt the idea that Maya inscriptions and cities were intimately connected to contemporary Mayan languages and people, who were the descendants of those who had built the extraordinary cities of Mexico and Central America.

## Interdisciplinary archaeological projects

In the 1960s and '70s Processual Archaeology or New Archaeology called for more attention to cultural systems and development, including studies of economic infrastructure, agriculture, the environment and various levels of society.[46] Following the model established by Willey's studies of settlement patterns, more projects conducted settlement surveys and investigated residential structures, as well as examining monumental architecture in site centres. Major projects were at Dzibilchaltun, Yucatan, which studied Formative to colonial-period occupations, and at sites in Guatemala such as Altar de Sacrificios and Ceibal.[47] Many scholars also began substantial studies of materials and artefacts. Anna Shepard, an innovative researcher of Maya ceramics, studied their materials and manufacture, using various techniques including microscopy and petrography and combining these analyses with information from ethnography and archaeology. Additional studies of stone tools, particularly those from Belize, and obsidian blades and cores have contributed new data about Maya economics and the trade of raw materials and finished products across Mesoamerica.[48] Through both direct exploration and continued exploitation of the rainforest, cave archaeology has also come to the fore, with caves, cenotes and underwater aquifers being explored in Belize, Guatemala and Mexico, with attention not only to their physical aspects but to the religious importance of caves as openings in the sacred, animate earth.[49]

The archaeologist David Pendergast coined the phrase the 'Blossoming of Belize' archaeology because of the increase in archaeological projects beginning in the 1970s, before the nation's independence from Britain. These were conducted mostly by foreign teams, but also by the Belize Department of Archaeology, and included studies of Cuello, Ambergris Caye and Lamanai, which had a long occupation that continued into the colonial period. Several projects researched Cerros and contributed in substantive ways to understanding of the Late Preclassic period, and archaeology at Caracol revealed the complexity of that large city and its interaction with other powerful Late Classic kingdoms.[50] Belize also hosts many projects serving as archaeology field schools, exposing a multitude of foreign students to archaeological techniques and the ancient Maya.

In the second half of the century in Mexico, a new generation of INAH archaeologists excavated sites across the Maya realm. In the 1960s and '70s Jorge Acosta investigated Palenque (and other sites across Mesoamerica), and Arnoldo González Cruz excavated at Palenque in the 1990s, finding a queen's tomb adjacent to the Temple of the Inscriptions and many buried censers on the Temple of the Cross. In the early 1970s the German archaeologist Jürgen K. Brüggemann led stratigraphic excavations at Yaxchilan,[51] and

Drawing 21 of ballplayer, Naj Tunich, Peten, Guatemala, 8th century CE, carbon on cave wall.

Roberto García Moll directed a major project at the site in the 1980s and uncovered several tombs, although the findings were never fully published. In Campeche, Ramón Carrasco Vargas led a multi-year project at Calakmul that uncovered Preclassic buildings with modelled polychrome plaster inside Structure II and a small building covered with painted murals in the Chiik Nahb sector.[52] In Quintana Roo, Enrique Nalda researched Dzibanche, now known to have been the Early Classic seat of the Kaanul dynasty.[53] In Yucatan, Peter Schmidt and Rafael Cobos directed major long-term projects at Chichen Itza, with special attention to Puuc-style architecture and the chronology of the site.

An essential change in the second half of the twentieth century was the growing involvement of archaeologists from Guatemala, Honduras and Belize, who have served as project directors and governmental administrators in charge of archaeological sites in their home countries. Ricardo Agurcia Fasquelle served as director of IHAH and led projects at Copan, one of which revealed the Rosalila Structure, whose polychrome stucco decoration honours the ancestral ruler K'inich Yax K'uk' Mo'. Jorge Ramos excavated at Copan and directs a project at nearby El Rastrojón. Harriot Topsey served as archaeological commissioner of Belize, and Jaime Awe and John Morris are the former and current directors of the Institute of Archaeology, in Belize's National Institute of Culture and History. Awe has also led projects at sites across Belize, including Caracol, Cahal Pech and Xunantunich, where his team found a major tomb and carved panels that shed light on the Kaanul dynasty and political intrigue with other sites.[54]

During this period increased attention was paid to the professional training of Guatemalan archaeologists, with many attaining scholarly degrees of *licenciado*, Masters and PhD. These archaeologists directed, co-directed or otherwise participated in national and international collaborative projects. For instance, in the late 1970s and '80s the Guatemalan government established archaeological projects at Tikal and Uaxactun that were led by Guatemalan archaeologists, and which trained a new generation. Two pioneers were Juan Pedro Laporte and Juan Antonio Valdés. At Tikal, Laporte and his collaborators excavated the Lost World

'Ballcourt Marker', from Group 6c-xvi, Tikal, Peten, Guatemala, 4th century CE, limestone.

Group and Group 6c-xvi, both of which demonstrated significant connections with Teotihuacan and were revelatory about the Early Classic period. Valdés also excavated in Tikal, Kaminaljuyu and Uaxactun, and wrote about the dynastic history of Uaxactun in relation to the site's architecture and tombs. The Tikal National Project, which began in 1979, also served as a training ground for new archaeologists who later established their own projects in other sites, constituting a crucial change from the decades of primarily foreign research into Maya archaeology in Guatemala. Both Laporte and Valdés also trained archaeologists in their roles as professors at the Universidad de San Carlos de Guatemala and the Universidad del Valle, both in Guatemala City.[55] Vilma Fialko also collaborated with Laporte and Valdés, and has since directed a project at Naranjo, which had been heavily looted.

The next generations of Guatemalan archaeologists have excavated throughout Guatemala. Bárbara Arroyo, Oswaldo Chinchilla Mazariegos and Héctor Escobedo Ayala worked together – along with u.s. graduate students – on the Petexbatun Regional Archaeological Project in the 1990s, directed by Arthur Demarest of Vanderbilt University in Nashville, Tennessee, which investigated Dos Pilas, Tamarindito and Aguateca.[56] They went on to establish or co-direct other excavations at Piedras Negras, El Perú-Waka', Kaminaljuyu and El Baúl (on the Pacific Coast, a region formerly at the margins of study). In addition, all have served important functions in IDAEH or the Museo Popol Vuh, Guatemala City. Many other Guatemalan archaeologists have taken up the mantle of the Archaeological Atlas of Guatemala, continuing to document the country's archaeological heritage, and have served as archaeologists, administrators and laboratory directors at sites across the country.[57] In addition, Maya archaeologists such as Iyaxel Cojti Ren, a K'iche' archaeologist who trained in Guatemala and at Vanderbilt University, have established new field projects.[58]

Another central development has been the exploration, uncovering and better understanding of the Late Preclassic period throughout the Maya world. Some sites were abandoned at the end of the Preclassic, leaving that architecture more accessible for study, as at Cerros or El Mirador. But in sites where the Preclassic buildings had been buried, improvements in tunnelling technology have allowed archaeologists to search for earlier phases of art and architecture. Excavations at Ceibal have revealed monumental architecture from as early as 1000 BCE and shed light on relationships between the Maya and Olmec, which has added to research at other sites, such as Cival, in the illumination of Middle Preclassic Maya material culture. Airborne LiDAR surveys have also aided in understanding the Preclassic, both in exposing more about known sites, such as Izapa, and in revealing previously unknown settlements, including the extraordinary early Middle Classic monumental architecture at Aguada Fénix.[59]

At Copan, a multidisciplinary project with many partners including IHAH, Harvard University, the University of Pennsylvania and Pennsylvania State University used tunnel excavations to study monumental architecture in the Acropolis. The work exposed layers of architecture from the Early and Late Classic periods, which researchers correlated with dynastic rulers based on epigraphy, ceramic chronologies and architectural styles. Their studies revealed that information from eighth-century texts aligned with that of earlier periods, indicating that the ancient Maya were tracking historical information as part of legitimizing power. In addition, investigations of the larger settlement and environmental conditions of the Copan Valley addressed questions of environmental pressure and the collapse of the Classic Maya.

Excavations in Peten in the late twentieth and early twenty-first century have also expanded our understanding of ancient Maya history and politics. Much of Peten was inaccessible for research for many years during Guatemala's civil war (1960–96). After the end of the conflict, several archaeological projects were established in sites across Peten, some of which had been ravaged by looting. At San Bartolo, a looter's tunnel exposed a section of an astonishing Late Preclassic mural. Subsequent excavation uncovered two walls bearing murals related to the Maize God's life cycle, as well as countless fragments of additional paintings that had been ripped from the walls in antiquity.[60] The archaeologist and artist Heather Hurst carefully documented the murals' proportions, lines and colours in order to recreate the murals accurately in watercolour, as she had done for Bonampak, and examined pigment recipes for evidence of individual ancient artists' hands, revealing fundamental information about Preclassic Maya artistic practice.[61] Another hallmark of these more recent projects is the extensive collaboration with Guatemalan archaeologists.

New political dynamics can now be assessed, including the fact that many sites held key and disparate roles in the Kaanul dynasty in the Late Classic. An archaeological team initially directed by David Freidel and Héctor Escobedo Ayala investigated El Perú-Waka', whose stone sculptures had been looted in the 1960s.[62] Their excavations revealed several elite tombs, including that of a royal queen, Ixik K'abel, a Kaanul princess who married into the El Perú-Waka' royal family.[63] Excavations at La Corona provided further insight about the Kaanul dynasty and affiliated sites. In the 1960s small distinctively carved panels, some with ballplayer figures, appeared on the art market; the archaeologist Peter Mathews hypothesized that many had come from the same place, nicknamed Site Q, for *qué?* (which?), since their place of origin was unknown. The place was identified as La Corona, where excavations found new panels and inscriptions in situ and revealed information that made a crucial contribution to understanding the Kaanul dynasty's diplomatic and expansionist endeavours.[64]

In the second half of the century, archaeologists conducted more research in the Northern Lowlands that probed various historical periods and chronological relationships with southern Classic Maya cities. These included studies of the Preclassic and Early Classic occupations at Oxkintok and Yaxuna, providing new insight into Yucatan's long-term chronology, which was essential, since much twentieth-century scholarship had focused on its Postclassic history.[65] Excavations on the Acropolis at Ek' Balam uncovered the stunning zoomorphic portal on the building containing the royal tomb of Ukit Kan Le'k Tok', and decipherment exposed details of his life from the inscriptions.[66] The architecture of the Puuc and Río Bec regions has also been intensively studied; similarities among those buildings and ones in Maya sites in the Southern and Northern Lowlands indicate that there was not an abrupt break or shift, as earlier scholars had suggested. Mayapan has also been the site of continued archaeological projects.[67] Especially transformative research in the Yucatan Peninsula has involved coastal and island sites such as Jaina Island and maritime trade in antiquity.[68]

Panel 1 (detail), from Hieroglyphic Stairway 2, La Corona, Peten, Guatemala, 677 CE, limestone.

## Late twentieth- and early twenty-first-century documentation and decipherment

As in earlier decades, documentation efforts continued, inspired by the desire to document sites and inscriptions before they were lost to new settlement, looting and erosion. The goals of the Corpus of Maya Hieroglyphic Inscriptions (CMHI), founded in 1968 by Ian Graham and taken on after his retirement by the archaeologist and illustrator Barbara Fash, were to record stone monuments before erosion or looters damaged them; to document them with attention to detail for epigraphic use; and to highlight archaeological and epigraphic riches to encourage their protection and study. Epigraphers and artists worked with Graham to produce drawings that were published in books and online. The artist and teacher Merle Greene Robertson established a project making rubbings of Maya sculptures and documenting polychrome stuccoes at Palenque, which was especially crucial because they were deteriorating.[69] Trained first as an artist, Linda Schele, who documented Palenque and Copan images and inscriptions, became a prominent epigrapher and champion of Maya studies, organizing the annual Maya Meetings in Austin, Texas, that attracted a large following and which Maya linguists and tour guides from Guatemala and Mexico attended.

Guatemalan and Mexican projects also focused on large-scale documentation. The Archaeological Atlas of Guatemala set out to record sites throughout Guatemala and served as a significant training ground for Guatemalan archaeologists. The Prehispanic Mexican Painted Mural Project, founded by Beatriz de la Fuente of UNAM's Institute of Aesthetic Investigations, planned to record all painted pre-Hispanic murals in the Mexican nation, including at Maya sites in Yucatan and Chiapas. Their approach has been both documentary and interpretive, involving iconographic studies, stylistic analysis and scientific studies of materials and techniques.[70]

The documentation and dissemination efforts allowed decipherment to progress apace, both in terms of decoding phonetic readings and revealing historical content. Since Knorozov's essay on phoneticism in 1952 and Proskouriakoff's essay of 1960 on the

Piedras Negras rulers, epigraphers have deciphered many syllables and logograms and have rediscovered countless details to unravel the complexities of Classic-period Maya geopolitics.[71] Progress in decipherment has been an international endeavour, with contributions from researchers in Mexico, Guatemala, the United States and various European countries. Epigraphic discoveries have taken place in diverse locales: archaeological sites, universities, conferences such as the Palenque Mesa Redonda and the Maya Meetings in Austin, and people's houses.[72] Schele and Federico Fahsen, an architect and Guatemalan ambassador to the United States, also organized workshops in Guatemala to teach hieroglyphs to speakers of Mayan languages. Workshop participants included Maya linguists and other scholars and students from the Asociación Oxlajuuj Keej Maya Ajtziib (OKMA) and Sak Chuwen, who made contributions about vocabulary, grammar, decipherment and other topics (see also Chapter Eight).

There have been several avenues of research in the continuing decipherment of Maya writing. One has been the teasing out of dynastic histories, following in Proskouriakoff's path. In 1974 at the Palenque Mesa Redonda, epigraphers began to reconstruct the dynastic history of that ancient city.[73] In later years others continued to decipher Palenque's inscriptions and also contributed to the decipherment of dynastic history at Yaxchilan, Dos Pilas, Cancuen and Tikal, as well as sites in the Northern Lowlands including Ek' Balam and Chichen Itza.[74] In recent years, epigraphic study has contributed greatly to understanding the history and politics of the Kaanul dynasty at Calakmul and of Dzibanche as the Early Classic home of the Kaanul dynasty, furthering the understanding that Emblem Glyphs refer not to places but to polities or dynasties that could move around.[75] Other studies have made significant contributions regarding Maya history, religion and philosophy.[76] Further advances have been in phonetic decipherment, following in the path of Knorozov and Kelley. David Stuart's *Ten Phonetic Syllables* (1987) is a model of deploying the evidence for the decipherment of ten syllables using principles of substitution; this short study is both an essential contribution regarding those syllables and a model methodological approach.[77] Stuart has since made countless other contributions to understanding Maya writing, the calendar and political history.

The linguistics and grammar of Maya writing are a significant area of research that has involved collaborations between epigraphers and linguists, including native Maya speakers. Linguists have determined that the language of the writing system is an ancestor of contemporary Mayan languages; called 'Common Mayan' today, it was a prestige language related to Ch'orti' and Ch'olti'.[78] Progress has also continued in creating dictionaries and understanding contemporary Mayan languages, through the work of organizations such as the Proyecto Lingüístico Francisco Marroquín and the Asociación Oxlajuuj Keej Maya Ajtziib in Guatemala. Some linguists from those organizations, including Lolmay García Matzar,[79] participate regularly in hieroglyphic workshops around the world, and organizations such as Sak Chuwen in Guatemala organize workshops for Maya speakers in various countries. In addition to the individuals named here, many others have contributed to deciphering syllables and logograms, teasing out dynastic history and understanding the grammar of ancient Maya writing.[80]

## Art history and iconography

The discipline of art history has increased our understanding of Maya art, artists and other aspects of Maya culture. Art historians have addressed artistic style, following Proskouriakoff's tome on Maya sculpture; iconography, following Paul Schellhas; and materials and materiality. Clemency Coggins wrote her dissertation on the painting and drawing styles of Tikal, studying murals and ceramic painting and carving on bones and stone.[81] Her analysis was insightful, particularly in considering change over time and investigating artistic styles and exchanges with Teotihuacan and Kaminaljuyu.

Many art-historical studies focus on one medium from a particular site or period, addressing topics such as iconography, style and political context or working to recreate the ancient viewer's experience of buildings, places, artworks and landscapes.

A number of art-historical books address Maya painting, sculpture or architecture, including Early Classic sculpture; painting at Bonampak and the Naj Tunich cave; sculpture at Copan, Izapa, Piedras Negras, Quirigua and Yaxchilan; and architecture at Uxmal. These cover varied topics such as style, iconography and materiality.[82] Some programmes, such as the Bonampak Documentation Project, have incorporated multispectral imaging in order to recover information about pigments or effaced lines.[83] Also prevalent are focused articles and books on specific themes or aspects of iconography, including dance, Maya deities and mythological narratives, and the meaning of materials such as jade.[84]

Art historians and archaeologists have organized major museum exhibitions and published associated catalogues about Maya art. These include general introductions to Maya art and focused shows addressing particular places, such as the Chichen Itza cenote, or on thematic topics such as the birth of Maya rulership, Maya ritual practices, the art of Maya courts and Maya relationships with the sea.[85]

The study of Maya polychrome painted ceramic vessels is another rich area of research that was advanced by the Maya Vase books and Justin Kerr's online database of rollout photographs. The dissemination of photographs of nearly 2,000 vessels allowed many more people to see and study them, including those in countries such as Mexico and Guatemala, which encouraged the internationalization of their study. Many of those painted ceramics lack archaeological context, reducing their scientific value, but scholars have made crucial iconographic and epigraphic discoveries by studying them, recognizing in Maya polychrome ceramics the greatest extant repository of ancient Maya mythology. Comparisons of those painted ceramics with ones that have been excavated by archaeologists are also fruitful; an extraordinary deposit of codex-style sherds from Calakmul bear fragments of scenes painted on complete vessels in museum collections.[86] The whole vessels allow archaeologists to discern what the fragments may have portrayed, and the excavated sherds provide opportunities to compare materials and artists' hands, and even give insight into the looted vessels' sites of origin.

## Materials science and biological science

Materials and biological sciences have enriched archaeological and art-historical research, focusing on ancient Maya sites, artefacts, human remains and plant and animal specimens from excavations and museum collections. Following in Anna Shepard's footsteps are scholars studying Maya ceramics, researching topics such as the technical aspects of their production.[87] The Maya Ceramics Project of the Smithsonian Institution has used Instrumental Neutron Activation Analysis to discern the chemical make-up of Maya ceramics in relation to regional styles of ceramic production, and this approach has been useful in studying the gifting of ceramics and in connecting looted objects to possible places of origin.[88] Other analyses study residues, most notably with the discovery of chemical traces of chocolate in a vessel from a Río Azul tomb.[89] Prominent ceramics projects have been conducted in museums to learn about painted ceramics, both ones found in archaeological excavations and those that were obtained through the art and antiquities market.[90] More recent studies of ceramics have attempted to move beyond the approaches from Processual Archaeology. Indeed, regarding her research into ceramic production at Motul de San José, Guatemala, Antonia Foias emphasizes that she is not dealing simply with datasets but with individual people and their products, articulating a distinction between twenty-first-century ceramics studies and Processual studies of decades earlier.[91]

Bioarchaeology is another research area that has illuminated ancient diets, pathology and disease, violence and migration through analysis of human remains, using visual and microscopic analysis and analytical techniques such as measuring oxygen and strontium stable isotope ratios.[92] Some analysis was inspired by questions posed from the archaeological or epigraphic records. For example, based on inscriptions and imagery from Tikal and Copan, some scholars had hypothesized that the Tikal ruler Yax Nuun Ahiin and the Copan ruler Yax K'uk' Mo' had come from Central Mexico, but isotopic studies show that they grew up in the Maya area.[93] Other research has settled the dispute between epigraphy and earlier physical anthropological studies by concluding that the person buried in the Palenque Temple of the Inscriptions tomb, named K'inich Janaab Pakal, was that of an elderly man. This allowed researchers to dismiss earlier speculation that the interred person was a younger man, an idea that had denigrated the epigraphic record as royal propaganda. Furthermore, research has found genetic connections between persons interred at Dzibanche and Calakmul, which aligns with epigraphic research indicating the Kaanul dynasty's presence at both sites.[94]

Zooarchaeology and archaeobotany have also become fundamental to ancient Maya archaeological research. Zooarchaeology addresses how humans engage with animals for diet, ceremony or other reasons. Kitty Emery, a pioneer in ancient Maya zooarchaeology, not only intricately examines animal bones but incorporates questions of ritual, economics and politics, and considers the use of animal remains by different social groups.[95] Another generation of zooarchaeologists has continued to make significant contributions across the Maya region. Archaeobotany or paleoethnobotany investigates relationships between humans and plants, considering agriculture and food consumption as well as the ceremonial use of plants. Such studies may also address politics, meaning, social interaction and gender in considering human–plant interaction, thus moving beyond Processual studies of humans in relation to their environment.[96]

### New technology and forms of documentation

Since the late twentieth century, new technology has been adopted to document Maya objects, buildings and settlements. The Alliance for Integrated Spatial Technologies at the University of South Florida in Tampa has used three-dimensional laser scanning to document Maya objects from national museums and private collections. CMHI also uses laser scanning as an addition to photography and drawing to document Maya inscriptions. For the Copan Hieroglyphic Stairway, CMHI scanned each block and made a three-dimensional model of the stairway with the blocks in the correct order, allowing scholars to manipulate in a non-invasive

Digital reconstruction of Upper Temple of the Jaguars, Chichen Itza, Yucatan, Mexico, by the cultural heritage group INSIGHT.

manner this vital monument whose blocks had been jumbled a century before.[97]

Three-dimensional scanning has also been applied to Maya sites for the purpose of public education. The Institute for the Study and Integration of Graphical Heritage Techniques (INSIGHT), working in collaboration with the Chabot Space and Science Center in Oakland, California, scanned Chichen Itza buildings and sculptures for a full-dome film for public distribution, *Tales of the Maya Skies*, focusing on ancient Maya astronomy. In making the models, INSIGHT collaborated with archaeologists and conservators regarding the buildings, textures and colours. Working with skills from the film and video-game industries, INSIGHT recreated the buildings in full colour, reflecting Chichen Itza both in its florescence and after its decline. The data from these scans were made available online for download, allowing others to manipulate the models and create their own reconstructions.[98]

Laser scanning has also been used in airborne systems along with NASA imagery and Geographic Information System to advance the study of settlements. LiDAR has been used at individual Maya sites such as Caracol and Izapa, showing archaeologists that these cities covered a greater expanse than had previously been realized.[99] More recent large-scale LiDAR surveys of the Maya Biosphere Reserve in Peten have offered a transformative view of the extent of Maya cities and settlement patterns, and revealed agricultural systems that had gone unrecognized. In addition, LiDAR surveys in southern Mexico have uncovered monumental artificial plateaus from the early Middle Preclassic, transforming the understanding of Preclassic Maya chronology.[100]

## Public dissemination and the involvement of Maya communities

For the past century, several magazines have been fora for the popular dissemination of archaeological discoveries. *National Geographic* has covered Maya archaeology extensively, particularly under George Stuart, staff archaeologist and editor for decades beginning in 1960. In the mid-twentieth century the Archaeological Institute of America began to publish *Archaeology* magazine, covering archaeology worldwide. *Arqueología Mexicana*, a Spanish-language magazine about Mexican archaeology, launched in 1993. Articles about Maya archaeology also appear in the *New York Times*, albeit infrequently, and newspapers in Mexico and Guatemala regularly cover Maya excavations. These are notable for circulating information and generating interest in the ancient Maya, which has encouraged tourism and support of scholarship. The dissemination of knowledge among the general public has been useful in combating erroneous narratives about lost continents, diffusion and aliens.

Another essential and transformative development in the late twentieth century was the increased involvement of Maya people and communities in archaeological projects. Some projects, such as that directed by Robert Carmack at Q'umarkaj, the K'iche' capital, involved Maya people as active participants in archaeological research, beginning with research design and including fieldwork and the dissemination of knowledge. Archaeologists across the Maya realm have worked to disseminate results to local people, allowing those communities to take ownership of the sites and to participate in further diffusion of information in local schools and through tourism; some sites are managed in collaboration with local communities.[101] This provides economic opportunities, allowing communities to take advantage of the increased tourism arising from the popularization of archaeological discoveries. Furthermore, organizations such as INHERIT: Indigenous Heritage Passed to Present collaborate with Indigenous communities to create research projects and educational materials relating to archaeology and cultural heritage. The Sustainable Preservation Initiative has worked to help Indigenous communities, including those near Kaminaljuyu in Guatemala City, to develop businesses associated with archaeological sites. There is great need for continued engagement and emphasis on the agency of Maya communities in making decisions about their communities and their heritage.

Knowledge of the ancient Maya was transformed in the twentieth and twenty-first centuries. Because of the astounding amount of research that has been done, this summary has been unavoidably selective and incomplete, characterizing trends in scholarship rather than serving as an exhaustive repository. The ancient Maya are now known to have been a civilization with complex politics and history, and both ancient Maya geopolitics and individual biographies have been reconstructed (with more to come, certainly). Scholars have diversified topics of study, seeking to understand all levels of society. In addition are many innovations in using technology at large and small scales, ranging from LiDAR surveys documenting immense settlements to pollen studies analysing minuscule remains. Both types of study produce more knowledge about ancient Maya life and the climate they experienced.

Studies of the ancient Maya have become more democratic and international, and not just carried out in a few elite institutions. Furthermore, more Maya people have become involved in these efforts, whether participating in collaborative decision-making about sites and archaeological projects; or working as archaeologists, linguists, epigraphers and museum professionals. Even so, there is work still to do as Maya people continue to advocate for the restoration of their rights and agency over their ancestral heritage, as discussed in Chapter Eight.

# SIX

# COLLECTING AND EXHIBITING THE ANCIENT MAYA IN THE TWENTIETH AND TWENTY-FIRST CENTURIES

People who acquired Maya objects in the twentieth and twenty-first centuries did so for various reasons and in diverse ways, as in earlier centuries. Latin American nation states generally collected items from cultures within their borders, whereas universal museums and private collectors outside those countries acquired Maya objects along with material from other world cultures. In the twentieth century, divisions arose between archaeology and collecting. Changing antiquities laws professionalized archaeological excavations, requiring permits and limiting the export of found items. Objects from permitted excavations at Maya sites in Mexico and Central America were subsequently accessioned into governmental institutions and museums, but those in national collections were frequently loaned to foreign museums for research or display. Despite these laws and policies, looting increased, especially between the 1950s and the 1980s, when thousands of Maya objects were illicitly removed from archaeological sites and sold to private collectors and museums, a practice that devastated many ancient Maya sites and buildings. In the late twentieth and into the twenty-first century, governments and international treaties have endeavoured to stop looting and the collecting practices that supported such behaviour. In many cases, objects seized from smugglers have been incorporated into national collections.

## Ancient Maya materials in museums in the first half of the twentieth century

Before about 1950, Maya objects were displayed mostly in national museums in Latin America (as in Mexico) or in natural-history or anthropological museums outside of Latin America, called here 'foreign museums' for brevity's sake. Mexican and Guatemalan national museums began as multifaceted collections, comprising history (including archaeology), natural history and geology. These originated in viceregal or early republican governmental collections and were further developed by universities, historical societies, governments and international exposition committees focused on knowing, documenting or disseminating the countries' historical, cultural and natural resources (discussed in Chapter Four). Before the Mexican Revolution, there were some Maya objects in the National Museum in Mexico City, including the Chichen Itza chacmool discovered by Augustus Le Plongeon and the Palenque Tablet of the Cross panel, whose three parts entered the museum in 1884, 1908 and 1909. Still, the Mexico City collections mostly held items from Central Mexico, with fewer items from the Maya area and other regions within the nation.

As the collections of the Mexican National Museum – housed at the old mint in the first half of the twentieth century – grew and specialized, and as ideology changed, the museum was divided into departments, and these began to separate from the whole (a pattern seen outside Mexico, too). The natural-history collections separated to form the National Museum of Natural History, which moved in 1913 to El Chopo, a former exposition building, and the museum at the old mint was renamed the National Museum of Archaeology, History and Ethnography.[1] In 1939 History separated to form the National Museum of History, installed at Chapultepec Castle, and the museum at the old mint, holding archaeological and ethnographic material, was renamed the National Museum of Anthropology. This was the same year that the National Institute of Anthropology and History (INAH) was founded, marking a crucial development in the specialization and professionalization of anthropology in Mexico.[2]

In the 1920s and '30s, after the Mexican Revolution, archaeology and anthropology advanced considerably in Mexico, and museum collections grew, too, with more attention paid to contextualizing materials within the discipline of anthropology, in line with Manuel Gamio's promotion of archaeology and ethnography as part of the revolutionary project. Researchers and other staff at INAH and the National Museum worked to diversify research and collections to encompass more regions across Mexico. Mexican projects in Yucatan and Quintana Roo in the 1920s and '30s – and in subsequent decades in Chiapas – uncovered material that entered national collections. But internal correspondence in the National Museum archives attempted to address the relative paucity of Maya materials in the museum. A letter from museum archaeologists and anthropologists to the Secretary of Public Education in 1936 cites the need to hire a competent archaeologist and make a 'dignified' Maya collection: 'the Maya culture is shamefully under-represented, when we could have the best collection in the world.'[3]

Guatemala was also building its national collections in these years, and in 1930 a new iteration of the National Museum opened. The museum's archaeological collection was built with pieces excavated by foreign projects. For example, the Carnegie work at Uaxactun and the University of Pennsylvania Museum's investigations in Piedras Negras found items that entered Guatemala's national collections. In 1946 Guatemala established the Institute of Anthropology and History (IDAEH), dedicated to research, publication and protection of archaeological sites and collections, analogous to Mexico's INAH.[4]

In the United States, the institutions that collected ancient Maya and other objects from the Americas were generally natural-history and anthropology museums. The American Museum of Natural History, founded in 1869 in New York City, originated as a natural-history museum, but hired Frederic Ward Putnam and later Franz Boas as anthropology curators and acquired objects relating to Indigenous cultures of the Americas, including the Maya. The museum has retained its primary focus on natural history, while also displaying items from Indigenous peoples from the United States and Latin America. Some U.S. museums were developed in the wake of international expositions. The Field Columbian Museum in Chicago was created with objects from the 1893 World's Columbian Exposition, devoted to art, archaeology, science and history.[5] The museum continued to amass natural-history and anthropological collections, and curators made expeditions to Yucatan and elsewhere to seek artefacts from the ancient Maya and other cultures. For museums derived from nineteenth-century practices of displaying ancient artefacts and ethnographic materials alongside natural-history specimens such as insects and gemstones, the juxtaposition of such materials conveys a sense that Indigenous people and their cultural heritage are resources to be mined or otherwise used, as opposed to being representatives of esteemed and enduring cultural traditions.

There were also Maya collections in museums devoted to anthropology or to Indigenous peoples of the Americas. The Museum of the American Indian, established in New York in the 1910s by George Gustav Heye, and the Southwest Museum in Los Angeles, founded by Charles Lummis in 1907, amassed materials from Indigenous peoples from across the Americas, ancient to modern, by conducting excavations, receiving donations, trading with other museums and purchasing objects. Anthropology museums in Europe included the Trocadéro Museum in Paris, which acquired some of Claude-Joseph-Désiré Charnay's collections, and the Leiden National Museum of Ethnology, which procured the famed Leiden Plaque. Erwin Paul Dieseldorff, a German coffee-planter and merchant in Coban, in Alta Verapaz, Guatemala, collected Maya pieces from locals and excavated at Chamá, from where he obtained more objects. He gave part of those collections to the Royal Museum for Ethnology in Berlin, now the Ethnological Museum (and after his death, his son gave the rest of his collection to the National Museum of Archaeology and Ethnology in Guatemala City).[6] Also active in obtaining Maya materials were university museums such as Harvard's Peabody Museum and the Penn Museum, which received artefacts from archaeological projects, accepted donations and exchanged with other museums. For instance, archaeologists at Copan shipped excavated works to the

Peabody Museum, as permitted by the Honduran government. But the Peabody also accepted artefacts from the dredging in 1904–10 of the Chichen Itza Sacred Cenote, exported without permission. Mexico later claimed those objects, and the Peabody returned a part of the collection to Mexico, but other items remained.[7]

Universal museums and art museums in Europe and the United States also acquired Maya and other pre-Hispanic objects through excavations, donations and purchases. The British Museum obtained Yaxchilan lintels from Alfred Maudslay and pieces from Thomas Gann's excavations in Belize. A relatively small number of Maya works were exhibited in art museums in the first half of the twentieth century. In 1912 the Boston Museum of Fine Arts displayed items from Copan, Piedras Negras and other sites from Harvard's Peabody Museum, selected to be 'of interest to the visitors of an art museum' and deemed 'worthy of the name of art'.[8] 'American Sources of Modern Art' at the Museum of Modern Art (MOMA) in New York in 1933 juxtaposed art of the ancient Americas with modern American art. Borrowing from museums in the United States, Europe, Mexico, and Central and South American countries, this exhibition was geographically diverse. The curator Holger Cahill, acting director of MOMA, extolled the Maya objects for their formal and aesthetic qualities, claiming that they should be considered not 'primitive' but the 'art of high civilizations'.[9]

Ancient Maya and other pre-Hispanic objects were again exhibited at MOMA and categorized as 'art' in the exhibition 'Twenty Centuries of Mexican Art' co-organized by INAH in 1940.[10] This collaboration was part of U.S. President Franklin Roosevelt's Good Neighbor Policy, which encouraged better relations with Mexico and other Latin American countries. Among the Mexican curators were the archaeologist and INAH director Alfonso Caso and the artist Miguel Covarrubias; the president of MOMA, Nelson Rockefeller, also played a crucial role. The exhibition presented antiquities from Mexican national collections, ancient to contemporary, including modern and folk art. Ancient Maya objects, including the chacmool that Le Plongeon had excavated, were displayed in the same exhibition as modern paintings by Diego Rivera, and the works were called 'Mexican art', an umbrella of aesthetic value.

This exhibition established a framework for displaying ancient and modern Mexican art that would continue for several decades. Mexico adopted it for many mid-century international expositions, curated by the famed Mexican museographer Fernando Gamboa for display in cities throughout Europe, and in Los Angeles.[11] It also provided a model or inspiration for U.S. art museums to collect and display pre-Hispanic objects. In the MOMA show and subsequent exhibitions, pieces were displayed against minimal backgrounds, without contextual images, photos or models (thus unlike earlier international expositions), presented primarily as aesthetic products for visual appreciation.

In the late 1930s and early 1940s university and municipal museums in the United States showed ancient Maya and other pre-Hispanic materials and called them 'art'. This took place in 1937 at the Baltimore Museum of Art, in 1940 at Harvard's Fogg Art Museum and the Los Angeles County Museum, and in 1942 at the Santa Barbara Museum of Art.[12] The Baltimore exhibition borrowed mostly from U.S. museums but also from the Pierre Matisse Gallery. The Fogg exhibition displayed pieces from Mexico's National Museum, U.S. museums, collectors including Mildred and Robert Woods Bliss, and dealers, thus exhibiting both Mexican national collections and those in foreign hands. The Los Angeles exhibition, on the other hand, displayed only objects from U.S. collections – from art dealers Earl Stendahl and Joseph and Ernest Brummer, collectors such as Bliss and Walter and Louise Arensberg, and institutions including Tulane University's Middle American Research Institute in New Orleans, the Cleveland Museum of Art and the Penn Museum. The Santa Barbara exhibition had a similar array of lenders, including U.S. collectors, dealers and museums.[13]

These exhibitions brought to light the growing market in the United States for arts of the ancient Americas, which were sold by dealers in Europe and the States such as Brummer and Stendahl. The latter, for example, began selling European art in 1911, and started to sell pre-Hispanic pieces in the late 1930s.[14] Numerous private collectors and art, anthropology and cultural-history museums built collections of pre-Hispanic objects through the art market.

Bliss, a diplomat and ambassador to Argentina, purchased objects from throughout Latin America. In 1935 he travelled to Maya sites with Connecticut senator and Carnegie board member Frederic Walcott, visiting the Chichen Itza project and meeting Sylvanus Griswold Morley and Alfred Kidder. Bliss acquired his first Maya objects two years later. He purchased from dealers such as Stendahl and received some items as exchanges with other institutions, receiving a Copan stone head from the Peabody Museum in 1952.[15] From 1947 to 1962 Bliss displayed his collection in the National Gallery of Art in Washington, DC, later donating it to Harvard for display at Dumbarton Oaks. The art historian and curator Joanne Pillsbury recounts that he 'was adamant that his own collection of ancient American art be seen as fine art'.[16] Rockefeller, who collected widely from across the Americas, Africa and Oceania, also promoted calling these materials '*art* with aesthetic merit rather than . . . specimens more suitable for a natural-history museum'.[17] He offered to donate his collections to the Metropolitan Museum of Art, but the Met resisted; in response, he founded the short-lived Museum of Primitive Art in 1954. In 1969 the Met finally relented and accepted his collections, which went on display there in 1981.

These prominent collectors and exhibitions were part of changing trends that increased the estimation of ancient Maya art. One might say that this was positive, for the pieces were valued for their inherent qualities, but, when they were displayed to highlight their aesthetic qualities, the cultural meaning was frequently stripped away, divorcing the pieces from the people and societies who made them. Also, objects in private collections and foreign museums outside of Latin America generally lacked archaeological provenience, meaning that they had not been scientifically excavated and so, generally, were clandestinely entered into the art and antiquities market. Art dealers trying to sell pieces for profit and create new markets encouraged such acquisitions, and their businesses grew in the second and third quarters of the twentieth century.[18] Stendahl Galleries sold to individuals and museums across the United States and Europe, including university museums and municipal museums, and to dealers who in turn sought new clients.

Why did they collect? Some were intrigued by the forms of objects or by ancient makers, and others wanted connections with Indigenous artists or with Mexico or other Latin American countries. The Stendahls and their collaborators expressed admiration for Mexico's artistic traditions and articulated the desire to educate about 'the great cultural heritage of our own continent'.[19] The actor Vincent Price, a Stendahl client, raved about the artists' vitality and creativity:

> Before Columbus and almost up to now Europe fed the spirit of the world, and only now do we repay that debt by lending back a force of Art more vital, more pertinent to modern man than any since the rediscovery of ancient Greece and Rome during the Renaissance. The Arts and Crafts of the Indians of the Americas are fresh. They concern themselves with our own forms, arising as they do from our own earth.[20]

Price and the Stendahls may have deeply appreciated these materials, but their activities also contributed to the looting of sites in Mexico and other countries.

Meanwhile, in the mid-twentieth century, private collectors in Mexico also acquired ancient Maya art. Mexican collectors had been buying pre-Hispanic art for decades; Diego Rivera and Frida Kahlo bought Central and West Mexican ceramics, popular in the 1930s and '40s, and Aztec pieces, and Rivera also collected Jaina-style figurines, now at the Anahuacalli Museum in Mexico City. The German-born collector Kurt Stavenhagen, who donated his collection to UNAM, collected Jaina-style figurines and other objects. The Mexican economist Josué Sáenz and his wife, Jacqueline, began collecting pre-Hispanic art in 1944 and became prominent collectors in the second half of the century. They bought pieces inside and outside Mexico, including in Munich, encountering the most prominent objects – including Maya stone sculptures – outside their native country. They stopped collecting in 1972, when Mexican law designated pre-Hispanic art national patrimony; their collection is now in the Amparo Museum in Puebla, Mexico.[21]

One of the galleries dedicated to the ancient Maya in the Museo Nacional de Antropología, Mexico City.

## Ancient Maya materials in museums in the second half of the twentieth century

While foreign museums and collectors were buying ancient Maya and other pre-Hispanic objects, Mexico endeavoured to build its national collections and prepared to open a new National Museum of Anthropology in Chapultepec Park, Mexico City. One approach to expanding collections was through sanctioned excavation. One of the most important mid-century INAH excavations, at Palenque, exposed K'inich Janaab Pakal's tomb, which offered a new understanding of Maya rulership and funerary practices, and these extraordinary materials subsequently entered the National Museum. In the middle of the century (c. 1940–64), Hugo Moedano Koer, Miguel Ángel Fernández and Román Piña Chan conducted focused excavations on Jaina Island, both to understand the island

and to obtain figurines for the National Museum.[22] The Mexican authorities also seized, purchased and received donations of private collections both from Mexican collectors such as Covarrubias and from expat collectors and dealers such as William Spratling.[23]

National Museum collections were enriched by continuing to take items from other regions, including Maya objects from Chiapas and Yucatan, but this practice was maligned. Álvar Carrillo Gil, a doctor and collector of modern art who was born in Yucatan, denounced the transfer of objects from Yucatan to Mexico City for the new museum.[24] Likewise, a newspaper article of 1964 characterized the central government's taking of antiquities from states, specifically citing the removal of Maya collections from Yucatan, as *saqueo* (looting).[25] Carrillo Gil also condemned the government's neglect of antiquities and the pillage of Maya archaeological sites, and he purchased antiquities (primarily Maya ones) to prevent their sale outside the country.[26] These complaints about the centralization of Mexico's cultural heritage were valid, especially since Mérida had long had a museum that stored and displayed Maya antiquities. But the authorities needed new items for the National Museum of Anthropology in Chapultepec Park, Mexico City.

Mexico planned for three new museums – of anthropology, colonial art and modern art – to open in 1964. Before their inaugurations, a touring exhibition was organized of hundreds of pieces from those collections. They appeared in the 1958 Expo in Brussels and toured in 1959–64 to more than a dozen European cities, as well as Los Angeles. Curated by Gamboa, 'Master Works of Mexican Art' followed 'Twenty Centuries' in exhibiting a range of Mexican arts, from ancient to contemporary, as if a continuum of artistic traditions across the ages. The collections, from both national and private Mexican collections, represented Indigenous and non-Indigenous artists, and all the works – including those from the Palenque tomb – were displayed under the 'Mexican art' rubric. After this tour, the pre-Hispanic objects were installed along with ethnographic works in the new anthropology museum in Chapultepec Park, and the colonial and modern works went to the art museums. The Stendahl Galleries held simultaneous exhibitions in Europe and Los Angeles, and in some European cities the two exhibitions merged, but many of the Stendahl objects were for sale, leading to a permanent rupture.[27]

Both the exhibitions organized by Mexico and those created by dealers promoted sales by increasing awareness of these materials and the appetite to own them. This brought about a dramatic increase in private and art museums' collecting of Maya and other pre-Hispanic art in the second half of the twentieth century. Private collectors donated pieces to museums, but museums also purchased directly from dealers. Sotheby's, Christie's and other auction houses in the United States and Europe also sold pre-Hispanic objects to museums and private clients. This trend coincided with a changing perception of ancient Maya objects, and with the desire of art museums to expand the definition of 'art' and become more encyclopaedic or universal, to encompass the world.

## Mid-twentieth-century looting and legislation

This increasing hunger for ancient Maya art was met largely through looting and smuggling. The countries encompassing the ancient Maya ancestral lands passed laws prohibiting the export of antiquities at various points in the nineteenth and twentieth centuries, but smuggling continued. In response, those countries created stricter laws, enforced them more dutifully and enacted agreements with other countries to prohibit the export and import of archaeological materials. But it took decades to mitigate the looting, as people found ways around such laws or agreements, for instance by smuggling objects out of forested regions by plane, boat or mule, bribing customs agents, or having 'runners' (who smuggle items across borders) conceal them as modern objects.

The crisis in looting reached fever pitch with the fragmentation of Maya stone sculptures in the 1960s. In particular, the sculptures of several sites in Peten and Campeche, including Piedras Negras, El Perú-Waka', Machaquila and Calakmul, were cut into pieces and smuggled out of Guatemala and Mexico. Other sculptures originated in sites that had not yet been identified, such as Site Q, which is now known to be La Corona. Looters cut the monuments into sections that would fit on the backs of mules or into small

Giles G. Healey, Jose Pepe, Raul Pavón Abreu and Nabor with Stela 1 from Lacanja, Chiapas, Mexico, in April 1946, published in *Archaeology*, III (1950).

aeroplanes or suitcases, in the process slicing through ancient texts and images. They also thinned monuments to reduce their weight, leaving fragments behind as detritus, whether the 'carcass', from which carved portions had been cut, or pieces whose carvings were damaged during fragmentation.[28] Ian Graham recalled in his autobiography, 'Even before I had returned to Guatemala, early in 1965, I had become seriously concerned about the surge of looting in Petén. At several sites I had found the sliced-up remains of previously undamaged monuments – and later, advertisements in art magazines for splendid Maya monuments of unknown origin.'[29]

Dealers, private collectors and museums in Mexico, Central America and beyond acquired these fragments. For instance, Graham reports seeing Naranjo Stela 8 in 1966 in May's Department Store on Wilshire Boulevard, next to the Los Angeles County Museum of Art.[30] Teobert Maler had documented it in 1905, but Everett Rassiga, aeroplane pilot turned antiquities dealer, was involved in its illicit removal from Guatemala in the 1960s. Rassiga sold the stela to Morton D. May, who displayed it at his store but then loaned it to the Saint Louis Art Museum (SLAM). May ultimately returned legal ownership of the stela to Guatemala, and it remained on loan to SLAM until it was repatriated to Guatemala's National Museum of Archaeology and Ethnology (MUNAE) in 2015.[31] Also in 1966, Maya sculptures from Peten and Chiapas appeared for sale in the Galerie Jeanne Bucher, a Paris gallery specializing in modern painting that tried to enter the Maya antiquities market, although it did not sell all the sculptures, which remain in storage there.[32]

At around the same time, respected U.S. politicians and diplomats purchased Maya monuments. Bliss acquired a sculpted stone panel from the Lacanha region (that was named the Kuna-Lacanha panel) in 1960 from the dealer John Stokes, and Rockefeller bought a La Pasadita lintel in 1962 from Rassiga. Rockefeller, the Brooklyn Museum and the Minneapolis Institute of Arts also bought Piedras Negras stelae or fragments in the 1960s.[33] Other sculptures were removed by rogue adventurers. Dana and Ginger Lamb – who spun wild stories about their jungle adventures, the veracity of which has been questioned – photographed two ancient Maya lintels in their 'Lost City', which they named Laxtunich, though they did not identify its location (probably in Peten). The lintels were smuggled out of the region and ended up in the possession of the Maine collector William Palmer III; they are now in other private hands.[34]

Such acquisitions drew recrimination from parties in Mexico and Guatemala. Following the publication in 1963 of the Kuna-Lacanha panel in *Handbook of the Robert Woods Bliss Collection of Pre-Columbian Art*, writers in the Mexican press criticized the acquisition. In June 1965 César Lizardi Ramos asserted that the panel was part of Mexico's 'cultural patrimony' and had been stolen.[35] Another article in that same year condemned the presence of the panel in the Bliss collection and referred to the 'moral obligation' to return it to the Mexican nation.[36] The panel was not returned. In 1966 the Guatemalan historian Jorge Luján Muñoz denounced the presence of two Piedras Negras stelae in New York City museums, and asserted that they should be returned to Guatemala.[37] Rockefeller responded by returning Stela 5's title to Guatemala, but negotiated a loan to the Museum of Primitive Art and subsequently the Met. In addition, Rafael Morales of Guatemala's Pre-Hispanic Monuments worked with colleagues to form Operación Rescate (Rescue Operation) to save stela fragments that had been left behind, holding an exhibition in 1971 at MUNAE to raise awareness about the depredation.[38]

Other Maya materials were looted during this period, including figurines from Jaina Island and elsewhere. Bliss purchased several Maya figurines, ceramic vessels and carved jades before 1962.[39] Michael Coe's exhibition 'The Maya Scribe and His World' at the Grolier Club in New York in 1973 displayed Maya ceramic vessels without archaeological provenience, including a codex-style vessel with an elaborate supernatural underworld court scene, now at Princeton. Also displayed was the *Maya Codex of Mexico* (formerly the *Grolier Codex*), which was allegedly found in a cave. Sáenz purchased it in 1966 and later donated it to the library of Mexico's National Museum of Anthropology.[40] Rassiga was also involved, along with the American dealer Lee Moore and others, in removing a massive stucco facade from Placeres, Campeche, which was offered to the Metropolitan Museum of Art, but the Met's director reported it to the Mexican government. Mexico forced the dealers to return the facade to Mexico, and it was subsequently sent to the National Museum of Anthropology, where it remains today.[41]

In the United States, Graham and Clemency Coggins became staunch anti-looting activists, exposing the systems and individuals carrying out looting and criticizing museums or scholars that accepted or published looted materials.[42] Graham founded the Corpus of Maya Hieroglyphic Inscriptions to document sites and inscriptions before they were lost, and both advocated for strengthening antiquities laws. Although the various countries of origin had laws prohibiting the export of pre-Hispanic antiquities, the countries to which they were smuggled did not have laws against importing them, and thus the countries of origin had difficulties reclaiming looted objects. In 1970 the UNESCO Convention on the Means of Prohibiting and Preventing the Illicit Import, Export and Transport of Ownership of Cultural Property, an international treaty, was drafted to attempt to stop looting by prohibiting the import of antiquities, although it took years for countries to ratify it; the United States did not pass the appropriate legislation until 1983. In 1972 Mexico instituted its Federal Law on Archaeological, Artistic and Historic Monuments and Areas, which strengthened the protection of Mexican antiquities within and outside Mexico. Also in 1972, the United States passed the Pre-Columbian Art Act, which prohibited the import of monumental sculpture, murals and other architectural pieces, but it did not cover portable items. Another effective measure was to try dealers in u.s. courts. The FBI investigated the dealer Clive Hollinshead, who had smuggled two Machaquila stelae into the United States, and convicted him under federal stolen property law in 1973 for illegal import and transportation.[43] The stelae were returned to Guatemala, but other monuments that had not been documented in situ remained in collections in the United States.

These activities helped to reduce the looting of Maya monumental sculpture, but looting was redirected to portable material, especially ceramics from Peten, which was especially vulnerable during Guatemala's civil war. Before this period, some collectors had bought Maya ceramics, but the numbers increased drastically in the 1970s and '80s as more dealers and collectors desired to own them or profit from their sale. Río Azul was heavily looted from 1976 to 1981, when looters destroyed many Early Classic tombs. The archaeologist Richard Adams learned that the looting was commissioned by a wealthy Guatemalan collector who paid workers – as many as eighty at a time – to make trenches and tunnels in the buildings; finds were flown out of the jungle in small planes. Adams reported finding at least 125 open trenches and tunnels, and 28 looted tombs. His team also excavated unlooted tombs, and those grave goods – including extraordinary Early Classic ceramics – were submitted to Guatemala's National Museum. However, many ceramics, jade items and other materials looted from the site remain in foreign collections.[44]

During this time, many private collectors amassed Maya fine polychrome ceramics. Among them were Jorge Castillo in

Guatemala, who later donated his collection to the Universidad Francisco Marroquín in Guatemala City, which used the collection to form the Museo Popol Vuh in 1977–8. Gillett Griffin acquired Maya pieces as part of his vast Mesoamerican collection, which he donated to the Princeton University Art Museum, where he was curator. John Fulling amassed many items, called the November Collection, which he sold to Landon Clay, who donated it to the Boston Museum of Fine Arts in 1988. Francis Robicsek focused on acquiring codex-style ceramics, many of which are now in the Mint Museum in Charlotte, North Carolina. Jay Kislak donated his collection, which included fine Maya ceramics and early American maps, to the U.S. Library of Congress. Another major collector was Lewis Ranieri, whose collection of polychrome ceramics and other items was acquired by the Los Angeles County Museum of Art (LACMA) in 2010. Many of these polychrome ceramics probably come from Peten, and scholars have connected particular vessels to certain sites or regions by studying their inscriptions and painting styles.[45] Another area that experienced major looting was the Department of Escuintla, on Guatemala's Pacific Coast; complex sculpted censers from this region are now in many U.S. museums.[46]

New legislation and the criticism of museum practices have mitigated such devastating looting and site destruction. In 1991 the United States – responding to a request from Guatemala – took emergency action to prohibit the import of Maya archaeological artefacts from Peten; this was formalized with a Memorandum of Understanding in 1997.[47] Museums have also changed their collecting policies, especially following the Association of Art Museum Directors guidelines of 2008, which encourage museums not to collect antiquities without clear documentation of the fact that they were outside their country of origin by 1970, the date of the UNESCO Convention. These new policies have limited what museums can acquire and consequently what private individuals buy, thereby reducing the market for pre-Hispanic antiquities in the United States.

In the twenty-first century museums will need to respond to these histories and decide if and how to make up for past actions. For instance, they may return ownership or possession of objects to the countries of origin or work towards restitution in other ways, supporting archaeological projects or the construction of museums in those countries or collaborating in research and exhibitions. The process will be challenging for the thousands of looted sculptures, vessels and figurines that may be from Mexico, Guatemala, Belize or Honduras, and whose illicit removal has left their findspots a mystery. For even in cases in which an inscription, painting style or chemical signature indicates one archaeological site and thus one country, the piece may have been traded to or deposited in another site in what is now another country, since the exchange of items was crucial to ancient Maya social networking and diplomacy. This happened with the Buenavista Vase, which was painted in a style from Guatemala but found in a tomb in Belize.[48] Such uncertainty will cloud attempts to repatriate Maya antiquities, but this could be solved by agreements among the countries occupying the Maya ancestral homelands. Or perhaps such objects could be returned to a supranational organization or trust run by and benefiting Maya people living in several countries.

Museums may move away from collecting and instead organize exhibitions featuring excavated materials from source countries. The recent blockbuster exhibition 'Teotihuacan: City of Water, City of Fire' (2017–19) at the de Young Museum in San Francisco, LACMA and the Phoenix Art Museum featured new finds from Mexican and foreign archaeological teams, and 'Golden Kingdoms: Luxury and Legacy in the Ancient Americas' (2017–18), at the Getty Museum and the Metropolitan Museum of Art, displayed excavated objects from more than a dozen Latin American countries (in addition to some pieces that were not excavated by archaeologists).[49] In the future, museums would do well to use funds to promote sanctioned excavations, loans, exhibitions and collaborative research and foster relationships with Indigenous communities, as opposed to purchasing items without archaeological provenience.

Another significant trend in the care and display of ancient Maya objects has been the development of site and regional museums in Mexico and Central America, where pieces from that place or region are held and displayed. These include site museums at Palenque, Tonina, Tikal and Copan; the Miraflores Museum in Guatemala City, which displays artefacts from the southern part of Kaminaljuyu; and regional museums such as the Museo Regional Mundo Maya in Flores and the Museo Maya de Cancún. Spread across the Maya world, these museums allow local people as well as visitors to see and appreciate items from each respective region. The genre of the Euro-American museum, generally engaged in collecting items from many cultures and displaying them together, is historically based on colonial enterprises that endeavoured to keep and know the resources of the colonial dominion. In some ways, the development of Mexico's National Museum followed such a trend, building collections from throughout their territory. Such nationalizing of culture has been criticized, but another perspective is that such collections productively promote a nation's multicultural identity.[50] The development of more regional, local and site museums partially addresses such criticism, offering opportunities for local people to experience the material culture of their region and benefit from sustainable tourism. Although Maya sites were ravaged as looting increased to support the art market in the third quarter of the twentieth century, improved laws and international treaties, better enforcement of laws and treaties, changing museum acquisition practices, and efforts to support and involve communities near archaeological sites have reduced looting and engaged communities in protecting sites, but there is still work to do. Today and in the future, museums must confront the history of their collections. It will not be easy, but dialogue with governments and communities of origin is a place to start. It is time to pivot, to join with contemporary Maya people in preserving and protecting the legacy of their ancestors.

# SEVEN

# ANCIENT MAYA IN POPULAR CULTURE, ARCHITECTURE AND VISUAL ARTS

O ver the past several centuries, ancient Maya designs have appeared in myriad ways in architecture, popular culture and visual arts. Some architects and artists have used Maya imagery and architecture for reasons of personal, civic or religious identity, for instance to create a national or regional identity and connect with an actual or desired ancestral past, often participating in broader appropriations of the ancient Maya as predecessors of larger groups such as Yucatecans, Mexicans or Guatemalans. Furthermore, people from the United States have at times claimed affiliation with the ancient Maya because of the shared location in the Americas and a desire to develop a true 'American' art, defined broadly. This was especially relevant for Maya Revival architecture in California, which James Oles argues was related 'to the search for a unique regional identity', comparable to efforts in Yucatan, even though the Maya ruins were far from California.[1] U.S. artists and architects also adopted ancient Maya motifs to promote Mexican culture in the United States, or for the purposes of business, entertainment or tourism. Examples of the above can be especially problematic if they involve appropriating the ancient Maya legacy while disassociating it from contemporary Maya people. In contrast, some artists have used Maya forms to criticize earlier appropriations of ancient Maya culture, and their works constitute a call to action that complements the cultural and political activism of contemporary Maya people.

## Neo-Maya architecture

In the late nineteenth and early twentieth centuries, many archi-tects, politicians and archaeologists from Mexico, Central America, the United States and Europe looked to ancient Maya architecture as inspiration for new buildings. Some were temporary structures, made for a single international exposition; others were more per-manent, made as a civic building or theatre; and some were used in expositions but retained afterwards. These comprise a style called 'Maya Revival' or 'Neo-Maya', defined as modern buildings that evoke ancient Maya architecture, which first appeared in Yucatan and Southern California in the early twentieth century. This style is part of a larger 'Pre-Hispanic Revival' style that engages other cultures, including Aztec, Zapotec and Inka.[2] Maya motifs were frequently mixed with other pre-Hispanic motifs, because the architects either did not know the difference or preferred to mix styles.

One manifestation of this engagement with ancient Maya and other pre-Hispanic architecture was in European and u.s. inter-national expositions, where casts, copies or motifs from Maya buildings represented Mexico or the Americas or, alternatively, the discipline of anthropology. The pavilions' experiential nature was important, and organizers used media in many scales – includ-ing architecture, sculptures, wall paintings, architectural models and artefacts – to convey a sense of place, country or identity and create immersive environments. Expositions were one forum for Mexico to present itself to the world, and the choice to use pre-Hispanic motifs conveyed its unique history and contributed to larger efforts to build a national identity after Independence. Projects generated in Central Mexico generally chose the Mexica or Aztec civilization as inspiration.[3] Two significant examples of Mexico engaging with pre-Hispanic Central Mexican architectural styles are the international expositions in Paris in 1867 and 1889, described in Chapter Four.

The first known use of ancient Maya architecture came from outside Mexico, in the 1893 World's Columbian Exposition in Chicago, which celebrated Christopher Columbus's arrival in the

Cast of a portion of Uxmal's Palace of the Governor, World's Columbian
Exposition, Chicago, 1893.

Americas. But this Maya architecture was associated with a pavilion dedicated not to Mexico but to anthropology. Casts of Maya architecture from Labna and Uxmal were installed outside the fair's Anthropological Building to showcase the people who were in the Americas when Columbus arrived.[4] Thus the pre-Hispanic buildings symbolized pre-Hispanic Maya people, but they were presented as an architectural folly, in ruin, with growing plants and loose stones toppled off the buildings, gesturing to researchers' exploration and discovery of lost or neglected archaeological sites.[5] As with other fairs, the interior of the pavilion was filled with media at many scales, including artefacts, sculpture casts, and photographs by Alfred Maudslay and Teobert Maler of sites across the Maya region. Honduras lent Maya sculpture fragments for display, and European and American museums lent artefacts, too. Indeed, the French anthropologist Ernest-Théodore Hamy wrote proudly that the pieces sent from the Trocadéro in Paris encompassed all the regions of the New World, emphasizing the extensive collections of French museums.[6]

This exposition, like the 1889 Exposition Universelle in Paris, established a problematic relationship between the architecture of the ancient Americas and contemporary Indigenous people. An exhibition publication remarked that the ancient Maya buildings were 'the architecture of a forgotten and mysterious race'.[7] Such a statement omitted or bypassed the connections to contemporary Indigenous people of the Americas. Furthermore, nearby were outdoor exhibits with living people, including Kwakwaka'wakw people from Fort Rupert, British Columbia, who performed ceremonies and daily routines while on public display, exposed to touristic consumption and contrasted with the cultures of technology and modernity exhibited elsewhere in the fair.[8]

Mexican architects later constructed Neo-Maya buildings (either temporary or permanent) as expressions of national or regional pride. The first Maya Revival buildings in Mexico were temporary arches emulating Chichen Itza's Nunnery Annex. These were built as if new, not in ruin. One ephemeral arch, designed by Leopoldo Batres, was constructed in Mexico City in 1899 to represent Yucatan, amid other arches sponsored by various Mexican states to celebrate Independence and honour Porfirio Díaz. A comparable arch based on the Nunnery Annex but topped with allegorical sculptures representing progress and modernity was constructed in the main plaza of Mérida in 1906, commemorating Díaz's visit.[9] This type of arch derives from ancient Roman and European triumphal arches celebrating conquests, a practice that was adopted in New Spain. Some earlier arches appropriated European and pre-Hispanic Central Mexican motifs, but the Maya portals expressed Yucatan's unique history and culture. However, they were built during and just after the Caste Wars and the brutal suppression of Maya communities fighting for autonomy. The architect and archaeologist Juan Antonio Siller observes that this use of ancient Maya architecture for political purposes contrasted with the disregard or disdain for contemporary Maya people, many of whom had died during the Caste Wars or remained in servitude in henequen plantations.[10] Those in power thus appropriated ancient Maya architecture while celebrating the continued subjugation of Maya people. Such appropriation was perhaps made possible by continuing rhetoric that divorced contemporary Maya people from their ancestors' legacy and claimed it for the region, nation and hemisphere.

The first permanent Maya Revival building in Mexico was also in Mérida, but was made during the revolution that ousted Díaz. Manuel Amábilis Domínguez, an architect from Mérida who studied in Paris, designed a new facade for the seventeenth-century Templo del Dulce Nombre de Jesús church, which was changed into a Freemason lodge, beginning in 1915 and completed in 1918.[11] This change in function enacted a symbolic conversion of the Mexican Catholic and colonial past into a revolutionary future. The Maya-style facade, featuring a corbel vault for the central portal, pilasters with Chichen Itza-style serpent-head bases, and Puuc-style frets, crosses and zoomorphic masks, projected this transformation.

Amábilis also designed a Maya Revival building for Mexico's pavilion in the 1929 Ibero-American Exposition in Seville, in concert with the sculptor Leopoldo Tommasi López and the painter Victor M. Reyes.[12] The facade was adorned with Puuc-style bound

TEMPLO MASONICO.. MASONIC TEMPLE, MERIDA, YUC.

Manuel Amábilis, Templo Masónico (Masonic Temple): United Grand Lodge of the
Eastern Yucatan Peninsula, Mérida, Yucatan, Mexico, 1915, postcard.

Manuel Amábilis, Leopoldo Tommasi López and Victor M. Reyes, Mexican Pavilion, Ibero-American Exposition, Seville, Spain, 1929.

columns and flaring cornices, and the central portal combined Chichen Itza-style serpent columns and designs from the Nunnery Annex, but in the central cartouche was an eagle on a cactus with a serpent, marking the Maya architecture with the symbol of the Mexican flag and nation, originally an Aztec design. Copies of Chichen Itza chacmool sculptures crowned the roof, flanking an allegorical frieze portraying nude figures and women in Mexican clothing. In front were two 'Toltec' stelae, creative reinterpretations of Piedras Negras Stela 14 in which the ancient Maya ruler and his mother were transformed into male allegories of Labour and Spirituality.[13] Amábilis called them 'Toltec' (not Maya), and some aspects of the design appear to have been inspired by Masonic iconography.

As Amábilis recounted, engaging with the art and architecture 'of our grandparents' was a way to use Yucatan's unique identity to create post-Revolutionary Mexican forms to contrast with European styles and revive arts that had been suppressed during the colonial period and Díaz's dictatorship. Further, the pavilion countered exposition rhetoric claiming the colonies owed their birth and progress in the arts and culture to Spain.[14] Instead, Amábilis emphasized the superior qualities of pre-Hispanic architecture and stressed that these styles offered opportunities to improve European art and architecture. His preference for pre-Hispanic forms aligned with other Mexican endeavours to adopt Indigenous forms as national symbols after the Revolution. Indeed, Yucatan's socialist government, especially during the governorships of General Salvador Alvarado and Felipe Carrillo Puerto, implemented policies to better the conditions for Indigenous people through land reform and educational improvements. As governor, Carrillo Puerto elevated Maya language and culture, both for the state's identity and for the liberation of Indigenous people.[15] Luis Carranza argues that the Mexican pavilion's appropriation of Maya forms 'could be seen, therefore, as denouncing colonialist practices, as rejecting the objectification, stereotyping, and exotification of a diverse national culture, and as advocating class equality'.[16] Yet Amábilis resisted calling this sculpture and architecture 'Maya', and instead followed nineteenth-century writers in saying that the ancient cities were made by the 'Toltecs', who spread civilization in Mexico and beyond. Moreover, Amábilis expected European architects to understand and embrace pre-Hispanic Mexican forms in contemporary buildings because he believed that European and Maya architecture 'derived from the same root' (later specified as Atlantis).[17] Thus despite his contributions to elevating Indigenous architecture on a global scale, and his anti-colonialist rhetoric, the attribution of Maya designs to the legendary Toltecs continued the problematic appropriation of Indigenous forms that disconnected contemporary Maya people from them.

## Arts, nationalism and ethnic identity

In the 1920s and '30s several Mexican and Guatemalan artists used Maya or other pre-Hispanic imagery to create a collective identity for their nation or region. On an interior stairwell in the National Palace in Mexico City, Diego Rivera painted *The History of Mexico* (1929–35), which portrays Mexican history from before the Conquest to the present day. The pre-Hispanic section focuses on Quetzalcoatl, making reference to the legend that Hernán Cortés was the returned Aztec deity. This mural became a model that later artists in Guatemala and Yucatan emulated. In 1939–43 the Guatemalan painter Alfredo Gálvez Suárez painted for the Guatemalan National Palace a series of murals that were analogous to Rivera's in depicting the country's history in a government building, but which focused partially on Maya people and myths, including the K'iche' Maya *Popol Vuh*.[18]

In contrast to these scenes is the Mexican muralist David Alfaro Siqueiros's painting of a Maya pyramid in *América Tropical* (1932). Siqueiros was commissioned to paint a mural for Los Angeles's Olvera Street, a touristic location that presented a romantic image of Mexico. Siqueiros created not a romanticized Mexican scene but an image of resistance, for in front of the pyramid, overgrown with jungle, is an Indigenous man crucified on a double cross topped

Roberto Berdecio stands in front of Davíd Alfaro Siqueiros's *América Tropical* mural shortly after completion, Los Angeles, 1932.

Federico Mariscal, Chac relief in Palacio de Bellas Artes, Mexico City, 1934, marble and bronze.

by an eagle, symbolizing u.s. economic imperialism's devastation of Indigenous peasants. Siqueiros also portrayed Peruvian and Mexican revolutionaries aiming guns at the eagle.[19] The use of Maya imagery was thus not to elevate the ancient Maya but to decry the poor treatment of contemporary Indigenous people and criticize the United States. But his patrons, having expected a romanticized scene, soon whitewashed the mural.

Perhaps one of the most prominent buildings with Maya designs is the Palacio de Bellas Artes in Mexico City, but it was not planned this way, for the Maya motifs were part of a post-Revolution transformation of a pre-Revolution building. In 1934 Federico Mariscal completed the interior design, modifying the Neoclassical building that was begun during the Díaz dictatorship but left unfinished.[20] He clad the interior in eclectic Mexican symbols and Art Deco design, including Puuc-style zoomorphic masks, rendered in bronze and set in an Art Deco frame of pink marble, that cap enormous vertical pillars with embedded light fixtures, significant transformations from their original stone mosaics. On the front doors, Mariscal copied heads from the Teotihuacan Feathered Serpent Pyramid, and Oles asserts that the use of both Maya and Teotihuacan designs was a 'carefully considered gesture of national unification'.[21] Also fundamental to the building are the murals created by Rivera, Siqueiros, Rufino Tamayo and José Clemente Orozco, some of which convey significant moments in Mexico's history, including Siqueiros's dynamic mural of the torture of Cuauhtemoc, the heroic Aztec emperor who resisted Spanish invaders and whose actions resonated with those who fought the Porfiriato's authoritarian regime. The post-Revolution transformation of this building thus uses pre-Hispanic and later designs and narratives to establish a new visual history for Mexico.

## Maya architecture and design in the United States

One of the first permanent manifestations of u.s. architecture engaging with ancient Maya and other pre-Hispanic art and architecture was the Pan-American Union Building of 1910 in Washington, DC. The institution's mission was Pan-American unity, and the architecture – designed by Paul Philippe Cret and Albert Kelsey and funded by Andrew Carnegie – responds in some ways to this ideal. This was a European-style Neoclassical building, but adornments included Maya, Aztec, Zapotec and Inka designs, and the mixing of cultures was intended to display Pan-Americanism or the unity of the states.[22] Yet, as the architectural historian Robert Alexander González has observed, references to Indigenous people were only in details on a European-style building, and the selective references from Latin American nations excluded other groups, including Native Americans in the United States.[23]

More explicit engagements were prominent in Southern Californian expositions. In 1915 the Panama-California Exposition, held in Balboa Park, San Diego, celebrated California and Latin America, for San Diego was the first (or last) stop on the u.s. Pacific Coast for ships travelling the newly completed Panama Canal.[24] The interior of the California Building, curated by the anthropologist Edgar Lee Hewett, displayed ancient Panamanian artefacts, casts of ancient Maya sculptures and new media, including a relief map of Central America and photographs, models and paintings of Maya buildings. The artist Carlos Vierra, who travelled to Quirigua with Hewett and worked with Sylvanus Morley, painted romanticized scenes of Maya sites after their abandon-ment.[25] Another artist, Jean Cook-Smith, created bas-relief plaster sculptures with themes from Palenque, rendering them in a style evoking Classical Greek art that aligned with the adage that the Maya were the Greeks of the New World. A Chichen Itza-style Serpent Portal featured the exhibition's opening date, 1 January 1915, in Maya writing.[26] Hewett remarked that the goal was to show 'something of what Europeans saw when they first looked upon the new world'.[27] In an exposition publication, he wrote about the autochthonous development of the Maya: 'Fantastic theories about these people, their Oriental or Egyptian origin . . . all this may be dismissed. There is nothing mysterious about it. The ancient temple builders of Central America were American Indians.' Moreover, he stated that 'Some of us dare to hope that this is the beginning of a general awakening to the importance of a great people, possibly to the opening up of a veritable treasure-house of knowledge, long obscured but not destined to perpetual oblivion.'[28]

These objects evoking the pre-Hispanic world were held inside a building whose exterior, designed by Bertram Grosvenor Goodhue, was Spanish or Mexican Baroque. The interior and exterior thus emphasized the Indigenous and Spanish herit-ages of California. Yet the pavilion did not feature the Cahuilla, Kumeyaay, Luiseño, or other local Indigenous tribes; instead, it connected ancient Guatemala, Mexico and Panama to California, suggesting that Latin American heritage belonged to California – or that California belonged to Latin America. Furthermore, the pavilion rhetoric allowed Hewett to envision the Spanish and Native cultures in harmony because the 'golden age' had allegedly ended before the Spanish arrived:

It seemed especially fitting that the California Building should enshrine the memorials of a race that ran its course in America before the continent was seen by Europeans . . . The object of the exhibits in the California Building is to present a picture of the golden age of that race – a page of human history that is as worthy of study as are its great contemporaries of the old world.[29]

By emphasizing that the exhibition was about Native people who disappeared before the arrival of the Spanish, and presenting both groups contributing to California heritage, organizers sidestepped the sixteenth-century wars of conquest and later acts of genocide against Indigenous Americans.

Regardless, the installation's display of an antiquity for California that was separate from Europe and distinctively American had a lasting effect on Maya Revival design, inspiring other architects and designers in California. The Southwest Museum, founded in 1907, moved in 1914 to its campus in Highland Park, Los Angeles, which featured Andalusian and California Mission-style buildings. In 1919–20 the director, Hector Alliot, hired the architectural firm Allison & Allison to modify the campus. The new plan featured many architectural styles, including a large Tikal-style pyramid on the hilltop above the Spanish and California Mission-style buildings, which together would have gestured to the museum's mission, encompassing the Southwestern United States and Latin America. That plan was not fully realized, but a Maya-style facade, modelled on the Chichen Itza Nunnery Annex, was built as a new entrance to the older building.[30]

Frank Lloyd Wright also emulated Maya architecture in his designs. He probably saw the Maya building casts at the Chicago fair in 1893, which may have sparked interests that he later explored by consulting publications of Maya sites.[31] The exterior of his A. D. German Warehouse in Richland Center, Wisconsin, designed in 1915 and constructed in 1917–20, has Chichen Itza and Puuc elements.[32] For example, the planar surfaces of the exterior brick walls and the patterned cast-concrete cornice evoke – but do not copy – Puuc architecture from Uxmal and Chichen Itza. But Wright integrated Maya forms more fully in the Hollyhock House (Alice Barnsdall House) in Hollywood. Built on a terraced hill, the house has a quadrangle organization similar to that of the Palenque Palace and Uxmal Nunnery. The smooth exterior plaster is comparable to Palenque and Puuc buildings, and the hip roofs resemble the architecture of Palenque and Yaxchilan.[33] In addition, the 'hollyhock' plant designs, abstracted into geometric forms that stud the exterior stairways, evoke Copan stelae. This

Frank Lloyd Wright, Hollyhock House, Hollywood, California, 1919–21.

house is unmistakably resonant with Maya architecture, but the quotations are not direct. Indeed, Wright said that his approach was one of emulating, rather than imitating, tradition.[34]

Wright was ambiguous about his use of ancient Maya and other cultures' architectural forms. In 1930, early in his career, he expressed admiration for the architecture of the Indigenous Americas, saying, 'I remember how, as a boy, primitive American architecture – Toltec, Aztec, Mayan, Inca – stirred my wonder, excited my wishful admiration. I wished I might have money someday to go to Mexico, Guatemala and Peru to join in excavating those long slumbering remains of lost cultures.'[35] Furthermore, he said, 'we may learn from them.'[36] In 1937 Wright again extolled the virtues of Maya architecture and decoration, suggesting that the reader

Grasp the simple force of the level grandeur of the primal Mayan sense of form and the Mayan enrichment of it. Grasp the cruel power of his crude Gods . . . then relate that to the extended plateau his terraces made and the mighty scale of his horizontal stone constructions. You will have in these trabeations the sense of might in stone. Even a Mayan 'decoration' was mighty.[37]

Thus it appears that Wright admired and cited Maya and other cultures' forms, but he later resisted being wed to them, insisting that his work sought universal forms: 'There never was an exterior influence upon my work either foreign or native.'[38] Indeed, he may have borrowed designs, but he abstracted them in order to universalize them, highlighting commonalities across cultures, as opposed to citing specific ones. Through such techniques, he created a unique American architecture whose forms shared qualities with Indigenous buildings but were blended with international styles in explicitly modern structures. Moreover, in denying the use of Indigenous sources, he distanced himself from the English architect Robert Stacy-Judd, who unambiguously quoted Maya designs. Nonetheless, others celebrated the Maya influences in Wright's buildings; for instance, Charles Ennis added Maya motifs in metalwork to his home, one of Wright's Textile-Block Houses in Los Angeles.[39]

Stacy-Judd, who had moved to Los Angeles in 1922, designed buildings that fancifully and explicitly evoked Maya architecture, first as another exotic style and later to connect to narratives of global diffusion from Atlantis. In his early years in Los Angeles, he worked in several revival styles, including European medieval, Mediterranean, Spanish, Egyptian and Islamic, but he ultimately focused on Maya Revival.[40] Stacy-Judd, who recalled that his interest in Maya architecture stemmed from reading John Lloyd Stephens and Frederick Catherwood, used George Oakley Totten's book of Maya architectural ornamentation (1926) and visited archaeological sites in Yucatan to seek ideas.[41] Contemporaneous descriptions of his architecture emphasize it as uniquely 'American'. In 1928 the journalist Edgar Lloyd Hampton described Stacy-Judd's Aztec Hotel in Monrovia, California (1924–5), as 'the only structure standing on the earth today that embodies exclusively the art, architecture, and decorative designs of our prehistoric past. In other words, it is the only building in the United States that is 100 per cent American.'[42] Granted, missing from the commentary are other structures with comparable characteristics, such as the Mayan Theatre in Los Angeles, designed by Francisco Cornejo and inaugurated in 1927.

Stacy-Judd's use of Maya elements changed over time. Early projects such as the Aztec Hotel (named as such because the Aztecs were better-known) applied decorative elements to street facades and interior public spaces.[43] Marjorie Ingle observes that the Maya ornamentation was a late decision, for earlier plans projected an Egyptian Revival building.[44] The designs invoked many sources, including Puuc-style bound columns on the cornices and motifs recalling Maya breath scrolls or featherwork around the entries, windows and building corners, but they are abstracted or stylized. However, later designs and buildings, including the Ventura First Baptist Church (1928–32), the Philosophical Research Society in Los Feliz (1935–7) and the Masonic Temple of North Hollywood (1948–51), incorporated Maya architectural features in a more integrated way. Especially notable are the tall Maya-style corbel vaults forming the front entries, similar to the vaults of Labna

Robert Stacy-Judd, Masonic Temple, North Hollywood, California, 1948–51.

Robert Stacy-Judd, *The Destruction of Atlantis*, 1936, rendering on board.

or the Uxmal Governor's Palace. In addition, interior rooms of the Philosophical Research Society are shaped like corbel vaults, and supporting columns in the courtyard are Chichen Itza-style Serpent Columns.

As well as designing Maya Revival buildings to create American designs in contrast to European styles, Stacy-Judd chose Maya Revival because of his own and his clients' interest in Freemasonry in terms of the potential connections of early societies across the world, a preoccupation that drew on nineteenth-century speculation about cultural diffusion.[45] In the late 1930s Stacy-Judd published ideas about mass migration from Atlantis. He referred to 'the much discussed Lost Atlantis, whence, I believe, the Mayas came', and argued that 'the Maya civilization in Central America arrived in that area fully developed, its origin and growth having taken place in some centre other than the American continent,' claiming that the Maya people, after fleeing Atlantis, colonized Central America. His evidence included perceived similarities in language, religion and architecture between the Maya and 'early civilizations of Europe and Asia Minor', but these were superficial or baseless.[46] Drawing on the earlier ideas of Charles-Étienne Brasseur de Bourbourg and Augustus Le Plongeon, Stacy-Judd argued that the references to great deluges in many civilizations derived from the flooding of Atlantis, and he supported these arguments by rendering Maya-style bodies and buildings when illustrating the flight from Atlantis.[47] In one painting, he portrays men in canoes amid rolling waves, while a volcano erupts in the background. The rising water engulfs buildings that emulate the structures of Uxmal, Palenque and Tikal, creating what Stacy-Judd may have imagined to be an ideal Maya city, but it also conveyed the idea that his own designs mixing styles and places originated in this lost city.

## Interior design in southern California

Several interior designers in southern California used Maya designs in houses and public buildings. *Southern California Business*, the magazine of the Los Angeles Chamber of Commerce, promoted Stacy-Judd's designs and those of companies producing Maya Revival items for the home. Edgar Lloyd Hampton described the 'exhaustless number of possibilities' to be derived from archaeologists' books that could provide inspiration for structural designs and decorative purposes, each offering the possibility of reciting 'some vital phase of the life history of an American prehistoric race'.[48] Ceramic tile companies produced Maya-inspired tiles, as well as Egyptian, Chinese and Persian styles. The Batchelder-Wilson Company's line of Maya Revival tiles included fireplaces, counters, plates and bookends.[49] CALCO Tiles, founded by Rufus Bradley Keeler, produced individual tiles and full fireplaces, including one in Keeler's own home. Flanking the firebox are standing figures from the Palenque Tablet of the Cross, which had been displayed in the San Diego exposition, and above is the earth zoomorph from the same panel. The tile and fireplace designers mixed and shuffled the designs, with little concern for verisimilitude in relation to their originals, but these pieces allowed homeowners in cities across the United States to engage with the Maya and other distant cultures.

Other notable designers were Francisco Cornejo and Henry Lovins, who used Maya and Aztec designs to create a 'modern' or 'true American art'. Lovins, who arrived in Los Angeles from New York and Denver in 1911, designed murals for the California

Building (1915) in San Diego that were colourful renditions of Yaxchilan and Palenque sculptures and became part of his design repertoire. Both artists expressed a desire to find inspiration for 'American art' from the ancient art forms of the Americas, rather than from the European tradition. Cornejo avidly promoted Mexican culture in Los Angeles, presenting illustrated lectures on ancient and contemporary Mexican culture and movies of Mexican ruins, folk songs and dances; in 1921 he brought an exhibition of ancient Mexican art to Los Angeles.[50]

Cornejo used Maya and other cultures' designs for private houses, clubs and theatres. For the Mayan Theatre (1927) in downtown Los Angeles, Cornejo – working under decorating contractor Richard Sobieraj and the architectural firm Morgan, Walls & Clements – mixed Maya motifs with other Mesoamerican and South American designs. He explained that the project borrowed and adapted 'the wealth of the ancient arts of the American style for their architectural and decorative qualities', but applied them to meet modern conditions.[51] According to Cornejo, the facade's entwined serpent and floral pattern, which was cast to resemble rough, weathered sandstone, was inspired by Uxmal and Chichen

CALCO (California Clay Products Company), Fireplace Surround, 1923–32, earthenware.

Francisco Cornejo (designer), Mayan Theatre exterior, Los Angeles, California, 1927.

Itza architecture, and the seated figures were like Zapotec censers. In the lobby, Cornejo used the corbel vault and the Palenque tre-foil-shaped vault to recall Maya buildings. Many designs in the lobby and theatre are based on monuments from Quirigua, Tikal and Chichen Itza, whose casts Cornejo saw in San Diego. On the lobby floor and walls are texts from Quirigua stelae, but they are repeated, reshuffled, or turned sideways or upside down. Inside the theatre, the proscenium arches draw on Quirigua Stela E, and the curtains of the side stages recall Palenque tablets, but none is a direct copy. The ceiling is an extraordinary evocation of the Aztec Calendar Stone, and other motifs derive from Central Mexican and Bolivian sculptures. It is truly Pan-American in scope.[52] Furthermore, the designs, made for a theatre – a place for fiction and fantasy – appropriate but wilfully transform and misunderstand their sources.

Contemporaneous reviews of the Mayan Theatre were positive. Announcing the opening in August 1927, Edwin Schallert of the *Los Angeles Times* wrote: 'It embodies ideas that are singularly artistic in its scheme of construction, and gives every promise of being warmly inviting.'[53] He also noted that the theatre would be particularly alluring for those who had studied American history, because of the antiquity of the Maya. Another critic viewed it as 'rugged and grotesque at times' but a 'most welcome relief from the stereotyped designs of the past which have shown repeated variations of the use of many of the classic and renaissance adaptations'.[54] Even so, in a recent critique, the artist Nina Höchtl calls the theatre an example of 'cultural transvestism' and the result of a 'coloniality of seeing'.[55]

Maya Revival theatres were built in other American cities in the same decade, including San Antonio, Detroit, Denver and New York City (in Queens), and skyscraper architects in San Francisco, Los Angeles and New York used Maya design elements, too. According to the British architect Alfred C. Bossom, Maya pyramids were the first American skyscrapers, and thus it made sense to cloak new skyscrapers in Indigenous American forms. Francisco Mujica, a Peruvian architect who worked in Mexico and the United States, promoted the study of Indigenous American architecture as inspiration for new, modern buildings.[56]

The trend of creating Maya Revival buildings in the United States was mostly stalled by the Great Depression, but there were two more expositions in the 1930s with Maya-style buildings, in Chicago and San Diego. The 1933 Chicago Century of Progress World's Fair celebrated the fortieth anniversary of the 1893 fair and included a 'Mayan Temple' based on the North Building of the Uxmal Nunnery. The Danish archaeologist Frans Blom, of Tulane University's Middle American Research Institute, travelled to Yucatan to collect photographs, moulds and film footage that were used to reproduce the North Building.[57] This structure was built whole and new – not as a ruin – and painted in polychrome.

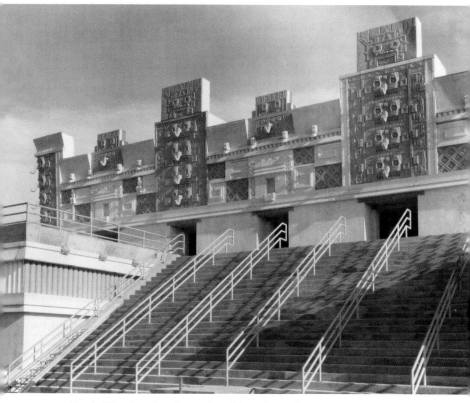

Exposition building based on the North Building of Uxmal's Nunnery, Century of Progress, Chicago, 1933.

The interior featured various media, but especially notable were the Piedras Negras sculptures that had been removed by Penn Museum archaeologists in earlier years. The actual sculptures, rare in the United States at the time, were thus contained within the simulacrum.

The 1935 California-Pacific International Exposition, held on the twentieth anniversary of the 1915 San Diego fair, reused some of the older fair's buildings, including the California Building, and created new ones. The 1935 fair promoted engagement with Latin American culture and countries as part of President Roosevelt's Good Neighbor Policy.[58] The Federal Building, designed by the architect Richard Requa and the Hollywood artist Juan Larrinaga, was a huge, rectangular modern building with a mostly plain exterior, but the central portal was in the shape of a corbel vault and decorated with zoomorphic masks similar to those on Uxmal's Palace of the Governor, but much larger in scale. It copied its source more faithfully than did earlier Maya Revival buildings, but it has been criticized for the way the Maya building's 'bold stonework' was turned 'into flimsy fibre-wallboard approximations . . . hung as a frieze on the exterior'.[59] Nearby, the Indian Village, which had '150 Indians from thirty tribes' making crafts, dancing and faking stagecoach hold-ups and attacks on covered wagons, belittled Native Americans and brought into relief the fact that the fair's display of Indigenous Americans exoticized and created difference between fair visitors and Indigenous people, as expositions had for decades.[60]

Tourism and entertainment initiated a new wave of Maya Revival buildings in the late twentieth and twenty-first centuries. EPCOT's World Showcase at Walt Disney World in Orlando, Florida, is the late twentieth-century version of an international exposition, with pavilions dedicated to various countries, but designed by an American corporation. The Mexico Pavilion features smoking volcanoes and two pyramids, one Maya and the other a mix of Mesoamerican forms. Nearby, Disney's Coronado Springs Resort reproduces a Tikal-style Maya pyramid wrapped in jungle vines next to a swimming pool, but most of the architecture in the resort is Spanish of some sort, whether Andalusian or Spanish colonial in style. Indeed, the Mesoamerican elements are contextualized within a frame of the Spanish Conquest, for the resort celebrates 'the daring spirit of the great Spanish explorers, artists, writers and architects'.[61] The juxtaposition of Spanish and Indigenous American architecture and the resort's advertising appropriate this traumatic episode of world history for entertainment and crass commercialism.

Maya architecture is also used for tourism and entertainment in Mexico and Central America. In the 'Mayan Village' of Xcaret Park in Playa del Carmen, Quintana Roo, not far from ancient Maya archaeological sites, are fake pyramids surrounded by jungle. Visitors can watch a Maya ballgame and dance performance, or visit Maya houses where women weave. Maya people are on display, and Maya culture is exoticized for commercial and entertainment purposes. This comes to the fore with the Xcaret website photo of a white couple watching costumed performers conduct a smoke-filled ceremony on a fake pyramid.[62] The alleged lost island of Atlantis has also become a trope in tourism. The Atlantis Resort on Paradise Island, Bahamas, advertises a 'Mayan Temple' with water slides, including one that travels through a tube in a shark-filled lagoon. Although intended for entertainment, it perpetuates the myth of Atlantis and exploits the Maya for commercial means.

## Diffusionism and New Age religions

Also persistent in the twentieth century were nineteenth-century speculations about the Maya and cultural diffusion from Atlantis or other transoceanic contact. Manuel Amábilis Domínguez and Robert Stacy-Judd promoted the speculation that the Maya (or Toltecs) had come from Atlantis. James Churchward followed this idea but argued that the lost continent was the Island of Lemuria or Mu in the Pacific Ocean.[63] Churchward asserted that tablets found in India and Mexico revealed transoceanic connections, and that all civilized peoples originated from Mu. He praised the people of Mu as 'highly civilized and enlightened', and claimed: '*There was no savagery on the face of the earth, nor had there ever been*, since all the peoples on earth were children of Mu and under the suzerainty of the motherland.' Furthermore, he stated that 'the dominant race in the land of Mu was a *white race*' who governed other races of yellow, brown and black.[64] Such statements recall nineteenth-century stories of Aryans spreading civilization across the world, and took agency away from Indigenous people in the Americas.

A new type of diffusion narrative beginning in the 1960s stated or implied that ancient Maya cities were built or influenced by aliens from outer space, a continuation of the nineteenth-century scepticism about whether Indigenous Americans could have built ancient cities without external assistance. Erich von Däniken wrote about aliens helping the Maya and other ancient cultures, and proposed that the image on K'inich Janaab Pakal's sarcophagus at Palenque depicted the Maya king as an astronaut piloting a spaceship.[65] Some New Age writers also associated the ancient Maya with extraterrestrials. José Argüelles asserted that the Maya calendar was a portal to other dimensions, to escape from modern society and transform thinking. His speculations concerned extraterrestrial contact, intergalactic travel and the alleged ability of the ancient Maya to communicate on an inter-galactic energy plane, and he claimed that one of the missions of this civilization 'was to place the Earth and its solar system in synchronization with a larger galactic community'.[66]

Argüelles denied connections between contemporary Maya people and the ancient Maya who built pyramids and established the calendar, even though twentieth-century scholarship had made that connection definitively. Indeed, it is clear that he had read part of that scholarship, for some of his ideas invoked the ninth-century collapse in the Southern Lowlands. However, instead of understanding the collapse as scholarship framed it, involving fragmented power structures and migration to other regions, Argüelles wrote about the collapse as if the Maya had simply dis-appeared, asking, 'Where did the Maya go following AD 830?' He concluded that the people who had built the pyramids and invented the calendar moved on: 'Their purpose was to codify and establish a system of knowledge, a science, and having codified it in stone and text, to move along.' Nonetheless, he said that some remained behind to oversee 'the Tzolkin, the harmonic matrix'.[67]

Argüelles also followed writers who used the Maya calendar to predict massive societal shifts, whether of global peace or apoca-lyptic destruction, at the end of the Maya *bak'tun* calendar cycle. One source was the mid-century writings of Domingo Martínez Parédez, a professor at UNAM of Yucatec Maya descent who advanced the idea that the ancient Maya practised monotheism, using the concept of 'Hunab Ku' (One God) – a phrase applied to the Christian god in colonial-period Yucatan – and connecting this concept with Freemasonry in the path of Le Plongeon and others.[68] Another source was Frank Waters's book *Mexico Mystique* (1971), which predicted 'a shift in planetary consciousness, "The Coming

Sixth Age of Consciousness"', on 24 December 2011, fusing the Maya calendar with Aztec references to world destruction to make apocalyptic predictions.[69] In addition, Argüelles focused on an earlier date, 16–17 August 1987, for which he predicted a Harmonic Convergence, when 'Mayan sages' and 'the luminous wave-forms of Quetzalcoatl' would return as 'inner light' or 'feathered serpent rainbow wheels turning in the air', recalling sixteenth-century Central Mexican legends but amending them to fit the New Age imagination.[70]

Such predictions took varying shapes with the 2012 movement, which predicted either major disasters or improvements in consciousness via telepathy and visionary experiences. The writer and New Age Maya elder Hunbatz Men, who came from near Valladolid, Yucatán, and was one of Argüelles's inspirations, organized trips to Maya sites to train tourists to be shamans or daykeepers.[71] He and others also spoke of an alleged set of crystal skulls dispersed around the world, including ones in Tibet and with the Lacandon Maya in Chiapas, that would help mankind's awakening in a new era. As was announced during a winter solstice ritual on 21 December 2012,

> the skulls from all over the world are going to fulfil part of the prophecies of the new awakening of mankind and the ancient temples from all over the world are going to receive the energy from the universe retransmitted by the sacred crystal skulls from all over the world and universe.[72]

These speculations have been dismissed by ancient Maya specialists. David Stuart wrote that 'no Maya text – ancient, colonial, or modern – ever predicted the end of time or the end of the world.'[73] Nonetheless, their ideas seeped into popular culture through several paths, including the Hollywood film industry. *Indiana Jones and the Kingdom of the Crystal Skull* (2008), directed by Steven Spielberg, combines legends about the ancient Maya, aliens – said to be interdimensional beings, reminiscent of Argüelles's writings – and crystal skulls, thus disseminating such notions more widely than the New Age books.

Travel companies capitalized on the hype by creating special 2012 tour packages, and businesses and New Age practitioners organized spectacles and ceremonies on the solstices and equinoxes.[74] Yet these celebrations were part of a longer trend promoting tourism in the Maya region. Quetzil Castañeda describes the spring equinox events at Chichen Itza as a 'tourist ritual' or 'massive publicity event' staged by the state tourist industry since 1984. In the event in 1989, New Age 'Maya' spiritualists and 'Aztec' revivalists, who were in conflict with each other and with authorities from the National Institute of Anthropology and History, performed ceremonies. Castañeda asserts that such events are not beneficial for Maya people, for they do not draw on knowledge of ancient Maya history, and they exclude contemporary Maya 'from positions of respect, status, power, and legitimacy'. The Maya are an 'empty signifier' for what the practitioners want them to be, or for what they want themselves to be.[75] This is reminiscent of writers in earlier centuries who assigned a mythical identity to the Maya for their own self-aggrandizement.

## Artists in the 1970s and beyond: critique and call to action

Decades after Diego Rivera, Davíd Alfaro Siqueiros and José Clemente Orozco painted murals that contributed to building Mexican identity after the Revolution, muralists in Mérida and Los Angeles emulated their efforts. In the 1970s the Yucatecan artist Fernando Castro Pacheco painted murals about Maya history in the Governor's Palace in Mérida, cultivating a regional identity analogous to the national one, but with the Maya at its centre. His paintings are detailed, naturalistic shaded line drawings with added impressionistic colour. Some emphasize positive narratives such as Maya world creation, relationships with corn, and ancient artists carving monuments, but others highlight violence by Spanish conquistadors and later regimes, from Diego de Landa's burning of Maya effigies to Maya people labouring in henequen plantations. As with Guatemala's National Palace, the Maya are presented as both originators and victims of colonial and post-colonial culture, here Yucatecan.

Chicano Park Murals: Soccoro Gamboa, Felipe Adame and Roger Lucero, *Sueño Serpiente* (left); Tomás Castañeda and Roger Lucero, *Chicano Park Takeover* (right), 1978, renovated 1991, Logan Heights, San Diego, California.

Young artists of the Chicano Civil Rights Movement, which fought against institutionalized racism and anti-immigrant sentiment in American society to build pride in Mexican-American identity, also created public murals in the 1970s. Chicanx activists emphasized their rightful place in the United States because of the Mexica (Aztec) legend of Aztlan, the northern land from which the Mexica said they migrated before settling in their capital, Tenochtitlan (now Mexico City). They asserted that Aztlan was in U.S. territory, which made Mexican-American presence in the United States more salient. Their ideology was outlined in *El Plan Espiritual de Aztlán*, by Rodolfo 'Corky' Gonzales and Alurista (Alberto Urista), which was presented at the First Chicano Youth Conference in 1969. It stated,

> We, the Chicano inhabitants and civilizers of the northern land of Aztlan, from whence came our forefathers, reclaiming the land of their birth and consecrating the determination of our people of the sun, Declare that the call of our blood is our power, our responsibility, and our inevitable destiny.[76]

Chicanx artists designed, adopted and disseminated visual symbols for the movement through posters, prints and murals. They looked to the post-Revolutionary Mexican muralists, but in contrast to murals painted in government buildings, Chicanx artists painted in public locations in neighbourhoods where Chicanx people lived and worked, using freeway supports, overpasses and the walls of public housing as their canvases. The murals affirmed community identity and resisted dominant culture.[77] Many of these artists drew on ancient Mexican art because they felt familial, ancestral and cultural connections to it. The artist Judithe Hernández expressed her desire in those years to use ancient Mexican art to counter racism and connect to her heritage, finding sources by travelling to Mexico, studying books and attending exhibitions of Mexican art. She also taught, in order to expose a new generation of students and activists to their roots.[78]

Although Aztec imagery was predominant, some artists used Maya images as inspiration. In *Libertad* (1976), Ester Hernández portrays herself chipping away at the Statue of Liberty to reveal a Maya stela whose base is labelled 'Aztlan'. Hernández made this work in response to the U.S. Bicentennial to emphasize the 'deeper roots of the Americas' and as 'a little reminder that we must not forget the Americas were/are inhabited by mestizo/Native peoples', a message that was especially relevant while the United States was celebrating its formation but bashing immigrants. She transformed the male Maya warrior of the original stela into a female to emphasize women activists in the Chicano Civil Rights Movement.[79] The title, *Libertad*, claims Lady Liberty for Spanish-speakers and acknowledges Indigenous and Mexican people and origins as integral to the United States. Nonetheless, Chicanx artists – as with many other Mexican and Guatemalan artists – used other art styles, forms and motifs, too. Indeed, although I

Ester Hernández, *Libertad* (Liberty), 1987, etching, 32/50.

emphasize those with ancient Maya or other pre-Hispanic forms, their diverse practices also articulate with other traditions.

A more recent trend in artists' engagement with the ancient Maya, though, is to critique earlier engagements, including museum installations, Maya Revival architecture and portrayals in popular culture. These follow in the footsteps of American Indian Movement activists in the 1970s and '80s who challenged museum practices regarding Indigenous bodies and grave goods, calling for the cessation of archaeological projects uncovering Native American human remains and for the repatriation of the ancestors and grave goods to their descendants. Activists occupied the Southwest Museum in Los Angeles in 1971, demanding that human remains and sacred objects be taken off display.[80] In his *Artifact Piece* (1986), the performance artist James Luna lay inside a display case at the San Diego Museum of Man, where the 1915 and 1935 expositions had been held, to challenge the display of Native American bodies. These collective efforts worked. The Native American Graves Protection and Repatriation Act, passed in 1990, required museums to report and potentially repatriate human remains and grave goods. Nonetheless, it does not apply to those from Latin America, but Articles 11 and 12 of the United Nations Declaration on the Rights of Indigenous Peoples, adopted in 2007, provide a potential framework for systematic international restitution in the future.

In more recent years, several Latin American and Latinx artists have used ancient motifs from Latin America for contemporary critiques. For *A Brief History of Architecture in Guatemala* (2010), the Guatemalan performance artist Naufus Ramírez-Figueroa dressed three performers in foam-board costumes depicting an ancient Maya temple, colonial church and modern structure. The performers danced awkwardly in these costumes and eventually destroyed them. The piece comments on the use of pre-Hispanic, Colonial and Modern architecture to represent Guatemalan national identity and the history of exploitation in each period.[81]

The Mexican-born printmaker and professor Enrique Chagoya creates contemporary screenfold codices whose collaged images mix pre-Hispanic and sixteenth-century designs with American

Naufus Ramírez Figueroa, *Breve Historia de la Arquitectura en Guatemala* (Short History of Architecture in Guatemala), performance for video (also exists as live performance), commissioned by One Torino, for exhibition at Castello di Rivoli, filmed in Guatemala City, 2010–13.

Enrique Chagoya, *Abenteurer der Kannibalen Bioethicists*, detail, 2001, amate paper and pigments.

icons. In the *Codex Espangliensis* (2000), Indigenous figures from Central American codices are portrayed as superheroes who battle Superman. The odd juxtapositions are humorous and criticize the Spanish Empire, the Mexican and U.S. governments, the Catholic Church and popular culture. For *The Adventures of the Bioethicist Cannibals* (2001), another screenfold book on *amate* (bark) paper, Chagoya mixed Maya imagery from the *Dresden Codex* and other sources with images from contemporary American art and popular culture. On one page, he takes a Maya figure from a painted ceramic vessel (no.1599 in Justin Kerr's Maya Vase Database, and now at LACMA), dresses him in a tuxedo and puts him at a dinner table with an elegant woman in a cocktail dress; the bowl before them holds a human head and hand, suggesting that they are cannibals. In Chagoya's fictional world, this Maya man wears both his pre-Hispanic and Euro-American garb because the Maya were not conquered by the Spanish but instead conquered them; further, the reference to cannibals is a criticism of Western culture's appropriation of Indigenous forms.[82]

Diego Romero, *Space Madness*, 2007, ceramic.

Clarissa Tossin, *Ch'u Mayaa* (Maya Blue), commissioned by the City of Los Angeles Department of Cultural Affairs for the exhibition *Condemned to be Modern* as part of Getty Foundation's *Pacific Standard Time: LA/LA*. Choreography/performer: Crystal Sepúlveda, 2017.

Diego Romero, a Cochitl Pueblo artist, also uses humour to criticize the appropriation of Maya history. For *Space Madness* (2007), he created a ceramic bowl shaped and painted like ancient Mimbres bowls from the American Southwest. At its centre are two figures wearing Maya-style earflares and space helmets, but these are the Chongo Brothers, Southwest Native men who appear in many of Romero's vessels. The cartoon-style captions exclaim 'Mayans from Mars?' and 'Flying Saucers'. He thus makes light of those who claim that Maya people were from outer space as a way to criticize portrayals of Indigenous people in the Americas, while also connecting to his ancestors' material culture, which has also been appropriated by Euro-American society and museums.

Others comment on Maya Revival architecture. Clarissa Tossin, a Brazilian artist living in the United States, focused on Los Angeles buildings by Frank Lloyd Wright and Francisco Cornejo for artworks commissioned as part of the Getty Foundation's

Pacific Standard Time: Latin America/Los Angeles initiative. Interested in the performative nature of ancient Maya architecture, she activated the newer, Maya Revival buildings with performance. She also critiqued appropriations and mistranslations in buildings that had engaged Maya designs but not Indigenous people. For *Ch'u Mayaa* (Maya Blue; 2017), filmed outside Wright's Hollyhock House, she collaborated with the dancer Crystal Sepúlveda, whose movements were inspired by Classic-period Maya images. Tossin said that she wanted to make the building 'Mayan' again, since she saw insufficient recognition of its Maya origins. But she also seems to criticize Wright's appropriative gesture, for Sepúlveda's costume, a cheap jaguar bodysuit and shiny blue tennis shoes, calls attention to the superficiality of the twentieth-century appropriation. Tossin's *The Mayan* (also 2017) more explicitly criticized the Mayan Theatre downtown. She cast selected passages from the lobby in silicone and was happy to learn that many texts and images were shuffled or turned on their sides, for she was interested in '(mis)representation' and '(mis)translation'.[83] She arranged some casts with painted plaster casts of her hands and feet in dancing poses and displayed others with fake quetzal feathers, jaguar fur and boa skin. The addition of faux materials suggests that artificiality is again being used to comment on earlier appropriations of Maya designs that ignored contemporary Maya people.

Yet not all contemporary artists engage with the ancient Maya and other pre-Hispanic cultures to criticize contemporary culture. The Mexican artist Pablo Vargas Lugo celebrates Maya artists' artistry and calligraphy by placing new versions of Maya books, inscriptions and paintings in contemporary contexts. But his works often create strange juxtapositions that encourage us to look at Maya art and contemporary places in new ways. For *Bonampak News* (2006), he created separate pages of the *Dresden Codex* in fibreglass, forming them as if crumpled newspaper pages on the ground, blown by the wind. Is this a fictional world in which Maya writing has continued into the present, so common as to be used for newspapers? Or does it imply contemporary society's casting off of the older written records? Vargas Lugo is deliberately ambiguous, preferring to keep the interpretation open and layered.

Pablo Vargas Lugo, *Bonampak News*, 2006, decals on fibreglass and paper.

For *Naj Tunich* (2018), he distorted Maya texts and imagery from the painted cave of Naj Tunich and spread them across the gallery, including on a lamp post, as if neo-Maya graffiti artists had tagged the gallery. He juxtaposed these with a marble copy of a stalactite from the cave set on the edge of a black-and-white chequerboard pattern, made to evoke Freemason lodge floors, as if the Freemasons had brought this cave trophy into their lodge. Meanwhile, a film on continuous loop, moving from the deepest cave recesses to the exterior, contrasted the cave and jungle colours with the black-and-white inscriptions and Masonic floor. Both the cave and the lodge are places of secrecy and inaccessibility, and his merging of the two sheds light on both spaces, questioning what we know and how we feel in them.

Contemporary Maya artists also engage with ancient Maya forms in many ways. Their works are included in Chapter Eight, in order to contextualize them within broader patterns of cultural revitalization and activism in the Maya world today.

For diverse reasons, artists, architects and writers have been inspired by ancient Maya and other pre-Hispanic forms, in some ways analogous to other artists looking to Egyptian, Greek, Roman and other historical forms. Some worked to research the ancient Maya by following contemporary scholarship, whereas others intentionally ignored that information and preferred to shape their own understanding. For some, the choice to engage with the ancient Maya was deliberate and meaningful for displaying identity, whereas for others, the ancient Maya style was one decorative form among others that could be used to create an exotic atmosphere. Among these examples are also varying relationships with contemporary Maya people, some appropriating ancient Maya forms while disconnecting from contemporary Maya people, and others challenging such appropriation and using their voice to call for change. The number of artists and architects engaging with the ancient Maya (not all mentioned here) demonstrates the enduring power the ancient Maya have had in the modern and contemporary world.

# EIGHT

# Contemporary Maya Arts, Education and Activism

'We are threads of an ancient glory that cause shame to those who don't know our history and admiration for those that value our culture.'

FROM 'THE OIL LAMP', BY ANTONIO L. COTA GARCÍA,
TRANSLATED BY VICTOR MONTEJO

The Jakaltek Maya poet Antonio L. Cota García wrote 'The Oil Lamp' in a Mexican refugee camp in 1988, during the Guatemalan civil war of 1960–96.[1] Proclaiming connections to the ancient past, Cota García refers to Maya people as threads of an ancient glory, using a textile metaphor that is especially apt because of the exemplary and diverse Maya textile traditions dating back more than a millennium. Responding to and recovering from the tragedy of the civil war, Maya people of Guatemala have worked to revitalize their culture. A major strategy has been to form coalitions of various Maya groups to promote ancient and contemporary Maya culture and identity. This final chapter focuses on the interests that Maya people in the late twentieth and twenty-first century have had in recovering and reinterpreting information about the past, and its use in the present for political purposes and the formation of identity. Earlier chapters addressed the contributions of Maya people to understanding the ancient Maya past in cases where we know them, but this is an incomplete history, and there is more work to be done to acknowledge their wisdom and contributions. What we do know is that countless

Maya people, not always named, have been involved in many ways over the centuries in retaining and building knowledge of the past.

## Ancient and contemporary Maya

Many Maya groups have recognized ancient sites as sacred locales. As discussed in Chapter Four, Lacandon Maya people have called centres such as Palenque and Yaxchilan 'the dwelling-places of the gods'. Likewise, Kaqchikel Maya people have affirmed that the archaeological site of Iximche', the capital of the Kaqchikel kingdom, is sacred and imbued 'with the spirits of their ancestors', and they perform ceremonies in certain parts of the site.[2] Other archaeological sites and carved sculptures are also ceremonial loci. Judith Maxwell and Ajpub' Pablo García Ixmatá surveyed the sacred landscape of Iximche' and surrounding regions, including more than fifty sites – both abandoned and active – sacred to Kaqchikel people. The sites varied from natural to man-made or modified locales, including caves, rivers and mountaintops as well as modern cemeteries and archaeological sites. At one active altar in front of a Postclassic stela and tenon head at Xek'owil, Santa Apolonia, people make offerings of fire and food. The shrine is especially significant because of its proximity to the town's water source.[3]

Earlier chapters addressed some of the many examples of writers over the centuries who tried to disassociate Maya people from the legacy of their ancestors and rob them of the right to maintain their ancestors' sacred sites. This rhetoric interrelates with the paradox of writers extolling the advanced state of the ancient Maya and using them to symbolize a country or region, but denigrating contemporary Maya people. Indeed, the Jakaltek scholar Victor Montejo decries the racism inherent in calling the ancient Maya 'extraordinary beings' and the contemporary Maya 'just a hazy reflection of their ancestors'.[4] Such rhetoric has been used to expropriate Maya lands and remove ancient monuments. But many authors and activists – both Maya and non-Maya – reject these notions definitively. Maya cultural revitalization and revindication embrace the connections between ancient and contemporary Maya people and culture, and celebrate both.

Altar in front of Postclassic stela and tenon head, Xek'owil, Santa Apolonia, Chimaltenango Department, Guatemala.

Even so, such disconnection may also have been in play in cases in which the outside world paid more attention to discoveries about the ancient Maya than to the plight of contemporary Maya people. For example, looting in Guatemala's Department of Peten, which wreaked havoc on the cultural heritage of Maya people and of Guatemala, was heightened in the 1970s and '80s during the civil war, including at Río Azul. Archaeologists and governmental authorities successfully halted looting at Río Azul and mounted a project to excavate royal tombs. A *New York Times* article in 1984 celebrated the discovery of Tomb 19 and remarked that the Guatemalan military was guarding the tomb. However, in a letter to the editor of the same newspaper, the anthropologist Beatriz Manz criticized the celebration of the military guarding ancient Maya bones while victimizing contemporary Maya people:

> While we glory in the ancient Mayas, we often disregard the fact that their descendants are being victimized by the same army that was described as so thoughtfully guarding the ruins of the past. How will the four million Mayas in Guatemala receive the news of the discovery? Too many are grieving over fresh tombs of kinsmen recently killed. Tens of thousands hiding in the mountains and jungles will not hear of the discovery for some time. Thousands more in crowded refugee camps in Mexico are being moved yet further away from their homelands.[5]

Indeed, the press, trying to commend the suspension of the destruction of cultural heritage, missed a greater tragedy happening in the same territories. Moreover, the museums that hold collections deriving from looting in this period may well use those collections to laud the ancient Maya, but must face the fact that they were obtained during this war.

Another aspect of such disconnection may be a lack of consultation with Maya people in the management of cultural resources, and Maya authors have advocated for more agency in the telling and interpretation of the Maya past and present. Luis Enrique Sam Colop, a K'iche' Maya lawyer and linguist, criticized foreign anthropologists for not involving or empowering the Maya communities they study, urging foreign linguists working in Maya communities to practise reciprocity and empowerment by involving the communities in their research plans and ensuring that collaborations benefit them.[6] Likewise, Avexnim Cojti Ren, a K'iche' Maya sociologist, affirms the need to involve Maya people in the management of archaeological research and interpretation: 'we want to relate to our history rather than being treated as objects, historical resources for the public and for the market. We want to speak on our own behalf; we want to tell our own

history.[7] Demetrio Cojtí Cuxil, a Kaqchikel Maya social communication scholar, Guatemalan government official and activist,
also has criticized the Guatemalan government regarding Maya
people's access to archaeological sites. In 1996 he published a list
of demands for Maya revindication that included territorial, political, jurisdictional, linguistic, educational and cultural rights, for
which the overarching themes were increasing Maya autonomy
and strengthening equality while celebrating ethnic difference in
Guatemala. Among the cultural demands are 'Recognizing the
value of Maya ceremonial centers' as places of religious significance to the Maya. He affirmed that charging Maya people to enter
these centres and treating them poorly in those places is 'further
proof that the Maya are foreigners not only in their own country
but also in their own homes'.[8] According to Cojtí Cuxil, archaeological sites are the homes not only of deities and ancestors, but
of living Maya people.

Following the Guatemalan Peace Accords, signed in 1996, a
ministerial agreement of the Ministry of Culture and Sports from
2002 acknowledged ancient Maya archaeological sites as sacred to
Maya spirituality, permitting free entry for Maya spiritual guides
and Maya people accompanying them, and allowing them to
perform ceremonies in designated areas of archaeological sites.
Indeed, at Tikal, Maya spiritual leaders worked with archaeologists to identify areas to be used for contemporary ceremonies,
including in the Great Plaza.[9]

## The pan-Maya movement: cultural revitalization and human rights

Cultural revitalization has been a long-term effort in which Maya
people have endeavoured to overcome significant discrimina-
tion, racism, poverty and other forms of oppression. As Montejo
recounts, 'In Guatemala 3 percent of the population own 70 percent of the arable land, one of the most inequitable systems of land
tenure in Latin America. Mayas, who for the most part are agricultural people, suffer from extreme poverty and landlessness.'[10]
Maya people were also severely affected by the Guatemalan civil

war, which engulfed much of the country in violence. A United Nations-sponsored study released in 1999, the 'Commission for Historical Clarification', determined that genocide was carried out against the Maya people of Guatemala. The worst of the violence happened between 1981 and 1983, when attacks on Maya people were so severe that up to 1.5 million people – of Guatemala's population of 8 million – had to flee their homes, displaced and exiled within Guatemala or in other countries.[11]

Despite these decades of tragedy, Maya people across Guatemala and elsewhere in Mexico and Central America have continued to be resilient in myriad ways. Indeed, following the civil war, there was a resurgence of Maya identity as many Maya groups worked towards rebuilding their lives and revitalizing their culture in what has come to be known as the pan-Maya movement.[12] Yet this was not the first breath of a pan-Maya movement, for an earlier version was led in the 1940s after the Second World War by Adrián Inés Chávez, a K'iche' Maya scholar who translated and analysed the *Popol Vuh*, promoted bilingual and bicultural education in Guatemala, and worked on orthographic revision for writing in Mayan languages.[13]

The pan-Maya movement gained significant traction in the 1980s and '90s in Guatemala as one path to revitalize culture and reclaim connections to ancestral homelands. The movement also gained momentum in response to the quincentenary of Columbus's arrival in the Americas, in order to counteract the idea that that event was worthy of celebration. Instead, Indigenous people across the Americas affirmed their rights and traditions. As Montejo avows,

> For the Maya, as for all Indigenous peoples of the continent, the supposed celebration of the quincentenary (1492–1992) was a wake-up call for those who had been sleeping until then to organize a cultural and militant resistance against the celebration held in the colonized countries. The opposition of Indigenous leaders was so strong that they managed to avert a euphoric, unthinking celebration of genocide in the Americas.[14]

In the same years in Chiapas, Mexico, Maya people demanding greater political and cultural autonomy rose up against the Mexican government. Peaceful protests in the early 1990s demanded Indigenous rights, but there was no sufficient governmental response. On New Year's Eve 1994 the Zapatista Army of National Liberation (EZLN) engaged in armed rebellion, seizing town halls in several Chiapas cities. Named after the Mexican revolutionary Emiliano Zapata Salazar (1879–1919) and his followers, who advocated for agrarian reform in his home state of Morelos and beyond, the Zapatistas are a coalition of people from many Maya groups, including speakers of Tzeltal, Tzotzil, Chol, Tojolabal and Mam, as well as Spanish speakers. They denounced the poor treatment of Maya people by the government, and were concerned about how globalization affected Indigenous people, resulting in deterritorialization, fragmentation of social relations and deculturation, especially heightened with the passage of the North American Free Trade Agreement. Furthermore, Zapatistas were seeking – and continue to strive for – autonomy and self-governance over land and the right to control judicial and educational systems and make 'indigenous cultural premises central' in educational curricula.[15] In addition to focusing on Maya cultural premises, EZLN combatant preparation also involved studies of Mexican history and the writings of Karl Marx and his followers.[16] They also promoted the tenet of leadership following the will of the people. According to one EZLN communication, published in the Mexican newspaper *La Jornada* on 27 February 1994, 'Our path was always that the will of the many be in the hearts of the men and women who command. The will of the majority is the path on which he who commands should walk.'[17] The Zapatista movement has continued in various forms since then. They have developed 'autonomous rebel municipalities' called *caracoles* (spiral shells) in Chiapas that manage their own education, healthcare and justice systems.[18] In addition, at the Universidad de la Tierra, a Zapatista University in San Cristóbal de las Casas, Chiapas, students study Mayan languages, philosophy and history, and train for vocations.

Pan-Maya activists acknowledge the great diversity of Maya people across Mexico and Central America, but advocate for coalitions promoting Maya culture and history and improving conditions for all Maya people. As Montejo writes, 'To call ourselves "Mayas" is a political act.' He argues explicitly for connections to the ancient Maya past as a way to unify the diverse Maya communities: 'This generative term for our identity has millennia-old historical roots and unifies us through space and time: the ancient Maya, the contemporary Maya, and the Maya of the future.' Yet he also acknowledges and celebrates the multicultural and pluri-ethnic nature of the people encompassed by the term 'Maya'. Also important to this conception is the fact that Maya identity is not fixed or set in the past, but is continuing to be developed. Indeed, as Montejo states,

> I personally believe that the agenda of Maya scholars and activists is not to embellish ourselves with a romantic past or to wrap ourselves in ancient Maya garb, but to revitalize our Maya identity and weave back in the sections worn away by centuries of neglect. Contemporary Maya are constantly creating and recreating their Maya culture and redefining themselves.[19]

Creative revitalization is explicitly stated or implied by other Maya artists, authors and other cultural creators who innovatively mix elements of the Maya past with elements from other traditions in order to forge new paths and identities.

Maya leaders in Guatemala have expressed the fact that dealing with the trauma of the past is essential for cultural revitalization. Montejo, decrying the 'politics of forgetfulness', argues that Maya people and Guatemala must deal with past trauma, including the Spanish Conquest and the Guatemalan civil war, in order to move into the future.[20] One significant account of the violence of the civil war, *I, Rigoberta Menchú: An Indian Woman in Guatemala*, recounted by a K'iche' Maya woman, Rigoberta Menchú Tum, working with the Venezuelan anthropologist Elisabeth Burgos-Debray, tells of the horrors that Menchú and her community experienced during the war; it won Menchú the Nobel Peace Prize in 1992.[21] In 1999 the U.S. anthropologist David Stoll questioned the truth of her testimonies in a book in which he compared Menchú's text with information from interviews he conducted, finding discrepancies, for example, in the accounts of how Menchú's brother Petrocinio was murdered. He thus questioned Menchú's reliability as narrator or eyewitness in this episode and the entire narrative.[22] Others have defended Menchú based on the definition of the genre of the testimony, as well as other factors.[23] Regardless, her contributions have been essential to raising global consciousness of the violence, and the truth commission confirmed that the Guatemalan military carried out massacres and genocide against Maya people.[24]

Maya people have also initiated efforts to preserve and revitalize their languages and cultures, working as linguists, anthropologists, archaeologists and epigraphers. Indeed, Maya linguists and others have been at the forefront of recording information about Mayan languages for dictionary and grammar projects. The Academy for Mayan Languages of Guatemala, an autonomous state organization, was established to promote language revitalization and literacy training in Mayan languages and to systematize grammar

Hieroglyph workshop at Iximche', Chimaltenango Department, Guatemala, c. 1991–2. Pictured left to right: Linda Schele, Nikolai Grube, Gollo Rodriguez, Saqch'en Ruperto Montejo, José Tuch, Federico Fahsen (standing), Pakal B'alam Rodriguez, Lolmay García Matzar, Nikte' Juliana Sis Iboy, unidentified person, Saqijix Candelaria López.

and spelling.[25] Proyecto Lingüístico Francisco Marroquín and the
Asociación Oxlajuuj Keej Maya Ajtziib (OKMA) have also contributed to these endeavours, and their dictionaries, grammars and
children's books are essential resources for communities and outsiders. Activists have also advocated for bilingualism in elementary
education and the use of Mayan languages in the court system, so
that speakers of Mayan languages can take full advantage of their
rights to justice.[26] Other significant activities are workshops on
ancient Maya writing or narratives such as the *Popol Vuh*. Maya
linguists and epigraphers regularly lead workshops on Maya epigraphy, returning the writing of their ancestors to contemporary
Maya people. These workshops have been held by OKMA and Sak
Chuwen in Guatemala, Maya'on in Yucatan, and other groups.

Some artists are using the knowledge they have gained in such
workshops to create new forms of art and writing for a contemporary moment. These include the Kaqchikel Maya artist and

Walter Paz Joj, *Conejo*, 2018, digital image printed on stickers.

scribe Walter Paz Joj, who both copies ancient texts and images and makes new ones.[27] Paz Joj plays with the flexibility and graphic nature of the ancient script, particularly its ability to render syllables and logograms as full-figure glyphs to create complex images and texts. His images and calligraphic style are inspired primarily by ancient Maya painted ceramics, but he renders his designs in new media, including murals and stickers for distribution during public protests. Indeed, some of his works comment on contemporary Guatemalan politics, as with *Conejo*, produced in 2018 to protest Guatemalan government corruption, disseminated digitally and printed on stickers for wider distribution. Ancient texts, and ancient writing made contemporary, give form to and uplift an important artistic voice that is of the utmost relevance today.

### Arts, economics and tourism

Although this book's first chapters on ancient Maya art and architecture ended with the Spanish Invasion, Maya artists have continued to make works, and Maya arts persist today in many forms. Some are similar to those of the past but with transformations and innovations, and others are entirely new. Arts such as weaving and dance are essential forms of creative and cultural expression and can function to retain and display historical and cultural memory. Many Maya women continue to weave textiles on backstrap looms, as Maya women have done for more than a millennium, but with innovations in materials and designs. For a ceremonial *huipil* (blouse) from San Juan Comalapa, Guatemala, made in about 1925, the weaver used both natural cotton, a material used for centuries, and silk – imported after the Spanish invasion – to create geometric animal designs, evoking ancient textiles, and floral designs from European traditions. Maya women weave garments for themselves and their families, as well as for sale. Sna Jolobil is a weavers' cooperative in San Cristóbal de las Casas that sells exquisite crafts woven by Maya women, some using designs inspired by ancient sculpture such as the *huipil* designs from Yaxchilan Lintels 24 and 25. Maya people have also continued to use dance and performance as powerful historical mediums, in

*Ri'j po't* (ceremonial *huipil* [blouse]), *c.* 1925, San Juan Comalapa, Chimaltenango Department, Guatemala, cotton, silk, velvet and dyes.

which past and present are integrated.[28] For example, the Rabinal Achi, which is danced in Rabinal, Guatemala, recounts conflict between the people of Rabinal and the K'iche'.

Artists have painted murals in many Maya communities in southern Mexico and Guatemala as a way to display identity and address history. Some communities in Chiapas have painted murals related to the Zapatista movement depicting a range of subject-matter, including corn, Maya families, Zapatistas in their characteristic ski masks, and Emiliano Zapata and Che Guevara. A powerful mural in Oventic, Chiapas, portrays a person wearing a Zapatista-style mask, but it is made of corncobs, signalling the continuing importance of corn to Maya people.

In 2002 Kaqchikel Maya people in San Juan Comalapa painted a series of murals on the walls of the town cemetery as a way to grapple with history and memory in response to the civil war. The works portray the history of their town and nation, beginning with pre-Hispanic life and continuing through the colonial period and nineteenth century and up to the present, including the civil war, commenting also on poverty, racism, violence and economic justice.[29] One panel in the colonial-period section depicts dismembered Maya people juxtaposed with Spaniards writing on paper, disconnected from the Maya people's pain caused by

Panel of mural on cemetery wall, San Juan Comalapa, Chimaltenango Department, Guatemala, 2002, plaster and pigments.

the Spanish Conquest. Another portrays Maya women wearing distinctive textiles and weaving, carrying water and performing other activities against the backdrop of a lunar disc. Juxtaposed is a blue Maya deity wearing a serpent headdress and weaving; she is Chak Chel or Ixchel, deity of childbirth and weaving, whose depiction recalls those in the *Dresden Codex*, albeit modernized. David Carey and Walter Little interpret the presence of Maya deities in these murals as markers of continuity of Maya religion and resistance to Christian evangelization. Furthermore, they characterize the murals both as community creative pursuits and as 'visual protests' demonstrating Maya resistance and resilience in the face of oppression, poverty and violence. The murals also help to transform oral history into visual programmes, and participate in recovering historical memory and inspiring intergenerational discussion about the past, present and future.[30]

Mario González Chavajay, *Ajmaak*, 2013, oil on canvas.

Painters in Comalapa and other towns also make smaller paintings, both for their own use and for sale to tourists. This trend began in the 1920s in the Guatemalan highlands, in Comalapa, San Pedro La Laguna, Santiago Atitlan, Totonicapan and Patzicia, where artists painted people, landscapes, traditions and historical events of their community.[31] One painting by Mario González Chavajay, a Tz'utuhil artist from San Pedro La Laguna, depicts people lighting candles and making offerings of fruit around a shaped stone. It may depict an actual sacred site, such as the one in Santa Apolonia. The making of such paintings allows artists to explore their own identity and history and benefit financially from their sales.

Artists in Yucatan have created new artistic genres for sale, too. In and around Santa Elena, near the Puuc region archaeological sites, Yucatec Maya artists including Jesús Marcos Delgado Kú, Miguel Uc Delgado, Wilberth Vázquez and Angel Ruíz Novelo carve wooden sculptures for sale to tourists. The practice followed the rise of tourism in the Yucatan Peninsula in the last quarter of the twentieth century. They carve both copies of famous ancient Maya pieces such as the Yaxchilan lintels and new designs based on ancient imagery and inscriptions. Other woodcarvers in Piste have also created items for sale in nearby Chichen Itza.[32] Patricia Martin Morales in Muna carefully creates copies of ancient Maya ceramics and paints images from other media (such as carved stone sculpture) on to ceramic vessels. Her studio is filled with books of Maya ceramics from Mexican, Guatemalan and u.s. collections, in which she and her collaborators find inspiration for their reproductions and new creations.

Maya people have also sought ways to benefit from tourism to ancient Maya archaeological sites. For example, the Lacandon Maya community of Lacanja Chansayab controls transportation into Bonampak, in the Selva Lacandona. Vehicles must stop outside the park, and Lacandon men drive the tourists to Bonampak. Inside, Lacandon people sell crafts and offer guided tours. In addition, an eco-hotel at Lacanja Chansayab, run by people from the Lacandon community, allows visitors to get to know local people, archaeological sites and jungle resources. Through these

Lacandon boy climbing a staircase in Yaxchilan, Chiapas, Mexico, during a tour of the ancient Maya site, 2006.

opportunities, Lacandon Maya people can profit from the archae-ological tourism economy. Many other Maya cooperatives strive to benefit from the tourism economy while maintaining craft traditions.

Changing museum trends towards developing regional muse-ums can benefit Maya communities. In the late twentieth century and the twenty-first century, Mexico, Guatemala and Honduras have invested in regional and site museums such as the Alberto Ruz Lhuillier Site Museum at Palenque. As more foreign muse-ums and private collections repatriate objects to their countries of origin, questions will be raised about where those artefacts should go. Avexnim Cojti Ren criticized the repatriation of objects to national museums, rather than to the sites for which they were made or to the descendants of their makers.[33] It is to be hoped that in the future, repatriated items can be returned not only to their countries of origin but to their places of origin. Moreover,

Balam Ajpu, *Jun winaq' Kajawal Q'ij/Tributo a los 20 Nawales* (2015), album cover.

Montejo affirms the importance of involving Maya people in the Guatemalan Ministry of Culture so that they can help to conserve the materials of the past and assist in the repatriation of objects: 'This ancestral Maya culture gives our current nationalism roots; and this unifies the multi ethnic population of the country.'[34]

## New popular music in Mayan languages

Young Maya people are creating new art forms across Mexico and Central America. For example, young musicians are performing new music in Mayan languages such as Yucatec, Mam, Tzotzil, Tz'utujil, K'iche' and Kaqchikel, as well as in Spanish. They are embracing their ancestral languages and using them to create music that draws on local and international musical forms, including rap and hip hop, to create new musical genres. Groups include Sobrevivencia (Survival), who sang in Mam and other Mayan languages; and Slaje'm K'op, who sing in Tzotzil Maya.[35] Jesús Pat Chablé, also known as Pat Boy, from José María Pino Suárez, Quintana Roo, performs in Yucatec Maya and Spanish and expresses his pride in his Maya roots, saying, 'We should be proud, not embarrassed. We built Chichén Itzá.' He also affirms that his music connects him to those roots: 'Through rapping in Maya, I better understand my culture.' Through his music, he wants to show people that the Maya still exist, and that although people may say that the Maya collapsed, they are still here, doing new things, emphasizing both persistence and innovation.[36]

The group Balam Ajpu performs in several Mayan languages of Guatemala. One member is Rene Dionisio, also known as Tzutu Kan, who raps in Tz'utujil Maya (his maternal language), K'iche' and Kaqchikel; another is Yefry Pacheco (M.C.H.E.), who raps in Spanish.[37] By choosing to rap in Mayan languages, Tzutu asserts his desire to move away from Guatemalan folk music such as the marimba, which he sees as 'colonial' and 'another form of oppression'. Hip hop, instead, can be a new form of expression of Maya culture, particularly in the era following the completion of the thirteenth *bak'tun* in 2012.[38] The year 2012 thus provided another inspiration for Maya cultural revitalization and innovation.

The members of Balam Ajpu also incorporate Maya spirituality into their music. One album is based on the twenty days of the 260-day *tzolk'in* calendar, and the lyrics are derived from Maya spiritual guides. By performing in Mayan languages and engaging with Maya spirituality, this group demonstrates persistence and innovation in Maya culture. The linguist Rusty Barrett writes: 'In bringing Maya culture and hip hop together, Balam Ajpu challenges the view that Maya culture is a relic of a primitive past.' The cover of one of the band's albums features ancient Maya writing; calendar symbols form a circle, and at the centre are the heads of a jaguar and a human, to represent Balam and Ajpu.[39] Between the heads, 'Hip Hop' is written in Maya writing above the words 'Maya Hip Hop'. The album cover thus engages in graphic pluralism to connect both to ancient Maya cultural traditions and to contemporary hip-hop culture. The creativity of this graphic pluralism echoes that of the sixteenth-century scribes discussed in Chapter Three.

Because of the challenges they have faced over the centuries, many Maya people have migrated from their ancestral homelands. Major migrations took place during the Guatemalan civil war, when many Maya people left Guatemala for Mexico or the United States.[40] Although many returned after a period of exile, others stayed and created new lives in those countries. While I was writing this book, there was another major wave of migration of Maya and other Indigenous people from Guatemala, Honduras and other Central American countries to Mexico and the United States, where people were seeking asylum from violence and poverty, although their movements were limited by then U.S. president Donald Trump's cruel policies and the COVID-19 pandemic.

In *Maya Intellectual Renaissance*, Montejo quotes a passage from the *Popol Vuh*:

> Oh, our children! We are going, we are returning; we leave you with healthy recommendations and wise advice . . . We are going to begin the return, we have completed our mission, our days are finished. Think, then, of us, and do not erase us from your memory nor forget us.[41]

These are words uttered by the Hero Twins before they are transformed into the sun and moon. Montejo interprets this passage as a reminder of the importance of ancestry in ancient and contemporary Maya culture. Although ancestors die or pass to another dimension, they must be remembered. He asserts that contemporary Maya people must remember both the heritage of their ancient ancestors and the atrocities Maya people have experienced over the last five centuries, and endeavour to recognize and write histories from their own perspective as they strive to revitalize Maya culture.

Indeed, although I have attempted to characterize Maya artistic and cultural production and contributions to understanding the Maya past, my words and efforts are inevitably insufficient. I hope this book is followed by the work of Maya writers who continue to record and commemorate Maya people's contributions to understanding their past and their innovations in the present and future. The world would benefit greatly from such efforts.

## 1 Art and Architecture

1 For more thorough analyses of the ancient Maya world, the reader is encouraged to consult other general publications addressing ancient Maya archaeology and art history, for example: Michael D. Coe and Stephen D. Houston, *The Maya*, 9th edn (London, 2015); Stephen D. Houston and Takeshi Inomata, *The Classic Maya* (Cambridge and New York, 2010); Simon Martin and Nikolai Grube, *Chronicle of the Maya Kings and Queens: Deciphering the Dynasties of the Ancient Maya*, 2nd edn (London, 2008); Mary Ellen Miller and Megan E. O'Neil, *Maya Art and Architecture*, 2nd revd edn (London, 2014); Robert J. Sharer and Loa P. Traxler, *The Ancient Maya*, 6th edn (Stanford, CA, 2005).

2 Matthew Restall, *The Maya World: Yucatec Culture and Society* (Stanford, CA, 1997), pp. 2, 13–20; Matthew Restall, *Maya Conquistador* (Boston, MA, 1998).

3 Matthew Restall, 'Maya Ethnogenesis', *Journal of Latin American Anthropology*, IX/1 (2004), pp. 65–7, 82, doi: 10.1525/jlca.2004.9.1.64.

4 Nora C. England, 'Mayan Languages', *Oxford Research Encyclopedia of Linguistics* (Oxford, 2017), doi: 10.1093/acrefore/9780199384655.013.60.

5 Preclassic dates from Takeshi Inomata et al., 'Monumental Architecture at Aguada Fénix and the Rise of Maya Civilization', *Nature* (3 June 2020), doi: 10.1038/s41586-020-2343-4.

6 Simon Martin and Erik Velásquez García, 'Polities and Places: Tracing the Toponyms of the Snake Dynasty', *PARI Journal*, XVII/2 (2016), pp. 23–33.

7 Stephen Houston and David Stuart, 'Of Gods, Glyphs and Kings: Divinity and Rulership among the Classic Maya', *Antiquity*, LXX/268 (1996), pp. 289–312, doi: 10.1017/S0003598X00083289; Megan E. O'Neil, *Forces of Nature: Ancient Maya Art from the Los Angeles County Museum of Art*, exh. cat., Shenzhen Museum, Shenzhen, Jinsha Site Museum, Chengdu, and Hubei Provincial Museum, Wuhan (Beijing, 2018).

8 David Stuart and George Stuart, *Palenque: Eternal City of the Maya* (London and New York, 2008), p. 173.

9  Simon Martin, 'Secrets of the Painted King List: Recovering the Early History of the Snake Dynasty', Maya Decipherment blog (5 May 2017), www.decipherment.wordpress.com.

10  Stephen D. Houston, 'Crafting Credit: Authorship among Classic Maya Painters and Sculptors', in *Making Value, Making Meaning: Techné in the Pre-Columbian World*, ed. C. L. Costin (Washington, DC, 2016), pp. 391–431.

11  Simon Martin, *Ancient Maya Politics: A Political Anthropology of the Classic Period 150–900 CE* (Cambridge, 2020), pp. 78–81.

12  Stephen Houston, John Robertson and David Stuart, 'The Language of Classic Maya Inscriptions', *Current Anthropology*, XLI/3 (2000), pp. 321–56, doi: 10.1086/300142.

13  David Stuart, *Ten Phonetic Syllables* (Washington, DC, 1987).

14  Michael D. Coe, *The Maya Scribe and His World* (New York, 1973); Mary Ellen Miller, *Maya Art and Architecture*, 1st edn (London, 1999), p. 82.

15  Houston, 'Crafting Credit', pp. 392–3.

16  Victoria Reifler Bricker, *The Indian Christ, the Indian King: The Historical Substrate of Maya Myth and Ritual* (Austin, TX, 1981), p. 8.

17  David Stuart, 'Hieroglyphs on Maya Vessels', in *The Maya Vase Book: A Corpus of Rollout Photographs of Maya Vases*, ed. J. Kerr (New York, 1989), vol. I, pp. 149–60.

18  Miller and O'Neil, *Maya Art and Architecture*, p. 45.

19  Evon Z. Vogt and David Stuart, 'Some Notes on Ritual Caves among the Ancient and Modern Maya', in *In the Maw of the Earth Monster: Mesoamerican Ritual Cave Use*, ed. J. E. Brady and K. M. Prufer (Austin, TX, 2005), p. 156.

20  Mary Ellen Miller and Stephen D. Houston, 'The Classic Maya Ballgame and Its Architectural Setting: A Study of Relations between Text and Image', *Res: Anthropology and Aesthetics*, 14 (1987), pp. 46–65.

21  Ibid.

22  David Stuart, 'Kings of Stone: A Consideration of Stelae in Ancient Maya Ritual and Representation', *Res: Anthropology and Aesthetics*, 29–30 (1996), pp. 148–71.

23  Karl A. Taube, 'The Symbolism of Jade in Classic Maya Religion', *Ancient Mesoamerica*, XVI/1 (2005), pp. 23–50, doi: 10.1017/S0956536105050017.

24  Karl A. Taube, 'Flower Mountain: Concepts of Life, Beauty, and Paradise among the Classic Maya', *Res: Anthropology and Aesthetics*, 45 (2004), pp. 69–98.

25  Prudence M. Rice, 'Late Classic Maya Pottery Production: Review and Synthesis', *Journal of Archaeological Method and Theory*, XVI/2 (2009), pp. 117–56.

26  Dean E. Arnold and Bruce F. Bohor, 'Attapulgite and Maya Blue: An Ancient Mine Comes to Light', *Archaeology*, XXVIII/1 (1975), pp. 23–9.

27  Bryan Just, *Dancing into Dreams: Maya Vase Painting of the Ik' Kingdom* (Princeton, NJ, 2012); Dorie Reents-Budet, *Painting the Maya Universe: Royal Ceramics of the Classic Period* (Durham, NC, 1994).

28  Oswaldo Chinchilla Mazariegos, *Art and Myth of the Ancient Maya* (New Haven, CT, and London, 2017); O'Neil, *Forces of Nature*.

29  Stephen D. Houston, *The Gifted Passage: Young Men in Classic Maya Art and Text* (New Haven, CT, 2018); Reents-Budet, *Painting*.

30  Michelle Rich, 'Archaeology at El Perú-Waka': A Maya Ritual Resurrection Scene in Broader Perspective', *Unframed* blog (21 September 2017), https://unframed.lacma.org.

31  William A. Saturno, David Stuart and Boris Beltrán, 'Early Maya Writing at San Bartolo Guatemala', *Science*, 311 (2006), pp. 1281–3; William A. Saturno, Karl A. Taube, David Stuart and Heather Hurst, *The Murals of San Bartolo, El Petén, Guatemala. Pt. 1: The North Wall*, Ancient America 7 (Barnardsville, NC, 2007); Karl A. Taube, William A. Saturno, David Stuart and Heather Hurst, *The Murals of San Bartolo, El Petén, Guatemala. Pt. 2: The West Wall*, Ancient America 10 (Barnardsville, NC, 2010).

32  Franco D. Rossi, William A. Saturno and Heather Hurst, 'Maya Codex Book Production and the Politics of Expertise: Archaeology of a Classic Period Household at Xultun, Guatemala', *American Anthropologist*, CXVII/1 (2015), pp. 116–32.

33  Simon Martin, 'Hieroglyphs from the Painted Pyramid: The Epigraphy of Chiik Nahb Structure Sub 1–4, Calakmul, Mexico', in *Maya Archaeology*, ed. C. Golden, S. Houston and J. Skidmore (San Francisco, CA, 2012), vol. II, pp. 60–81.

34  Sofía Martínez del Campo Lanz, ed., *El Códice Maya de México, Antes Grolier* (Mexico City, 2018).

35  Thomas A. Lee Jr, *Los Códices Mayas* (Provo, UT, 1985).

## 2 Places, Politics and History

1  Takeshi Inomata et al., 'Monumental Architecture at Aguada Fénix and the Rise of Maya Civilization', *Nature* (3 June 2020), doi: 10.1038/s41586-020-2343-4.

2  Francisco Estrada-Belli, *The First Maya Civilization: Ritual and Power Before the Classic Period* (Abingdon and New York, 2011); Richard D. Hansen, 'Cultural and Environmental Components of the First Maya States: A Perspective from the Central and Southern Maya Lowlands', in *The Origins of Maya States*, ed. L. P. Traxler and R. J. Sharer (Philadelphia, PA, 2016), pp. 329–416; Takeshi Inomata and Daniela Triadan, 'Middle Preclassic Caches from Ceibal, Guatemala', in *Maya Archaeology*, ed. C. Golden, S. Houston and J. Skidmore (San Francisco, CA, 2016), vol. III, pp. 56–91; Travis W. Stanton and Traci Ardren, 'The Middle Formative of Yucatan in Context: The View from Yaxuna', *Ancient Mesoamerica*, XVI (2005), pp. 213–28.

3  Estrada-Belli, *First Maya Civilization*; Inomata and Triadan, 'Middle Preclassic Caches'.

4  Julia Guernsey, *Ritual and Power in Stone: The Performance of Rulership in Mesoamerican Izapan Style Art* (Austin, TX, 2006).

5 Takeshi Inomata and Lucia Henderson, 'Time Tested: Re-Thinking Chronology and Sculptural Traditions in Preclassic Southern Mesoamerica', *Antiquity*, xc/350 (2016), pp. 456–71.

6 Edgar Suyuc and Richard Hansen, 'El Complejo Piramidal La Danta: Ejemplo del Auge en El Mirador', in *Millenary Maya Societies: Past Crises and Resilience*, ed. M.-C. Arnauld and A. Breton, pp. 217–34, electronic document, published online at Mesoweb (2013), www.mesoweb.com/ publications.

7 David A. Freidel and Linda Schele, 'Kingship in the Late Preclassic Maya Lowlands: The Instruments and Places of Ritual Power', *American Anthropologist*, xc/3 (1988), pp. 547–67.

8 William A. Saturno, Karl A. Taube, David Stuart and Heather Hurst, *The Murals of San Bartolo, El Petén, Guatemala. Pt. 1: The North Wall*, Ancient America 7 (Barnardsville, NC, 2007); Karl A. Taube, William A. Saturno, David Stuart and Heather Hurst, *The Murals of San Bartolo, El Petén, Guatemala. Pt. 2: The West Wall*, Ancient America 10 (Barnardsville, NC, 2010); William A. Saturno, 'Centering the Kingdom, Centering the King: Maya Creation and Legitimization at San Bartolo', in *The Art of Urbanism: How Mesoamerican Kingdoms Represented Themselves in Architecture and Imagery*, ed. W. L. Fash and L. López Luján (Washington, DC, 2009), pp. 111–34; Karl A. Taube, 'The Maya Maize God and the Mythic Origins of Dance', in *The Maya and Their Sacred Narratives: Text and Context in Maya Mythologies*, ed. G. Le Fort, R. Gardiol, S. Matteo and C. Helmke, Acta Mesoamericana 20 (Markt Schwaben, 2009), pp. 41–52.

9 Peter D. Harrison, *The Lords of Tikal: Rulers of an Ancient Maya City* (New York, 2000), pp. 60–66.

10 Estrada-Belli, *First Maya Civilization*; Inomata et al., 'Monumental Architecture'.

11 Hansen, 'Cultural and Environmental Components'.

12 James E. Brady et al., 'The Lowland Maya "Protoclassic": A Reconsideration of Its Nature and Significance', *Ancient Mesoamerica*, ix/1 (1998), pp. 17–38, doi: 10.1017/S0956536100001826; Bruce H. Dahlin, 'A Colossus in Guatemala: The Preclassic Maya City of El Mirador', *Archaeology*, xxxvii/5 (1984), pp. 18–25; Hansen, 'Cultural and Environmental Components'; Robert J. Sharer and Loa P. Traxler, *The Ancient Maya*, 6th edn (Stanford, CA, 2005), pp. 294–5, 301.

13 Stephen D. Houston, Sarah Newman, Edwin Román and Thomas Garrison, *Temple of the Night Sun: A Royal Tomb at El Diablo, Guatemala* (San Francisco, CA, 2015).

14 Ricardo Agurcia Fasquelle and Barbara W. Fash, 'The Evolution of Structure 10L-16, Heart of the Copán Acropolis', in *Copán: The History of an Ancient Maya Kingdom*, ed. E. W. Andrews and W. L. Fash (Santa Fe, NM, 2005), pp. 201–37; Robert J. Sharer et al., 'Early Classic Architecture Beneath the Copan Acropolis: A Research Update', *Ancient Mesoamerica*, x/1 (1999), pp. 3–23.

15  Francisco Estrada-Belli and Alexandre Tokovinine, 'A King's Apotheosis: Iconography, Text, and Politics from a Classic Maya Temple at Holmul', *Latin American Antiquity*, XXVII/2 (2016), pp. 149–68, doi: 10.7183/1045-6635.27.2.149.

16  Nawa Sugiyama et al., 'The Maya at Teotihuacan? New Insights into Teotihuacan-Maya Interactions from Plaza of the Columns Complex', in *Teotihuacan: The World Beyond the City*, ed. K. G. Hirth, D. M. Carballo and B. Arroyo (Washington, DC, 2020), pp. 139–72.

17  David Stuart, '"The Arrival of Strangers": Teotihuacan and Tollan in Classic Maya History', in *Mesoamerica's Classic Heritage: From Teotihuacan to the Aztecs*, ed. D. Carrasco (Boulder, CO, 2000), pp. 465–513.

18  Clemency Coggins, 'Painting and Drawing Styles at Tikal: An Historical and Iconographic Reconstruction', PhD diss., Harvard University, 1975; Diana Magaloni Kerpel, Megan E. O'Neil and María Teresa Uriarte, 'The Moving Image: Painted Murals and Vessels at Teotihuacan and the Maya Area', in *Teotihuacan*, ed. Hirth, Carballo and Arroyo, pp. 189–220.

19  Janet C. Berlo, 'Art Historical Approaches to the Study of Teotihuacán-related Ceramics from Escuintla, Guatemala', in *New Frontiers in the Archaeology of the Pacific Coast of Southern Mesoamerica*, ed. F. Bove and L. Heller, Anthropological Research Papers (Tempe, AZ, 1989), pp. 147–65; Claudia García-Des Lauriers, 'Gods, Cacao, and Obsidian: Multidirectional Interactions between Teotihuacan and the Southeastern Pacific Coast of Mesoamerica', in *Teotihuacan*, ed. Hirth, Carballo and Arroyo, pp. 409–34.

20  T. Douglas Price et al., 'Kings and Commoners at Copan: Isotopic Evidence for Origins and Movement in the Classic Maya Period', *Journal of Anthropological Archaeology*, XXIX/1 (2010), pp. 15–32, doi: 10.1016/j.jaa.2009.10.001.

21  Ellen E. Bell et al., 'Tombs and Burials in the Early Classic Acropolis at Copan', in *Understanding Early Classic Copan*, ed. E. Bell, M. A. Canuto and R. J. Sharer (Philadelphia, PA, 2004), pp. 132–57.

22  Andrea Stone, 'Disconnection, Foreign Insignia, and Political Expansion: Teotihuacan and the Warrior Stelae of Piedras Negras', in *Mesoamerica after the Decline of Teotihuacan*, ed. R. A. Diehl and J. C. Berlo (Washington, DC, 1989), pp. 153–72; Stuart, 'Arrival'.

23  Estrada-Belli, *First Maya Civilization*, pp. 138–9; Enrique Nalda, 'Prácticas funerarias en Dzibanché, Quintana Roo: Los entierros en el Edificio de los Cormorantes', *Arqueología*, XXXI (2003), pp. 25–37.

24  Christophe Helmke and Jaime Awe, 'Sharper than a Serpent's Tooth: A Tale of the Snake-head Dynasty as Recounted on Xunantunich Panel 4', *PARI Journal*, XVII/2 (2016), pp. 1–22; Simon Martin and Erik Velásquez García, 'Polities and Places: Tracing the Toponyms of the Snake Dynasty', *PARI Journal*, XVII/2 (2016), pp. 23–33.

25  Stephen Houston, 'Symbolic Sweatbaths of the Maya: Architectural Meaning in the Cross Group at Palenque, Mexico', *Latin American Antiquity*, VII (1996), pp. 132–51.

26 Mary Ellen Miller, *Maya Art and Architecture*, 1st edn (London, 1999); Merle Greene Robertson, *The Sculpture of Palenque*, vol. III: *The Late Buildings of the Palace* (Princeton, NJ, 1985).

27 Simon Martin and Nikolai Grube, *Chronicle of the Maya Kings and Queens: Deciphering the Dynasties of the Ancient Maya*, 2nd edn (London, 2008), p. 171.

28 Sharer and Traxler, *Ancient Maya*, p. 294.

29 Martin and Grube, *Chronicle*, p. 129; Carolyn E. Tate, *Yaxchilan: The Design of a Maya Ceremonial City* (Austin, TX, 1992), pp. 126–8.

30 Mary Ellen Miller and Claudia Brittenham, *The Spectacle of the Late Maya Court: Reflections on the Murals of Bonampak* (Austin, TX, 2013).

31 Stephen D. Houston, 'The Acropolis of Piedras Negras: Portrait of a Court System', in *Courtly Art of the Ancient Maya*, ed. M. E. Miller and Simon Martin, exh. cat., de Young Museum, San Francisco, and National Gallery of Art, Washington, DC (San Francisco and New York, 2004), p. 276.

32 Harrison, *Lords of Tikal*, pp. 119–20; Martin and Grube, *Chronicle*, pp. 39–43, 55–7; Simon Martin, *Ancient Maya Politics: A Political Anthropology of the Classic Period, 150–900 CE* (Cambridge, 2020).

33 Simon Martin, 'Of Snakes and Bats: Shifting Identities at Calakmul', *PARI Journal*, VI/2 (2005), pp. 5–15.

34 Marcello A. Canuto and Tomás Barrientos Q, 'La Corona: Un Acercamiento a las Políticas del Reino Kaan desde un Centro Secundario del Noroeste del Petén', *Estudios de Cultura Maya*, XXXVII (2011), pp. 11–43; Simon Martin, 'Wives and Daughters on the Dallas Altar', electronic document, published online at Mesoweb (2008), www.mesoweb.com.

35 Olivia C. Navarro-Farr, Keith Eppich, David A. Freidel and Griselda Pérez Robles, 'Ancient Maya Queenship: Generations of Crafting State Politics and Alliance Building from Kaanul to Waka', in *Approaches to Monumental Landscapes of the Ancient Maya*, ed. B. A. Houk et al. (Gainesville, FL, 2020), pp. 199–200.

36 Megan E. O'Neil, 'Ancient Maya Sculptures of Tikal, Seen and Unseen', *Res: Anthropology and Aesthetics*, 55–6 (2009), pp. 119–34.

37 Martin, *Ancient Maya Politics*, p. 242; Martin and Grube, *Chronicle*, p. 45; Stuart, 'Arrival'.

38 Martin and Grube, *Chronicle*, pp. 57–62; Mary Ellen Miller and Megan E. O'Neil, *Maya Art and Architecture*, 2nd revd edn (London, 2014).

39 Sharer and Traxler, *Ancient Maya*, p. 353.

40 William L. Fash, *Scribes, Warriors and Kings: The City of Copán and the Ancient Maya*, revd edn (London, 2001); David Stuart, 'A Foreign Past: The Writing and Representation of History on a Royal Ancestral Shrine at Copan', in *Copan*, ed. Andrews and Fash (Santa Fe, NM, and Oxford, 2005, pp. 373–94.

41 Matthew G. Looper, *Lightning Warrior: Maya Art and Kingship at Quirigua* (Austin, TX, 2003), pp. 4, 76–8; Martin and Grube, *Chronicle*, pp. 203–5, 218–19.

42 Fash, *Scribes*; Stuart, 'A Foreign Past'.

43  James J. Aimers, 'What Maya Collapse? Terminal Classic Variation in the Maya Lowlands', *Journal of Archaeological Research*, XV (2007), pp. 329–77, doi: 10.1007/s10814-007-9015-x; David Webster, *The Fall of the Ancient Maya: Solving the Mystery of the Maya Collapse* (New York, 2002).

44  Navarro-Farr et al., 'Ancient Maya Queenship'.

45  Miguel Rivera Dorado, *Los Mayas de Oxkintok* (Madrid, 1996).

46  William M. Ringle et al., 'The Decline of the East: The Classic to Postclassic Transition at Ek Balam, Yucatan', in *The Terminal Classic in the Maya Lowlands: Collapse, Transition, and Transformation*, ed. A. A. Demarest, P. M. Rice and D. S. Rice (Boulder, CO, 2004), pp. 485–516.

47  Alfonso Lacadena García-Gallo, 'The Glyphic Corpus from Ek' Balam, Yucatan, México', trans. Alex Lomónaco, FAMSI Grant Report (2003), pp. 99, 106; Leticia Vargas de la Peña and Víctor R. Castillo Borges, 'Las Construcciones Monumentales de Ek' Balam', in *The Archaeology of Yucatan*, ed. T. W. Stanton (Oxford, 2014), pp. 377–93.

48  Susan D. Gillespie, 'Toltecs, Tula, and Chichén Itzá: The Development of an Archaeological Myth', in *Twin Tollans: Chichén Itzá, Tula, and the Epiclassic to Early Postclassic Mesoamerican World*, ed. J. K. Kowalski and C. Kristan-Graham, revd edn (Washington, DC, 2011), pp. 61–92; Cynthia Kristan-Graham and Jeff Kowalski, 'Chichén Itzá, Tula, and Tollan: Changing Perspectives on a Recurring Problem in Mesoamerican Archaeology and Art History', in *Twin Tollans*, ed. Kowalski and Kristan-Graham, pp. 1–58; Benjamin Volta, Nancy Peniche May and Geoffrey E. Braswell, 'The Archaeology of Chichen Itza: Its History, What We Like to Argue About, and What We Think We Know', in *Landscapes of the Itza: Archaeology and Art History at Chichen Itza and Neighboring Sites*, ed. L. H. Wren, C. Kristan-Graham, T. Nygard and K. R. Spencer (Gainesville, FL, 2018), pp. 28–64.

49  Mary Ellen Miller, 'A Re-Examination of the Mesoamerican Chacmool', *Art Bulletin*, LCVII/1 (1985), pp. 7–17, doi: 10.2307/3050884.

50  Carlos Peraza Lope et al., 'The Chronology of Mayapan: New Radiocarbon Evidence', *Ancient Mesoamerica*, XVII (2006), pp. 172–3.

51  Anthony P. Andrews, 'Late Postclassic Lowland Maya Archaeology', *Journal of World Prehistory*, VII/1 (1993), pp. 35–69.

52  Susan Milbrath and Carlos Peraza Lope, 'Mayapán's Chen Mul Modeled Effigy Censers', in *Ancient Maya Pottery: Classification, Analysis, and Interpretation*, ed. J. J. Aimers (Gainesville, FL, 2014), pp. 203–28.

53  Grant D. Jones, *The Conquest of the Last Maya Kingdom* (Stanford, CA, 1998); Timothy W. Pugh, José Rómulo Sánchez and Yuko Shiratori, 'Contact and Missionization at Tayasal, Petén, Guatemala', *Journal of Field Archaeology*, XXXVII/1 (March 2012), pp. 3–19.

54  Thomas F. Babcock, *Utatlán: The Constituted Community of the K'iche' Maya of Q'umarkaj* (Boulder, CO, 2012); Robert M. Carmack, *The Quiché Mayas of Utatlán: The Evolution of a Highland Guatemala Kingdom* (Norman, OK, 1981), p. 193.

### 3 Contact and Conquest, Resistance and Resilience, in the Sixteenth to Eighteenth Centuries

1 Frances Karttunen, *Between Worlds: Interpreters, Guides and Survivors* (New Brunswick, NJ, 1994), p. 89; Matthew Restall, *Maya Conquistador* (Boston, MA, 1998), p. 144.
2 Constance Cortez, 'New Dance, Old Xius: The "Xiu Family Tree" and Maya Cultural Continuity after European Contact', in *Heart of Creation: The Mesoamerican World and the Legacy of Linda Schele*, ed. Andrea Stone (Tuscaloosa, AL, 2002), p. 202; Diego de Landa, *Yucatan Before and After the Conquest*, trans. William Gates (Baltimore, MD, 1937); Karttunen, *Between Worlds*, pp. 92, 113; Matthew Restall and John F. Chuchiak IV, 'A Reevaluation of the Authenticity of Fray Diego de Landa's *Relación de las Cosas de Yucatan*', *Ethnohistory*, XLIX/3 (2002), pp. 651–69, at p. 653.
3 Cortez, 'New Dance'.
4 Restall and Chuchiak, 'A Reevaluation'; Alfred M. Tozzer, *Landa's Relación de las Cosas de Yucatan: A Translation* (Cambridge, MA, 1941).
5 Landa, *Yucatan Before and After*, pp. 82–3.
6 Rolena Adorno, 'Discourses on Colonialism: Bernal Diaz, Las Casas, and the Twentieth-Century Reader', *MLN*, CIII/2 (March 1988), pp. 239–58; Matthew Restall, *Seven Myths of the Spanish Conquest* (Oxford and New York, 2003), p. 12.
7 Restall, *Maya Conquistador*, pp. 30–37, 44, 56, 82–3.
8 Inga Clendinnen, *Ambivalent Conquest: Maya and Spaniard in Yucatan, 1517–1570* (Cambridge, 1987), pp. 3–4.
9 Ibid., pp. 9–10; Bernal Díaz del Castillo, *The Discovery and Conquest of Mexico, 1517–1521*, ed. G. García, trans. A. P. Maudslay (London, 1928), pp. 44–51.
10 Díaz del Castillo, *Discovery*, pp. 60–67.
11 Clendinnen, *Ambivalent Conquest*, p. 16.
12 Ibid., p. 17; Díaz del Castillo, *Discovery*, pp. 90–91; Landa, *Yucatan Before and After*, p. 4.
13 Díaz del Castillo, *Discovery*, pp. 110–16; Camilla Townsend, *Malintzin's Choices: An Indian Woman in the Conquest of Mexico* (Albuquerque, NM, 2006), pp. 25–6.
14 Grant D. Jones, *The Conquest of the Last Maya Kingdom* (Stanford, CA, 1998), pp. 29–34.
15 Thomas Benjamin, 'A Time of Reconquest: History, the Maya Revival, and the Zapatista Rebellion in Chiapas', *American Historical Review*, CV/2 (2000), pp. 429–31, doi: 10.2307/1571458.
16 Matthew Restall and Florine G. L. Asselbergs, *Invading Guatemala: Spanish, Nahua, and Maya Accounts of the Conquest Wars* (University Park, PA, 2007); David Stuart, *The Order of Days: The Maya World and the Truth about 2012* (New York, 2012), p. 161.
17 Matthew Restall, *The Maya World: Yucatec Culture and Society* (Stanford, CA, 1997), p. 3; Restall, *Maya Conquistador*, pp. 6–7.

18  Ralph L. Roys, *The Book of Chilam Balam of Chumayel*, Carnegie Institution of Washington Publication 438 (Washington, DC, 1933), p. 83.

19  Restall, *Maya World*, pp. 3–5.

20  Clendinnen, *Ambivalent Conquest*, pp. 20–28.

21  Ian Graham, *Alfred Maudslay and the Maya: A Biography* (Norman, OK, 2002), p. 158.

22  Clendinnen, *Ambivalent Conquest*, pp. 28–32.

23  Karttunen, *Between Worlds*, p. 90.

24  Bartolomé de Las Casas, *A Short Account of the Destruction of the Indies*, trans. N. Griffin, reprint (New York, 2004), p. 6.

25  Ibid., pp. 12, 54–5, 57, 73.

26  Restall, *Maya Conquistador*, pp. 132–3.

27  John F. Chuchiak IV, 'Writing as Resistance: Maya Graphic Pluralism and Indigenous Elite Strategies for Survival in Colonial Yucatan, 1550–1750', *Ethnohistory*, LVII/1 (2010), pp. 89–90; Clendinnen, *Ambivalent Conquest*, pp. 73–6.

28  John F. Chuchiak IV, 'The Images Speak: The Survival and Production of Hieroglyphic Codices and their Use in Post-Conquest Maya Religion (1580–1720)', in *Continuity and Change: Maya Religious Practices in Temporal Perspective: 5th European Maya Conference, University of Bonn, December 2000*, ed. D. Graña Behrens et al., Acta Mesoamericana 14 (Markt Schwaben, 2004), pp. 171–5.

29  John F. Chuchiak IV, 'Papal Bulls, Extirpators, and the Madrid Codex: The Content and Probable Provenience of the M. 56 Patch', in *The Madrid Codex: New Approaches to Understanding an Ancient Maya Manuscript*, ed. G. Vail and A. F. Aveni (Boulder, CO, 2004), pp. 57, 72; John F. Chuchiak IV, 'De Extirpatio Codicis Yucatecanensis: The 1607 Colonial Confiscation of a Maya Sacred Book – New Interpretations on the Origins and Provenience of the Madrid Codex', in *Sacred Books, Sacred Languages: Two Thousand Years of Ritual and Religious Maya Literature: Proceedings of the 8th European Maya Conference, Madrid, November 25–30, 2003*, ed. R. Valencia Rivera and G. Le Fort, Acta Mesoamericana 18 (Markt Schwaben, 2006), pp. 113–15.

30  Michael D. Coe and Justin Kerr, *The Art of the Maya Scribe* (London, 1997), pp. 175, 179.

31  John B. Glass and Donald Robertson, 'A Census of Native Middle American Pictorial Manuscripts', *Handbook of Middle American Indians* (Austin, 1975), vol. XIV, part 3, pp. 81–252, at pp. 153–4; Gabrielle Vail and Anthony F. Aveni, 'Research Methodologies and New Approaches to Interpreting the Madrid Codex', in *Madrid Codex*, ed. Vail and Aveni, p. 3.

32  Landa, *Yucatan Before and After*, p. 85.

33  Ibid., p. 86.

34  Amara Solari, *Maya Ideologies of the Sacred: The Transfiguration of Space in Colonial Yucatan* (Austin, TX, 2013), pp. 11, 13.

35 Jesper Nielsen, 'The Memory of Stones: Ancient Maya Spolia in the Architecture of Early Colonial Yucatan', *PARI Journal*, xx/3 (Winter 2020), pp. 1–15.

36 Graham, *Alfred Maudslay*, pp. 133, 158; Norman Hammond, 'Lords of the Jungle: A Prosopography of Maya Archaeology', in *Civilization in the Ancient Americas: Essays in Honor of Gordon R. Willey*, ed. R. M. Leventhal and A. L. Kolata (Albuquerque, NM, 1983), p. 7.

37 Benjamin Keen, 'The Old World Meets the New: Some Repercussions, 1492–1800', in *The Maya Image in the Western World: A Catalog to an Exhibition at the University of New Mexico*, ed. P. S. Briggs, University of New Mexico Art Museum and Maxwell Museum of Anthropology (Albuquerque, NM, 1986), p. 7.

38 Gonzalo Fernández de Oviedo, *Historia general y natural de las Indias*, ed. Juan Pérez de Tudela y Bueso, reprint (Madrid, 1992), p. 17; Jaime Gómez de Caso Zuriaga, 'Spanish Historians of the Sixteenth Century and the Prediscoveries of America', *Mediterranean Studies*, ix (2000), pp. 79–80, 83.

39 Richard H. Popkin, 'The Pre-Adamite Theory in the Renaissance', in *Philosophy and Humanism: Renaissance Essays in Honor of Paul Oskar Kristeller*, ed. E. P. Mahoney (New York, 1976), pp. 50–69.

40 Landa, *Yucatan Before and After*, p. 85.

41 Gregorio García, *Origen de Los Indios de El Nuevo Mundo, e Indias Occidentales*, 2nd edn (Madrid, 1729), pp. 41, 46, 79–81.

42 María del Carmen León Cázares, 'La Presencia del Demonio en las Constituciones Diocesanas de Fray Francisco Núñez de la Vega', *Estudios de Historia Novohispana*, xiii/13 (1993), p. 41; Francisco Nuñez de la Vega, *Constituciones Diocesanas del Obispado de Chiappa* (Rome, 1702), p. 9.

43 Heather McKillop and Jaime Awe, 'The History of Archaeological Research in Belize', *Belizean Studies*, xi/2 (1983), pp. 1–2.

44 Chuchiak, 'The Images Speak', pp. 171–5; Chuchiak, 'Writing as Resistance', p. 88.

45 Victoria Reifler Bricker and Helga-Maria Miram, *An Encounter of Two Worlds: The Book of Chilam Balam of Kaua*, Publication 68 (New Orleans, LA, 2002), pp. 10–11, 66–7; Chuchiak, 'Writing as Resistance', p. 106.

46 Laura Caso Barrera and Mario M. Aliphat Fernández, 'The Chilam Balam of Ixil: Text and Translation', in *Chilam Balam of Ixil: Facsimile and Study of an Unpublished Maya Book*, ed. L. Caso Barrera, trans. Q. Pope (Leiden and Boston, MA, 2019), pp. 218–19.

47 Chuchiak, 'Writing as Resistance', pp. 87–8.

48 Solari, *Maya Ideologies*, p. 103.

49 Stuart, *Order of Days*, p. 210.

50 Jones, *Conquest*, pp. 111–19.

51 Stuart, *Order of Days*, p. 30.

52 Victoria Reifler Bricker, *The Indian Christ, the Indian King: The Historical Substrate of Maya Myth and Ritual* (Austin, TX, 1981); Nelson A. Reed, *The Caste War of Yucatan*, revd edn (Stanford, CA, 2002); Paul Sullivan,

*Unfinished Conversations: Mayas and Foreigners between Two Wars*
(New York, 1989), p. 3; William F. Hanks, *Converting Words: Maya in
the Age of the Cross*, Anthropology of Christianity 6 (Berkeley, CA, 2010),
pp. 365–6; Joel W. Palka, *Unconquered Lacandon Maya: Ethnohistory
and Archaeology of Indigenous Culture Change* (Gainesville, FL, 2005),
p. 88. See Bricker and Miram, *Encounter of Two Worlds*, for more detailed
discussions of revolts and revitalization movements in Maya communities
across Mexico and Guatemala.

## 4 Exploration, Documentation and the Search for Origins in the Eighteenth and Nineteenth Centuries

1 Joel W. Palka, *Unconquered Lacandon Maya: Ethnohistory and Archaeology
of Indigenous Culture Change* (Gainesville, FL, 2005), p. 262.

2 Didier Boremanse, 'A Comparative Study in Lacandon Maya Mythology',
*Journal de la Société des Américanistes*, LXVIII (1982), p. 84.

3 Carlos Navarrete, 'Otra vez Modesto Méndez, Ambrosio Tut, y el
moderno descubrimiento de Tikal', *Historia y antropología de Guatemala:
Ensayos en honor de J. Daniel Contreras R.* (Guatemala City, 1982), pp.
157–70, at pp. 157–9; Peter D. Harrison, *The Lords of Tikal: Rulers of an
Ancient Maya City* (New York, 2000), p. 31; Palka, *Unconquered Lacandon
Maya*, p. 148.

4 Oswaldo Chinchilla Mazariegos, 'Archaeology in Guatemala: Nationalist,
Colonialist, Imperialist', in *The Oxford Handbook of Mesoamerican
Archaeology*, ed. D. L. Nichols and C. A. Pool (Oxford and New York,
2012), pp. 56–7.

5 Enrique Florescano, 'The Creation of the Museo Nacional de
Antropología of Mexico and Its Scientific, Educational, and Political
Purposes', in *Collecting the Pre-Columbian Past*, ed. E. H. Boone
(Washington, DC, 1993), pp. 83–103.

6 Quoted in Ignacio Bernal, *A History of Mexican Archaeology: The
Vanished Civilizations of Middle America* (London and New York, 1980),
pp. 74–5.

7 Florescano, 'Creation'; Khristaan David Villela, 'Montezuma's Dinner:
Precolumbian Art in Nineteenth-Century Mexico, 1821–1876', PhD diss.,
University of Texas at Austin, 2001, pp. 62–4, 96.

8 Robert L. Brunhouse, *In Search of the Maya: The First Archaeologists*
(Albuquerque, NM, 1974), p. 6; Michael D. Coe, *Breaking the Maya Code*
(London, 1992), p. 74.

9 Brunhouse, *In Search*, pp. 5–7, 11–13; Antonio del Río, 'Report of Antonio
Del Río to Don José Estachería', in *Description of the Ruins of an Ancient
City Discovered near Palenque, in the Kingdom of Guatemala, in Spanish
America, Translated from the Original Manuscript Report of Captain*

Don Antonio Del Rio, Followed by Teatro Crítico Americano; or, a Critical Investigation and Research into the History of the Americas, by Doctor Paul Felix Cabrera of the City of New Guatemala (London, 1822), pp. 1–21.

10 Del Río, 'Report', p. 14.

11 Gillett G. Griffin, 'Early Travelers to Palenque', in Primera Mesa Redonda de Palenque, Part 1, ed. Merle Greene Robertson (Pebble Beach, CA, 1974), p. 10; David Stuart, 'Notes on Palenque's "Del Rio Throne"', Maya Decipherment blog (21 October 2008), www.decipherment.wordpress.com.

12 Brunhouse, In Search, pp. 5, 16, 28; Guillermo Dupaix, 'Troisième Expédition', in Antiquités mexicaines: Relation des trois expéditions du colonel Dupaix, ordonnées en 1805, 1806, et 1807, par le roi Charles IV, pour la recherche des antiquités du pays, notamment celles de Mitla et de Palenque, avec les dessins de Castañeda, ed. Jean-Henri Baradère (Paris, 1834), vol. I, pp. 1–40; R. Tripp Evans, Romancing the Maya: Mexican Antiquity in the American Imagination, 1820–1915 (Austin, TX, 2004), p. 23; Edward King, Antiquities of Mexico: . . . Together with the Monuments of New Spain by Dupaix (London, 1831), vol. VI.

13 Charles Farcy, 'Discours Préliminaire: Appendice', in Antiquités mexicaines, ed. Baradère, vol. I, pp. xiii–xiv.

14 Evans, Romancing, p. 23.

15 Ibid.

16 Del Río, 'Report', p. 5.

17 Paul Felix Cabrera, 'Teatro Crítico Americano; or, A Critical Investigation and Research into the History of the Americans', in Description of the Ruins, pp. 36, 38–9, 45–6; Evans, Romancing, p. 34.

18 Griffin, 'Early Travelers', p. 10; Domingo Juarros and Ricardo Toledo Palomo, Compendio de la historia de la ciudad de Guatemala [1808–18] (Guatemala City, 2000).

19 Coe, Breaking, p. 80; Evans, Romancing, p. 35.

20 Evans, Romancing, pp. 89–94, 102.

21 Dupaix, 'Troisième Expédition', pp. 29–33.

22 This speculation arises from Mary Miller's mention (personal communication, 2020) that the Maya textile historian Walter 'Chip' Morris had observed that Catherwood's illustrations at Palenque were the first such illustrations. However, Dupaix's portrayals were earlier.

23 Evans, Romancing, pp. 35–6.

24 Alexandre Lenoir, 'Parallèle des anciens monuments mexicains avec ceux de l'Inde et du reste de l'ancien monde', in Antiquités Mexicaines, ed. Baradère, vol. II, pp. 1, 7, 77, 80, 82, author's translation.

25 David Bailie Warden, 'Recherches sur les antiquités de l'Amérique du Nord, l'Amérique du Sud, et sur la population primitive de ces deux continents', in Antiquités Mexicaines, ed. Baradère, vol. II, pp. 186, 207–9.

26 Villela, 'Montezuma's Dinner', p. 65.

27 Alexander von Humboldt and Aimé Bonpland, *Vues des Cordillères, et monumens des peuples indigènes de l'Amérique* (Paris, 1810), vol. II, f. 10, pp. 28, 44; Villela, 'Montezuma's Dinner', pp. 79–80.

28 Benjamin Keen, 'The Old World Meets the New: Some Repercussions, 1492–1800', in *The Maya Image in the Western World: A Catalog to an Exhibition at the University of New Mexico*, ed. P. S. Briggs, University of New Mexico Art Museum and Maxwell Museum of Anthropology (Albuquerque, NM, 1986), p. 10.

29 Villela, 'Montezuma's Dinner', pp. 23, 31, 95–6.

30 Bernal, *History*, pp. 135–6; Kevin M. Gosner, 'Rediscovering the Aztecs and Mayas: Field Exploration, Archaeological Exhibits, and National Museums', in *Oxford Research Encyclopedia of Latin American History* (Oxford, 2017).

31 Chinchilla Mazariegos, 'Archaeology in Guatemala', p. 58; Oswaldo Chinchilla Mazariegos, 'Just and Patriotic: Creating a National Museum in Guatemala (1831–1930)', *Museum History Journal*, IX/1 (2016), p. 61.

32 Oswaldo Chinchilla Mazariegos, 'Archaeology and Nationalism in Guatemala at the Time of Independence', *Antiquity*, LXXII (1998), pp. 383–4; Chinchilla Mazariegos, 'Just and Patriotic', p. 61.

33 Victor Montejo, *Voices from Exile: Violence and Survival in Modern Maya History* (Norman, OK, 1999), p. 33.

34 Palka, *Unconquered Lacandon Maya*, p. 86.

35 Coe, *Breaking*, pp. 76–7; Jean Frédéric Maximilien de Waldeck, *Voyage pittoresque et archéologique dans la province d'Yucatan (Amérique Centrale), pendant les années 1834 et 1836* (Paris, 1838).

36 Miruna Achim, 'Maleta de doble fondo y colecciones de antigüedades Ciudad de México, ca. 1830', in *Museos al Detalle: Colecciones, antiqüedades e historia natural, 1790–1870*, ed. M. Achim and I. Podgorny (Rosario, 2013), p. 117. See also Esther Pasztory, *Jean-Frédéric Waldeck: Artist of Exotic Mexico* (Albuquerque, NM, 2010).

37 Brunhouse, *In Search*, p. 69; Evans, *Romancing*, pp. 37–40; Waldeck, *Voyage*, p. 71.

38 Grafton Elliot Smith, *Elephants and Ethnologists* (London, 1924), p. 1.

39 Brunhouse, *In Search*, pp. 30–33; Coe, *Breaking*, p. 75.

40 Juan Galindo, 'Ruins of Palenque', *London Literary Gazette and Journal of Belles Lettres, Arts, Sciences, etc.*, 769 (October 1831), pp. 665–6.

41 Brunhouse, *In Search*, p. 40; Juan Galindo, 'The Ruins of Copan', *Archaeologia Americana: Transactions and Collections of the American Antiquarian Society*, II (1836), pp. 543–50.

42 Galindo, 'Ruins of Copan', p. 546.

43 Susan D. Gillespie, 'Toltecs, Tula, and Chichén Itzá: The Development of an Archaeological Myth', in *Twin Tollans: Chichén Itzá, Tula, and the Epiclassic to Early Postclassic Mesoamerican World*, revd edn,

ed. J. K. Kowalski and C. Kristan-Graham (Washington, DC, 2011); Cynthia Kristan-Graham and Jeff Kowalski, 'Chichén Itzá, Tula, and Tollan: Changing Perspectives on a Recurring Problem in Mesoamerican Archaeology and Art History', in *Twin Tollans*, ed. Kowalski and Kristan-Graham, pp. 1–58.

44 Galindo, 'Ruins of Copan', p. 546.

45 John Lloyd Stephens, *Incidents of Travel in Central America, Chiapas and Yucatan*, 2 vols (New York, 1841); John Lloyd Stephens, *Incidents of Travel in Yucatan*, 2 vols (London, 1843).

46 Evans, *Romancing*, p. 49.

47 Stephens, *Central America*, vol. I, pp. 159–60.

48 Ibid., vol. II, p. 442.

49 Ibid., vol. I, p. 137.

50 Merideth Paxton, 'Frederick Catherwood and the Maya: Reorientation of Nineteenth Century Perceptions', in *Maya Image*, ed. Briggs, pp. 11–12.

51 Khristaan Villela, 'Beyond Stephens and Catherwood: Ancient Mesoamerica as Public Entertainment in the Early Nineteenth Century', in *Past Presented: Archaeological Illustration and the Ancient Americas*, ed. J. Pillsbury (Washington, DC, 2012), p. 155.

52 Evans, *Romancing*, pp. 2–3, 67; Stephens, *Central America*, p. 105.

53 Stephens, *Central America*, vol. I, pp. 115–16. See pp. 126–8, regarding the purchase.

54 Adam T. Sellen and Lynneth D. Lowe, 'Las antiguas colecciones arqueológicas de Yucatan en el Museo Americano de Historia Natural', *Estudios de Cultura Maya*, XXXIII (2009), pp. 53–71; Villela, 'Beyond Stephens', pp. 155–6.

55 Griffin, 'Early Travelers', p. 14; Charles Rau, *The Palenque Tablet in the United States National Museum, Washington, DC* (Washington, DC, 1879).

56 Robert D. Aguirre, 'Agencies of the Letter: The Foreign Office and the Ruins of Central America', *Victorian Studies*, XLVI/2 (2004), pp. 285–6.

57 Quoted ibid., p. 287, emphasis added by Aguirre.

58 Bernal, *History*, p. 140.

59 Ernest Théodore Hamy and Musée de l'Homme, *Galerie Américaine du Musée d'Ethnographie du Trocadéro. Choix de pièces archéologiques et ethnographiques décrites et publiées par le Dr E.-T. Hamy* (Paris, 1897), pp. 48, 51; Lynneth S. Lowe and Adam T. Sellen, 'Una pasión por la antigüedad: La colección arqueológica de Don Florentino Gimeno en Campeche durante el siglo XIX', *Estudios de Cultura Maya*, XXXVI/1 (2010), p. 149; Adam Sellen, 'Fraternal Curiosity: The Camacho Museum, Campeche, Mexico', in *Nature and Antiquities: The Making of Archaeology in the Americas*, ed. P. L. Kohl, I. Podgorny and S. Gänger (Tucson, AZ, 2014), pp. 1–109.

60  Lowe and Sellen, 'Una pasión', p. 160.

61  Keith F. Davis, *Désiré Charnay: Expeditionary Photographer* (Albuquerque, NM, 1981); Ian Graham, *The Art of Maya Hieroglyphic Writing: January 28–March 28, 1971; An Exhibition in the Art Gallery, Center for Inter-American Relations, Sponsored Jointly by Peabody Museum of Archaeology and Ethnology, Harvard University, Cambridge, Massachusetts, and Center for Inter-American Relations, Inc., New York, New York* (Cambridge, MA, 1971), p. 15; Bryan R. Just, 'Printed Pictures of Maya Sculpture', in *Past Presented*, ed. Pillsbury, p. 363.

62  Désiré Charnay, 'Préface', in *Cités et ruines américaines: Mitla, Palenqué, Izamal, Chichen-Itza, Uxmal* (Paris, 1863), p. iii, author's translation.

63  Evans, *Romancing*, p. 111; Eugène-Emmanuel Viollet-le-Duc, 'Antiquités Américaines', in *Cités et ruines américaines*, p. 27.

64  Davis, *Désiré Charnay*, p. 30; Evans, *Romancing*, p. 104.

65  Kristan-Graham and Kowalski, 'Chichén Itzá, Tula, and Tollan', p. 5.

66  Matthew Restall and John F. Chuchiak IV, 'A Reevaluation of the Authenticity of Fray Diego de Landa's *Relación de las Cosas de Yucatan*', *Ethnohistory*, XLIX/3 (2002), p. 655.

67  Charles-Étienne Brasseur de Bourbourg, *S'il existe des sources de l'histoire primitive du Mexique dans les monuments egyptiens et de l'histoire primitive de l'ancien monde dans les monuments américains?* (Paris, 1864); Brunhouse, *In Search*, pp. 110, 114.

68  Brasseur de Bourbourg, *S'il existe*, pp. 128–9.

69  Erik Velásquez García, 'The Maya Flood Myth and the Decapitation of the Cosmic Caiman', *PARI Journal*, VII/1 (2006), pp. 5–7.

70  Lawrence Gustave Desmond, *Yucatan through her Eyes: Alice Dixon Le Plongeon, Writer and Expeditionary Photographer* (Albuquerque, NM, 2009), p. 25.

71  Lawrence Gustave Desmond and Phyllis Mauch Messenger, *A Dream of Maya: Augustus and Alice Le Plongeon in Nineteenth-Century Yucatan* (Albuquerque, NM, 1989), pp. 50–51.

72  Barbara Braun, 'Henry Moore and Pre-Columbian Art', *Res: Anthropology and Aesthetics*, 17–18 (Spring–Autumn 1989), pp. 180–84.

73  Augustus Le Plongeon, *Sacred Mysteries among the Mayas and the Quiches: The Story of Central American Antiquities and their Relations to the Sacred Mysteries of Egypt, Greece, Chaldea, and India* (New York, 1886), pp. 36–7.

74  Ibid., p. xii.

75  Evans, *Romancing*, p. 136; Le Plongeon, *Sacred Mysteries*, p. 113; Augustus Le Plongeon, *Queen Móo and the Egyptian Sphinx* (London, 1896).

76  Evans, *Romancing*, p. 136.

77  Ibid., pp. 127, 141–4; Le Plongeon, *Sacred Mysteries*, p. 40.

78  Le Plongeon, *Sacred Mysteries*, p. 22.

79 Villela, 'Montezuma's Dinner', p. 106.

80 Le Plongeon, *Sacred Mysteries*, p. xiii.

81 W. Scott-Elliot, *The Story of Atlantis: A Geographical, Historical, and Ethnological Sketch*, 2nd revd edn (London, 1914), p. 9.

82 Ibid., pp. 29, 34.

83 Christina Bueno, *The Pursuit of Ruins: Archaeology, History, and the Making of Modern Mexico* (Albuquerque, NM, 2016), p. 4.

84 Mechthild Rutsch, 'Natural History, National Museum and Anthropology in Mexico: Some Reference Points in the Forging and Re-Forging of National Identity', *Perspectivas Latinoamericanas*, I (2004), pp. 95–6.

85 Christiane Demeulenaere-Douyère, 'Le Mexique s'expose à Paris: Xochicalco, Léon Méhédin et l'exposition Universelle de 1867', *Histoire(s) de l'Amérique Latine*, III/3 (2009), pp. 3–4.

86 Ibid.

87 Arturo Taracena Arriola, 'El Museo Yucateco y la Reinvención de Yucatan: La Prensa y la Construcción del Regionalismo Peninsular', *Península*, II/1 (2007), pp. 13–46; Arturo Taracena Arriola, 'Nineteenth-Century Yucatan Regionalism and the Literary Press: El Museo Yucateco and El Registro Yucateco', *Voices of Mexico*, LXXXV (2009), pp. 50–52.

88 Taracena Arriola, 'El Museo Yucateco', pp. 25–8; Taracena Arriola, 'Nineteenth-Century Yucatan Regionalism'.

89 Lynneth S. Lowe and Adam T. Sellen, 'Introducción', in *Documentos del Museo Yucateco, 1870–1885*, ed. L. S. Lowe and A. T. Sellen (Mérida, 2019), pp. 9–16.

90 Bernal, *History*, pp. 139–40; Florescano, 'Creation'; Villela, 'Montezuma's Dinner', pp. 332–6.

91 Bueno, *Pursuit of Ruins*, pp. 2, 48–52, 81; Rutsch, 'Natural History', pp. 104–6.

92 Lowe and Sellen, 'Introducción', p. 19; Desmond and Messenger, *A Dream*, pp. 40–42, 50; Clementina Díaz y Ovando, 'Vicente Riva Palacio y la Arqueología, 1878–80', *Anales del Instituto de Investigaciones Estéticas*, XV/58 (1987), pp. 179–86, doi: 10.22201/iie.18703062e.1987.58.1347.

93 Villela, 'Montezuma's Dinner', pp. 306–7.

94 Bueno, *Pursuit of Ruins*, pp. 173, 177–9.

95 Luis E. Carranza and Fernando Luiz Lara, *Modern Architecture in Latin America: Art, Technology, and Utopia* (Austin, TX, 2015), pp. 47–8.

96 Mauricio Tenorio-Trillo, *Mexico at the World's Fairs: Crafting a Modern Nation* (Berkeley, Los Angeles, CA, and London, 1996), pp. xii–xiii, 65–6.

97 Curtis Hinsley, 'The World as Marketplace: Commodification of the Exotic at the World's Columbian Exposition, Chicago, 1893', in *Exhibiting Cultures: The Poetics and Politics of Museum Display*, ed. I. Karp and S. D. Lavine (Washington, DC, 1991), p. 346.

98 Tenorio-Trillo, *Mexico at the World's Fairs*, pp. 64, 82–3, 88.

99 Alfredo Chavero, *Homenaje á Cristóbal Colón: Antigüedades Mexicanas publicadas por la Junta Colombina de México en el cuarto centenario del descubrimiento de América* (Mexico City, 1892), pp. iii–iv.

100 Oswaldo Chinchilla Mazariegos, 'Historiografía de los Mayas en Guatemala: El Pensamiento de Manuel García Elgueta', *Mesoamérica*, 38 (1999), pp. 55–75.

101 Chinchilla Mazariegos, 'Archaeology in Guatemala', pp. 58–9, 62.

102 Graham, *Art of Maya Hieroglyphic Writing*, p. 17; Ian Graham, *Alfred Maudslay and the Maya: A Biography* (Norman, OK, 2002), pp. 135, 137, 220–22.

103 Carolyn E. Tate, *Yaxchilan: The Design of a Maya Ceremonial City* (Austin, TX, 1992), p. 8; 'Yaxchilan: Principal Investigations at the Site', Corpus of Maya Hieroglyphic Inscriptions website, Peabody Museum of Archaeology and Ethnology, accessed 22 June 2020, www.peabody.harvard.edu.

104 Mary F. McVicker, *Adela Breton: A Victorian Artist amid Mexico's Ruins* (Albuquerque, NM, 2005), p. 57.

105 Davis, *Désiré Charnay*, p. 107; Graham, *Art of Maya Hieroglyphic Writing*, p. 19; Just, 'Printed Pictures', p. 373.

106 Teobert Maler, *Researches in the Central Portion of the Usumatsintla Valley: Reports of Explorations for the Museum, 1898–1900* (Cambridge, MA, 1901–3).

107 Coe, *Breaking*, pp. 89–91, 107–8; Graham, *Art of Maya Hieroglyphic Writing*, pp. 16–19; David Stuart, *The Order of Days: The Maya World and the Truth about 2012* (New York, 2012), pp. 165–6.

108 Stephen D. Houston, Oswaldo Chinchilla Mazariegos and David Stuart, '"Key to the Maya Hieroglyphs", Cyrus Thomas', in *The Decipherment of Ancient Maya Writing*, ed. S. D. Houston, O. Chinchilla Mazariegos and D. Stuart (Norman, OK, 2001), p. 113; Eduard Seler, 'Does There Really Exist a Phonetic Key to the Maya Hieroglyphic Writing?', *Science*, XX/499 (26 August 1892), pp. 121–2.

109 Paul Schellhas, *Representation of Deities of the Maya Manuscripts*, trans. S. Wesselhoeft and A. M. Parker, 2nd revd edn (Cambridge, MA, 1904).

## 5 Rediscovering Maya Histories in the Twentieth and Twenty-First Centuries

1 Ian Graham, *Alfred Maudslay and the Maya: A Biography* (Norman, OK, 2002), pp. 193–4, 210; Stephen D. Houston, Barbara W. Fash and David Stuart, 'Masterful Hands: Morelli and the Maya on the Hieroglyphic Stairway, Copan, Honduras', *Res: Anthropology and Aesthetics*, 65–6 (2014), pp. 16–17; Alfred Percival Maudslay, *Biologia Centrali-Americana;*

*or, Contributions to the Knowledge of the Fauna and Flora of Mexico and Central America*: vol. v: *Archaeology*, ed. F. D. Godman and O. Salvin (London, 1889), p. 65.

2 British Museum, 'Collection Online', accessed 19 March 2019, www. britishmuseum.org; Heather McKillop and Jaime Awe, 'The History of Archaeological Research in Belize', *Belizean Studies*, xi/2 (1983), p. 2; David M. Pendergast, 'The Center and the Edge: Archaeology in Belize, 1809–1992', *Journal of World Prehistory*, vii/1 (1993), p. 4; J.E.S. Thompson, 'Thomas Gann in the Maya Ruins', *British Medical Journal*, ii/5973 (1975), pp. 741–3.

3 Diego de Landa, *Yucatan Before and After the Conquest*, trans. William Gates (Baltimore, MD, 1937), p. 90.

4 Helen Delpar, *The Enormous Vogue of Things Mexican: Cultural Relations between the United States and Mexico, 1920–1935* (Tuscaloosa, AL, 1992), pp. 105–6; Norman Hammond, 'Lords of the Jungle: A Prosopography of Maya Archaeology', in *Civilization in the Ancient Americas: Essays in Honor of Gordon R. Willey*, ed. R. M. Leventhal and A. L. Kolata (Albuquerque, NM, 1983), p. 17; Mary F. McVicker, *Adela Breton: A Victorian Artist amid Mexico's Ruins* (Albuquerque, NM, 2005), pp. 128–9.

5 Franz Boas, 'Summary of the Work of the International School of American Archeology and Ethnology in Mexico', *American Anthropologist*, xvii/2 (1915), p. 388; Ricardo Godoy, 'Franz Boas and His Plans for an International School of American Archaeology and Ethnology in Mexico', *Journal of the History of the Behavioral Sciences*, xiii/3 (1977), pp. 228–42; 'Prof. Tozzer at the International School of American Archaeology', *Pan American Notes*, xxxvii (1913), p. 707.

6 Stephen L. Black, 'The Carnegie Uaxactun Project and the Development of Maya Archaeology', *Ancient Mesoamerica*, i/2 (1990), pp. 257–76; Philip Phillips, 'Alfred Marsten Tozzer 1877–1954', *American Antiquity*, xxi/1 (1955), pp. 72–80; Alfred M. Tozzer, *Landa's Relación de las Cosas de Yucatan: A Translation* (Cambridge, MA, 1941).

7 Raymond Edwin Merwin and George Clapp Vaillant, *The Ruins of Holmul, Guatemala* (Cambridge, MA, 1932).

8 Mary Ellen Miller, 'The History of the Study of Maya Vase Painting', in *The Maya Vase Book: A Corpus of Rollout Photographs of Maya Vases*, ed. J. Kerr (New York, 1989), vol. i, pp. 128–45.

9 Enrique Florescano, 'The Creation of the Museo Nacional de Antropología of Mexico and its Scientific, Educational, and Political Purposes', in *Collecting the Pre-Columbian Past*, ed. E. H. Boone (Washington, DC, 1993).

10 Herbert Joseph Spinden, 'Portraiture in Central American Art', in *Holmes Anniversary Volume: Anthropological Essays Presented to William Henry Holmes in Honor of his Seventieth Birthday, December 1, 1916*, ed. F. W. Hodges [1916], reprint (New York, 1977), p. 442.

11 Sylvanus Griswold Morley, 'The Foremost Intellectual Achievement of Ancient America', *National Geographic Magazine*, XLI/2 (1922), p. 109.

12 Roger Fry, 'American Archaeology', *Burlington Magazine for Connoisseurs*, XXXIII/188 (1918), p. 157.

13 Elizabeth Hill Boone, 'Collecting the Pre-Columbian Past: Historical Trends and the Process of Reception and Use', in *Collecting the Pre-Columbian Past*, ed. Boone, pp. 331–42.

14 Fry, 'American Archaeology', pp. 155, 157.

15 Morley, 'The Foremost Intellectual Achievement', p. 109; Sylvanus Griswold Morley, *The Inscriptions of Petén* (Washington, DC, 1937–8), vol. III, p. 229.

16 Sylvanus Griswold Morley, 'Maya Civilization, 100% American', *Forum*, LXXVIII/2 (1927), p. 226.

17 Sylvanus Griswold Morley, *An Introduction to the Study of the Maya Hieroglyphs* (Washington, DC, 1915), p. 33; Morley, 'Foremost Intellectual Achievement', p. 125.

18 J. Eric S. Thompson, 'The Solar Year of the Mayas at Quirigua, Guatemala', *Field Museum of Natural History*, Publication 315, Anthropological Series, XVII/4 (1932), pp. 389–90; J. Eric S. Thompson, *The Rise and Fall of the Maya Civilization* (Norman, OK, 1954), pp. 3–11.

19 See Morley, *The Inscriptions of Petén*, vol. IV, pp. 250–52; Linda Schele and Mary Ellen Miller, *The Blood of Kings: Dynasty and Ritual in Maya Art* (New York and Fort Worth, TX, 1986), pp. 18–23.

20 Oswaldo Chinchilla Mazariegos, 'Archaeology in Guatemala: Nationalist, Colonialist, Imperialist', in *The Oxford Handbook of Mesoamerican Archaeology*, ed. D. L. Nichols and C. A. Pool (Oxford and New York, 2012), p. 61; McKillop and Awe, 'History', p. 8.

21 Hammond, 'Lords', pp. 20–28; McKillop and Awe, 'History', p. 3; Jason Yaeger and Greg Borgstede, 'Professional Archaeology and the Modern Maya: A Historical Sketch', in *Continuities and Changes in Maya Archaeology: Perspectives at the Millennium*, ed. C. W. Golden and G. Borgstede (New York, 2004), p. 240.

22 McKillop and Awe, 'History', p. 3; Kidder quoted in Robert Wauchope, 'Alfred Vincent Kidder, 1885–1963', *American Antiquity*, XXXI/2 (1965), pp. 158–9.

23 Richard E. W. Adams, 'Maya Archaeology 1958–1968, a Review', *Latin American Research Review*, IV/2 (1969), p. 5; Wauchope, 'Alfred Vincent Kidder', pp. 149, 156–8.

24 Daniel Schávelzon, 'Semblanza: Miguel Ángel Fernández y la Arquitectura Prehispánica (1890–1945)', *Cuadernos de Arquitectura Mesoamericana*, VIII (1986), pp. 85–6; Benjamin Volta, Nancy Peniche May and Geoffrey E. Braswell, 'The Archaeology of Chichen Itza: Its History, What We Like to Argue About, and What We Think We Know', in *Landscapes of the Itza:*

*Archaeology and Art History at Chichen Itza and Neighboring Sites*, ed.
L. H. Wren, C. Kristan-Graham, T. Nygard and K. R. Spencer (Gainesville,
FL, 2018), p. 33.

25  Quetzil E. Castañeda, *In the Museum of Maya Culture: Touring
Chichen Itza*, 2nd printing (Minneapolis, MN, 1997), p. 121; James Oles,
'Reviving the Pre-Hispanic Past, from Mexico to California', in *Found
in Translation: Design in California and Mexico, 1915–1985*, ed. W. Kaplan,
exh. cat., Los Angeles County Museum of Art (Los Angeles, CA, 2017),
p. 143.

26  Paul Sullivan, *Unfinished Conversations: Mayas and Foreigners between
Two Wars* (New York, 1989), pp. 29, 76–89.

27  Hermann Beyer, *Studies on the Inscriptions of Chichen Itza*, Contributions
to American Archaeology, vol. IV/21 (Washington, DC, 1937), pp. 36, 38–9,
figs 1–14; Robert Wauchope, 'Hermann Beyer', *American Antiquity*, IX/4
(April 1944), p. 439.

28  Sylvanus G. Morley, 'Archeology', *Carnegie Institution of Washington
Yearbook*, 14 (1916), p. 338.

29  Black, 'Carnegie Uaxactun Project'.

30  Chinchilla Mazariegos, 'Archaeology in Guatemala', p. 60.

31  Manuel Gamio, 'The Sequence of Cultures in Mexico', *American
Anthropologist*, XXVI/3 (1924), pp. 307–22; A. V. Kidder, 'Excavations at
Kaminaljuyu, Guatemala', *American Antiquity*, XI/2 (1945), pp. 65–6, 74–5;
Susan D. Gillespie, 'Toltecs, Tula, and Chichén Itzá: The Development
of an Archaeological Myth', in *Twin Tollans: Chichén Itzá, Tula, and the
Epiclassic to Early Postclassic Mesoamerican World*, revd edn, ed. J. K.
Kowalski and C. Kristan-Graham (Washington, DC, 2011), pp. 194–5;
Miller, 'History of the Study', p. 133.

32  Anthony P. Andrews, 'Late Postclassic Lowland Maya Archaeology',
*Journal of World Prehistory*, VII/1 (1993), p. 37; Alberto Escalona Ramos,
'Algunas Ruinas Prehispánicas en Quintana Roo', *Boletín de La Sociedad
Mexicana de Geografía y Estadística*, LXI (1946), pp. 513–628; Miguel
Angel Fernández, 'Exploraciones Arqueológicas en la Isla de Cozumel,
Quintana Roo', *Anales del Museo Nacional de México*, I (1945), pp. 107–20;
Schávelzon, 'Semblanza', pp. 90–91.

33  Robert Wauchope, 'Edward Wyllys Andrews, IV, 1916–1971', *American
Antiquity*, XXXVII/3 (1972), pp. 394–403, doi: 10.1017/s0002731600087783;
Andrews, 'Late Postclassic', pp. 38–9.

34  Mary Ellen Miller and Claudia Brittenham, *The Spectacle of the Late Maya
Court: Reflections on the Murals of Bonampak* (Austin, TX, 2013); Jillian
Steinhauer, 'Rina Lazo, Muralist Who Worked with Diego Rivera, Dies at
96', *New York Times* (18 December 2019), www.nytimes.com.

35  Agustin Villagra Caleti, *Bonampak: la ciudad de los muros pintados*
(Mexico City, 1949).

36  Alberto Ruz Lhuillier, 'Exploraciones Arqueológicas en Palenque: 1953',
    *Anales del Instituto Nacional de Antropología e Historia*, X/39 (1956),
    pp. 69–116.

37  Michael D. Coe, 'The Funerary Temple among the Classic Maya',
    *Southwestern Journal of Anthropology*, XII/4 (1956), p. 393.

38  Hammond, 'Lords', p. 25; McKillop and Awe, 'History', p. 4; Jeremy A.
    Sabloff, 'Looking Backward and Looking Forward: How Maya Studies
    of Yesterday Shape Today', in *Continuities and Changes*, ed. Golden and
    Borgstede, p. 14.

39  The detailed studies of excavations, architecture and artefacts include the
    following: William Coe, *Excavations in the Great Plaza, North Terrace,
    and North Acropolis of Tikal*, Tikal Report 14, University Monograph 61
    (Philadelphia, PA, 1990); H. Stanley Loten, *Miscellaneous Investigations in
    Central Tikal*, Tikal Report 23A (Philadelphia, PA, 2002); Hattula Moholy-
    Nagy, *The Artifacts of Tikal: Utilitarian Artifacts and Unworked Material*,
    Tikal Report 27B (Philadelphia, PA, 2003).

40  Heinrich Berlin, 'The Destruction of Structure 5D–33–1st at Tikal',
    *American Antiquity*, XXXII/2 (1967), pp. 241–2.

41  Yuriy V. Knorozov, 'The Problem of the Study of the Maya Hieroglyphic
    Writing', *American Antiquity*, XXIII/3 (1958), pp. 284–91, doi: 10.2307/
    276310.

42  Luis Luján Muñoz, 'El Doctor Heinrich Berlin en la Arqueología Maya:
    Homenaje', in *II Simposio de Investigaciones Arqueológicas en Guatemala,
    1988*, ed. J. P. Laporte et al. (Guatemala City, 1991), pp. 119–20.

43  Heinrich Berlin, 'El Glifo "emblema" de las Inscripciones Mayas', *Journal
    de La Société des Américanistes*, 47 (1958), pp. 111, 113, doi: 10.3406/
    jsa.1958.1153, author's translation.

44  Tatiana Proskouriakoff, *An Album of Maya Architecture* (Washington,
    DC, 1946); Tatiana Proskouriakoff, *A Study of Classic Maya Sculpture*
    (Washington, DC, 1950); Tatiana Proskouriakoff, 'Historical Implications
    of a Pattern of Dates at Piedras Negras, Guatemala', *American Antiquity*,
    XXV/4 (1960), pp. 454–75, doi: 10.2307/276633.

45  David H. Kelley, 'Fonetismo en la Escritura Maya', *Estudios de Cultura
    Maya*, II (1962), pp. 277–317; David H. Kelley, 'Kakupacal and the Itzas',
    *Estudios de Cultura Maya*, VII (1968), pp. 255–68.

46  Hammond, 'Lords', p. 32; McKillop and Awe, 'History'; Jeremy A. Sabloff,
    *The New Archaeology and the Ancient Maya* (New York, 1990), pp. 6–7.

47  Adams, 'Maya Archaeology', p. 13; Black, 'Carnegie Uaxactun Project',
    p. 259.

48  Thomas R. Hester and Harry J. Shafer, 'Exploitation of Chert Resources
    by the Ancient Maya of Northern Belize, Central America', *World
    Archaeology*, XVI/2 (1984), pp. 157–73; Anna O. Shepard, *Ceramics for the
    Archaeologist*, Publication 609 (Washington, DC, 1956).

49 James Brady, 'Uncovering the Dark Secrets of the Maya – The Archeology of Maya Caves', in *Maya: Divine Kings of the Rain Forest*, ed. N. Grube (Potsdam, 2012), pp. 296–307.

50 Arlen F. Chase and Diane Z. Chase, *Investigations at the Classic Maya City of Caracol, Belize, 1985–1987* (San Francisco, CA, 1987); Hammond, 'Lords', pp. 9–10, 18.

51 Yamile Lira López, 'Juergen K. Brueggemann (1942–2004)', *Anales de Antropología*, XXXVII (2003), pp. 335–7.

52 Ramón Carrasco Vargas, Verónica A. Vázquez López and Simon Martin, 'Daily Life of the Ancient Maya Recorded on Murals at Calakmul, Mexico', *Proceedings of the National Academy of Sciences*, CVI/46 (2009), pp. 19245–9, doi: 10.1073/pnas.0904374106.

53 Enrique Nalda, ed., *Los Cautivos de Dzibanché* (Mexico City, 2004).

54 Christophe Helmke and Jaime Awe, 'Sharper than a Serpent's Tooth: A Tale of the Snake-Head Dynasty as Recounted on Xunantunich Panel 4', *PARI Journal*, XVII/2 (2016), pp. 1–22.

55 Bárbara Arroyo, 'Juan Pedro Laporte (1945–2010)', *Journal de La Société des Américanistes*, XCVI/2 (2010), pp. 293–6; Chinchilla Mazariegos, 'Archaeology in Guatemala', p. 62; Liwy Grazioso Sierra, 'In Memoriam: Juan Antonio Valdés Gómez, 1954–2011', Mesoweb Reports and News, electronic document, published online at Mesoweb, accessed 22 February 2019, www.mesoweb.com; Juan Pedro Laporte, 'Thirty Years Later: Some Results of Recent Investigations in Tikal', in *Tikal: Dynasties, Foreigners, and Affairs of State*, ed. J. A. Sabloff (Santa Fe, NM, 2003), pp. 281–318; Juan Antonio Valdés, Hector L. Escobedo and Federico Fahsen, *Reyes, tumbas y palacios: La historia dinástica de Uaxactun* (Mexico City and Guatemala City, 1999).

56 Arthur Demarest, *The Petexbatun Regional Archaeological Project: A Multidisciplinary Study of the Maya Collapse* (Nashville, TN, 2006).

57 Lilián Argentina Corzo, 'El Atlas Arqueológico de Guatemala, Un Programa de Registro Nacional. Resultados de 25 Años de Trabajo', in *XXV Simposio de Investigaciones Arqueológicas en Guatemala, 2011*, ed. B. Arroyo, L. Paiz and H. Mejía (Guatemala City, 2012), pp. 1–11, www.asociaciontikal.com.

58 Iyaxel Ixkan A. Cojti Ren, 'The Emergence of the Ancient Kaqchikel Polity: A Case of Ethnogenesis in the Guatemalan Highlands', PhD diss., Vanderbilt University, Nashville, TN, 2019, http://hdl.handle.net/1803/13625.

59 Takeshi Inomata et al., 'Monumental Architecture at Aguada Fénix and the Rise of Maya Civilization', *Nature* (3 June 2020), doi: 10.1038/s41586-020-2343-4; Robert M. Rosenswig, Ricardo López-Torrijos, Caroline E. Antonelli and Rebecca R. Mendelsohn, 'Lidar Mapping and Surface Survey of the Izapa State on the Tropical Piedmont of Chiapas, Mexico', *Journal of Archaeological Science*, XL/3 (2013), pp. 1493–507, doi: 10.1016/j.jas.2012.10.034.

60  William A. Saturno, Karl A. Taube, David Stuart and Heather Hurst, *The Murals of San Bartolo, El Petén, Guatemala. Pt. 1: The North Wall*, Ancient America 7 (Barnardsville, NC, 2007); Karl A. Taube, William A. Saturno, David Stuart and Heather Hurst, *The Murals of San Bartolo, El Petén, Guatemala. Pt. 2: The West Wall*, Ancient America 10 (Barnardsville, NC, 2010).

61  Heather Hurst, 'Murals and the Ancient Maya Artist: A Study of Art Production in the Guatemalan Lowlands', PhD diss., Yale University, New Haven, CT, 2009.

62  David A. Freidel and Héctor L. Escobedo, 'Un Diseño de Investigación para el Perú-Waka: Una Capital Maya Clásica en el Occidente de Petén', in XVI *Simposio de Investigaciones Arqueológicas en Guatemala, 2002*, ed. J. P. Laporte, B. Arroyo, H. Escobedo and H. Mejía (Guatemala City, 2003), pp. 391–408; Olivia C. Navarro-Farr, Keith Eppich, David A. Freidel and Griselda Pérez Robles, 'Ancient Maya Queenship: Generations of Crafting State Politics and Alliance Building from Kaanul to Waka', in *Approaches to Monumental Landscapes of the Ancient Maya*, ed. B. A. Houk et al. (Gainesville, FL, 2020).

63  Freidel and Escobedo, 'Un Diseño de Investigación'; Navarro-Farr et al., 'Ancient Maya Queenship'.

64  Marcello A. Canuto and Tomás Barrientos Q, 'La Corona: Un Acercamiento a las Políticas del Reino Kaan desde un Centro Secundario del Noroeste del Petén', *Estudios de Cultura Maya*, XXXVII (2011), pp. 11–43.

65  Miguel Rivera Dorado, *Los Mayas de Oxkintok* (Madrid, 1996); Charles Suhler, Traci Ardren and David Johnstone, 'The Chronology of Yaxuna: Evidence from Excavation and Ceramics', *Ancient Mesoamerica*, 9 (1998), pp. 167–82.

66  Alfonso Lacadena García-Gallo, 'The Glyphic Corpus from Ek' Balam, Yucatan, México', trans. Alex Lomónaco, FAMSI Grant Report (2003); Leticia Vargas de la Peña and Víctor R. Castillo Borges, 'Las Construcciones Monumentales de Ek' Balam', in *The Archaeology of Yucatan*, ed. T. W. Stanton (Oxford, 2014), pp. 377–93.

67  Carlos Peraza Lope et al., 'The Chronology of Mayapan: New Radiocarbon Evidence', *Ancient Mesoamerica*, XVII (2006), pp. 153–75.

68  Antonio Benavides Castillo and Ernesto Vargas Pacheco, 'Jaina, Campeche: Temporada 2003 los hallazgos y el futuro próximo', in *El patrimonio arqueológico maya en Campeche: Novedades, afectaciones y soluciones*, ed. A. Benavides Castillo (Mexico City, 2007), pp. 47–82.

69  Merle Greene Robertson, *The Sculpture of Palenque*, vol. III: *The Late Buildings of the Palace* (Princeton, NJ, 1985); Merle Greene Robertson, Martha J. Macri and Christi Vieira, *Merle Greene Robertson's Rubbings of Maya Sculpture* (San Francisco, CA, 1993), pp. 3–4.

70 Beatriz de la Fuente and Leticia Staines Cicero, eds, *Pintura Mural Prehispanica en Mexico*, vol. II: *Area Maya. Bonampak* (Mexico City, 1998).

71 See, for example, Simon Martin and Nikolai Grube, *Chronicle of the Maya Kings and Queens: Deciphering the Dynasties of the Ancient Maya*, 2nd edn (London, 2008).

72 Federico Fahsen and Night Fire Films, transcript of filmed interview for *Breaking the Maya Code* (2005), www.nightfirefilms.org.

73 Peter Mathews and Linda Schele, 'Lords of Palenque: The Glyphic Evidence', in *Primera Mesa Redonda de Palenque, Part 1*, ed. Merle Greene Robertson (Pebble Beach, CA, 1974), pp. 63–76.

74 Erik Boot, *Continuity and Change in Text and Image at Chichén Itzá, Yucatan, Mexico: A Study of the Inscriptions, Iconography, and Architecture at a Late Classic to Early Postclassic Maya Site* (Leiden, 2005); Stephen D. Houston, *Hieroglyphs and History at Dos Pilas: Dynastic Politics of the Classic Maya* (Austin, TX, 1993); Ruth J. Krochock, 'Women in the Hieroglyphic Inscriptions of Chichén Itzá', in *Ancient Maya Women*, ed. T. Ardren (Walnut Creek, CA, 2002); Lacadena García-Gallo, 'Glyphic Corpus'; Peter L. Mathews, 'Sculpture of Yaxchilan', PhD diss., Yale University, 1988.

75 Simon Martin, 'Preguntas epigráficas acerca de los escalones de Dzibanché', in *Los Cautivos*, ed. Nalda, pp. 105–15; Simon Martin and Erik Velásquez García, 'Polities and Places: Tracing the Toponyms of the Snake Dynasty', *PARI Journal*, XVII/2 (2016), pp. 23–33; Erik Velásquez García, 'Los escalones jeroglíficos de Dzibanché', in *Los Cautivos*, ed. Nalda, pp. 79–103.

76 Mercedes de la Garza, *La Conciencia Histórica de los Antiguos Mayas* (Mexico City, 1975).

77 David Stuart, *Ten Phonetic Syllables* (Washington, DC, 1987).

78 Stephen D. Houston, 'Into the Minds of Ancients: Advances in Maya Glyph Studies', *Journal of World Prehistory*, XIV/2 (2000), pp. 157–64; Stephen Houston, John Robertson and David Stuart, 'The Language of Classic Maya Inscriptions', *Current Anthropology*, XLI/3 (2000), pp. 321–56, doi: 10.1086/300142.

79 Lolmay García Matzar and Night Fire Films, transcript of filmed interview for *Breaking the Maya Code* (2005), www.nightfirefilms.org.

80 More information is included in the histories of decipherment in Michael D. Coe, *Breaking the Maya Code* (London, 1992); Houston, 'Into the Minds'; and Martha J. Macri and Gabrielle Vail, 'Introduction', in *The New Catalog of Maya Hieroglyphs*, vol. II: *The Codical Texts* (Norman, OK, 2009), pp. 3–32.

81 Clemency Coggins, 'Painting and Drawing Styles at Tikal: An Historical and Iconographic Reconstruction', PhD diss., Harvard University, 1975.

82  Flora Simmons Clancy, *Sculpture in the Ancient Maya Plaza: The Early Classic Period* (Albuquerque, NM, 1999); Flora Simmons Clancy, *The Monuments of Piedras Negras, an Ancient Maya City* (Albuquerque, NM, 2009); Julia Guernsey, *Ritual and Power in Stone: The Performance of Rulership in Mesoamerican Izapan Style Art* (Austin, TX, 2006); Matthew G. Looper, *Lightning Warrior: Maya Art and Kingship at Quirigua* (Austin, TX, 2003); Jeff Karl Kowalski, *The House of the Governor: A Maya Palace at Uxmal, Yucatan, Mexico* (Norman, OK, 1987); Miller and Brittenham, *Spectacle*; Elizabeth Newsome, *Trees of Paradise and Pillars of the World: The Serial Stela Cycle of 18-Rabbit-God K, King of Copán* (Austin, TX, 2001); Andrea Stone, *Images from the Underworld: Naj Tunich and the Tradition of Maya Cave Painting* (Austin, TX, 1995).

83  Miller and Brittenham, *Spectacle*.

84  Oswaldo Chinchilla Mazariegos, *Art and Myth of the Ancient Maya* (New Haven, CT, and London, 2017); Ana García Barrios, 'El aspecto bélico de Chaahk, el dios de la lluvia, en el Periodo Clásico maya', *Revista Española de Antropología Americana*, XXXIX/1 (2009), pp. 7–29; Matthew Looper, *To Be Like Gods: Dance in Ancient Maya Civilization* (Austin, TX, 2009); Karl A. Taube, 'The Symbolism of Jade in Classic Maya Religion', *Ancient Mesoamerica*, XVI/1 (2005), pp. 23–50, doi: 10.1017/S0956536105050017.

85  Clemency Chase Coggins and Orrin C. Shane III, eds, *Cenote of Sacrifice: Maya Treasures from the Sacred Well at Chichén Itzá* (Austin, TX, 1984); Virginia M. Fields and Dorie Reents-Budet, *Lords of Creation: The Origins of Sacred Maya Kingship* (London and Los Angeles, CA, 2005); Daniel Finamore and Stephen D. Houston, *Fiery Pool: The Maya and the Mythic Sea* (Salem, MA, and New Haven, CT, 2010); Mary Ellen Miller and Simon Martin, eds, *Courtly Art of the Ancient Maya*, exh. cat., de Young Museum, San Francisco, and National Gallery of Art, Washington, DC (San Francisco and New York, 2004); Schele and Miller, *Blood of Kings*.

86  Ana García Barrios, 'Análisis Iconográfico Preliminar de Fragmentos de las Vasijas Estilo Códice Procedentes de Calakmul', *Estudios de Cultura Maya*, XXXVII (2011), pp. 65–97.

87  Prudence M. Rice, 'Late Classic Maya Pottery Production: Review and Synthesis', *Journal of Archaeological Method and Theory*, XVI/2 (2009), pp. 117–56.

88  Dorie Reents-Budet and Ronald L. Bishop, 'Classic Maya Painted Ceramics: Artisans, Workshops, and Distribution', in *Ancient Maya Art at Dumbarton Oaks*, ed. J. Pillsbury, R. Ishihara-Brito, M. Doutriaux and A. Tokovinine, Pre-Columbian Art at Dumbarton Oaks 4 (Washington, DC, 2012), pp. 288–99.

89  Grant D. Hall et al., 'Cacao Residues in Ancient Maya Vessels from Rio Azul, Guatemala', *American Antiquity*, LV/1 (1990), pp. 138–43, doi: 10.2307/281499.

90  These include projects at the Penn Museum, the Princeton University Art Museum and the Los Angeles County Museum of Art. See Lynn A. Grant, *The Maya Vase Conservation Project* (Philadelphia, PA, 2006); Bryan Just, *Dancing into Dreams: Maya Vase Painting of the Ik' Kingdom* (Princeton, NJ, 2012); Megan E. O'Neil, 'The Inside Story: Seeing Maya Vessels in a New Light', Unframed blog (29 August 2016), https://unframed.lacma.org.

91  Antonia E. Foias, 'The Past and Future of Maya Ceramic Studies', in *Continuities and Changes*, ed. Golden and Borgstede, p. 143.

92  Andrew K. Scherer, 'Bioarchaeology and the Skeletons of the Pre-Columbian Maya', *Journal of Archaeological Research*, XXV/2 (2017), pp. 133–84, doi: 10.1007/s10814-016-9098-3.

93  T. Douglas Price et al., 'Kings and Commoners at Copan: Isotopic Evidence for Origins and Movement in the Classic Maya Period', *Journal of Anthropological Archaeology*, XXIX/1 (2010), pp. 15–32, doi: 10.1016/j.jaa.2009.10.001; Scherer, 'Bioarchaeology', p. 149; Lori E. Wright, 'Identifying Immigrants to Tikal, Guatemala: Defining Local Variability in Strontium Isotope Ratios of Human Tooth Enamel', *Journal of Archaeological Science*, XXXII/4 (2005), pp. 555–66, doi: 10.1016/j.jas.2004.11.011.

94  Scherer, 'Bioarchaeology', p. 147; Vera Tiesler, 'Vida y muerte de Janaab' Pakal de Palenque: Hallazgos bioarqueológicos recientes', in *Janaab' Pakal de Palenque: Vida y muerte de un gobernante maya*, ed. V. Tiesler and A. Cucina (Mexico City, 2004), pp. 37–67.

95  Kitty F. Emery, 'Maya Zooarchaeology: In Pursuit of Social Variability and Environmental Heterogeneity', in *Continuities and Changes*, ed. Golden and Borgstede, pp. 193–217.

96  Maria C. Bruno and Matthew P. Sayre, 'Social Paleoethnobotany: New Contributions to Archaeological Theory and Practice', in *Social Perspectives on Ancient Lives from Paleoethnobotanical Data*, ed. M. P. Sayre and M. C. Bruno (Cham, Switzerland, 2017), pp. 1–13.

97  Barbara W. Fash, 'Beyond the Naked Eye: Multidimensionality of Sculpture in Archaeological Illustration', in *Past Presented: Archaeological Illustration and the Ancient Americas*, ed. J. Pillsbury (Washington, DC, 2012), pp. 449–50, 465.

98  Kevin Cain and Philippe Martinez, 'An Open Source Data Archive for Chichén Itzá', lecture given at the 79th Annual Meeting, Society for American Archaeology, Austin, TX (2014).

99  Arlen F. Chase et al., 'Airborne LiDAR, Archaeology, and the Ancient Maya Landscape at Caracol, Belize', *Journal of Archaeological Science*, XXXVIII/2 (2011), pp. 387–98, doi: 10.1016/j.jas.2010.09.018; Rosenswig et al., 'Lidar Mapping'.

100  Marcello A. Canuto et al., 'Ancient Lowland Maya Complexity as Revealed by Airborne Laser Scanning of Northern Guatemala', *Science*, CCCLXI/6409 (2018), doi: 10.1126/science.aau0137; Richard D. Hansen, Carlos Morales-Aguilar, Thomas Schreiner and Enrique Hernandez, 'El uso de LiDAR en la identificación de los antiguos sistemas agrícolas mayas

de la Cuenca Mirador', in *xxxi Simposio de Investigaciones Arqueológicas en Guatemala, 2017*, ed. B. Arroyo, L. Méndez Salinas and G. Ajú Álvarez (Guatemala City, 2018), pp. 583–90; Inomata et al., 'Monumental Architecture'; Rosenswig et al., 'Lidar Mapping'.

101 Arthur A. Demarest, 'Maya Archaeology for the Twenty-First Century: The Progress, the Perils, and the Promise', *Ancient Mesoamerica*, xx/2 (2009), pp. 253–63, at p. 260; Yeager and Borgstede, 'Professional Archaeology', p. 245.

## 6 Collecting and Exhibiting the Ancient Maya in the Twentieth and Twenty-First Centuries

1 Enrique Florescano, 'The Creation of the Museo Nacional de Antropología of Mexico and Its Scientific, Educational, and Political Purposes', in *Collecting the Pre-Columbian Past*, ed. E. H. Boone (Washington, DC, 1993), pp. 83–103.

2 Ignacio Bernal, *A History of Mexican Archaeology: The Vanished Civilizations of Middle America* (London and New York, 1980), pp. 139–40.

3 Juan Valenzuela et al., 'Letter to the Secretario de la Educación Pública' (22 July 1936), unpublished letter in INAH archives, author's translation.

4 Oswaldo Chinchilla Mazariegos, 'Archaeology in Guatemala: Nationalist, Colonialist, Imperialist', in *The Oxford Handbook of Mesoamerican Archaeology*, ed. D. L. Nichols and C. A. Pool (Oxford and New York, 2012), p. 61; Oswaldo Chinchilla Mazariegos, 'Just and Patriotic: Creating a National Museum in Guatemala (1831–1930)', *Museum History Journal*, ix/1 (2016), p. 70.

5 Oliver C. Farrington, 'A Brief History of the Field Museum from 1893 to 1930', *Field Museum News*, i/1 (1930), pp. 1, 3.

6 Mary Ellen Miller, 'The History of the Study of Maya Vase Painting', in *The Maya Vase Book: A Corpus of Rollout Photographs of Maya Vases*, ed. J. Kerr (New York, 1989), vol. i, p. 129; Mónica Alejandra Pérez Galindo, 'Dieseldorff Collection: Ceramic Corpus of the Terminal Classic Originating from Molds', trans. Kim Goldsmith, FAMSI Grant Report (2007).

7 Helen Delpar, *The Enormous Vogue of Things Mexican: Cultural Relations between the United States and Mexico, 1920–1935* (Tuscaloosa, AL, 1992), pp. 105–6; Norman Hammond, 'Lords of the Jungle: A Prosopography of Maya Archaeology', in *Civilization in the Ancient Americas: Essays in Honor of Gordon R. Willey*, ed. R. M. Leventhal and A. L. Kolata (Albuquerque, NM, 1983), p. 17.

8 A.M.T., 'Exhibition of Maya Art', *Museum of Fine Arts Bulletin*, x/56 (1912), pp. 13–14.

9 Holger Cahill, *American Sources of Modern Art* (New York, 1933), pp. 8–9, 21.

10 Museum of Modern Art, *Twenty Centuries of Mexican Art* (New York, 1940).

11 Fernando Gamboa, *Masterworks of Mexican Art from Pre-Columbian Times to the Present: Los Angeles County Museum of Art; October 1963–January 1964*, exh. cat., Los Angeles County Museum of Art (Los Angeles, CA, 1963); Megan E. O'Neil and Mary Ellen Miller, '"An Artistic Discovery of America": Mexican Antiquities in Los Angeles, 1940–1960s', in *Found in Translation: Design in California and Mexico, 1915–1985*, ed. W. Kaplan, exh. cat., Los Angeles County Museum of Art (Los Angeles, CA, 2017), pp. 162–7.

12 Maurice Ries, *Ancient American Art, 500 BC–AD 1500*, exh. cat., Santa Barbara Museum of Art (Santa Barbara, CA, 1942); *An Exhibition of Pre-Columbian Art*, exh. cat., William Hayes Fogg Art Museum, Harvard University (Cambridge, MA, 1940); *Pre-Columbian Art*, essay by Marion G. Hollenbach, exh. cat., Los Angeles County Museum of Art (Los Angeles, CA, 1940), n.p.; The Art of the Maya, exh. cat., Baltimore Museum of Art (Baltimore, MD, 1937).

13 Joanne Pillsbury and Miriam Doutriaux, 'Incidents of Travel: Robert Woods Bliss and the Creation of the Maya Collection at Dumbarton Oaks', in *Ancient Maya Art at Dumbarton Oaks*, ed. J. Pillsbury, R. Ishihara-Brito, M. Doutriaux and A. Tokovinine, Pre-Columbian Art at Dumbarton Oaks 4 (Washington, DC, 2012), pp. 14–15.

14 April Dammann, *Exhibitionist: Earl Stendahl, Art Dealer as Impresario* (Santa Monica, CA, 2011).

15 Pillsbury and Doutriaux, 'Incidents of Travel', pp. 6–10, 13.

16 Joanne Pillsbury, 'The Pan-American: Nelson Rockefeller and the Arts of Ancient Latin America', in *The Nelson A. Rockefeller Vision: Arts of Africa, Oceania, and the Americas* (New York, 2014), p. 20.

17 Ibid.

18 O'Neil and Miller, 'Artistic Discovery', pp. 164–6.

19 Dammann, *Exhibitionist*; Alfred Stendahl, 'Foreword', in *Pre-Columbian Art: An Exhibition Assembled and Installed by the Stendahl Gallery for the Pasadena Art Institute* (Pasadena, CA, 1952), n.p.

20 Vincent Price, 'Foreword', in *Pre-Columbian Sculpture* (La Jolla, CA, 1956), n.p.

21 Silvia Romeu Adalid, 'Entrevista con una coleccionista: Jacqueline Larralde de Sáenz', *Expresión Antropológica*, XLI (January–April 2011), pp. 6–25.

22 Marta Foncerrada de Molina and Amalia Cardós de Méndez, *Las figurillas de Jaina, Campeche en el Museo Nacional de Antropología* (Mexico City, 1988), p. 15; Daniel Schávelzon, 'Semblanza: Miguel Ángel Fernández y la Arquitectura Prehispánica (1890–1945)', *Cuadernos de Arquitectura Mesoamericana*, VIII (1986), pp. 85–6.

23 Miguel Ángel Fernández, *Historia de los museos de México* (Mexico City, 1988), p. 220.

24 Ana Garduño, *El poder del coleccionismo de arte: Alvar Carrillo Gil* (Mexico City, 2009), p. 328.

25 Fernando Moguel Cruz, 'El Saqueo Arqueológico Debe Ser Investigado: Acción y No Polémicas Piden en Mérida' (16 July 1964). Unidentified

newspaper clipping in the Biblioteca del Museo Nacional de Antropología e Historia, ED1233.

26  Garduño, *El poder*, pp. 326–7.

27  O'Neil and Miller, 'Artistic Discovery'.

28  Clemency Coggins, 'Illicit Traffic of Pre-Columbian Antiquities', *Art Journal*, XXIX/1 (1969), p. 94; Ian Graham, *The Road to Ruins* (Albuquerque, NM, 2010), pp. 301, 340; Rafael Morales Fernández, 'Recuento de Operación Rescate de Monumentos Precolombinos de Guatemala', *Utz'ib*, III/5 (2003), pp. 1–14.

29  Graham, *Road to Ruins*, p. 293.

30  Ibid., p. 315.

31  Matthew H. Robb, Daniel E. Aquino Lara and Juan Carlos Meléndez, 'La Estela 8 de Naranjo, Petén: Medio Siglo en el Exilio', in *XXIX Simposio de Investigaciones Arqueológicas en Guatemala*, ed. B. Arroyo, L. Méndez Salinas and G. Ajú Álvarez (Guatemala City, 2016), pp. 629–38.

32  Galerie Jeanne Bucher, *Sculpture maya. [Galerie] Jeanne Bucher, [décembre 1966–février 1967. Les Maya, postface par José Luis Franco]* (Paris, 1966).

33  Megan E. O'Neil, 'Carved Stone Panel from the Lacanha Region', in *Ancient Maya Art at Dumbarton Oaks*, ed. Pillsbury et al., pp. 58–63; Megan E. O'Neil, *Engaging Ancient Maya Sculpture at Piedras Negras, Guatemala* (Norman, OK, 2012), pp. 189–211; Pillsbury, 'Pan-American', p. 23; 'Relief with Enthroned Ruler', accessed 25 June 2020, www.metmuseum.org.

34  Dana and Ginger Lamb, *Quest for the Lost City* (New York, 1951); Andrew Scherer, Charles Golden, Stephen Houston and James Doyle, 'A Universe in a Maya Lintel I: The Lamb's Journey and the "Lost City"', *Maya Decipherment* blog (25 August 2017), www.mayadecipherment.com.

35  César Lizardi Ramos, 'Aparece un Monumento que Robaron a México', *Excelsior* (27 July 1965), p. 31.

36  'Obligación Moral: Que se Devuelva a México Grandiosa Reliquia Maya', *Novedades* (19 September 1965), sec. 'México en la Cultura' p. 4.

37  Jorge Luján Muñoz, *Dos estelas mayas sustraídas de Guatemala: Su presencia en Nueva York* (Guatemala City, 1966); O'Neil, *Engaging Ancient Maya Sculpture*, pp. 204–5.

38  Bárbara Arroyo, 'Anotaciones Adicionales a la Labor de Rafael Morales y Operación Rescate', *Utz'ib*, III/5 (2003), pp. 26–30; Morales Fernández, 'Recuento', p. 7.

39  Elizabeth P. Benson and Michael D. Coe, *Handbook of the Robert Woods Bliss Collection of Pre-Columbian Art* (Washington, DC, 1963).

40  Michael D. Coe and Justin Kerr, *The Art of the Maya Scribe* (London, 1997), p. 175.

41  David Freidel, 'Mystery of the Maya Facade', *Archaeology*, LIII/5 (2000), pp. 24–5; Graham, *Road to Ruins*, pp. 388–9.

42  For example, see Coggins, 'Illicit Traffic'.

43  Graham, *Road to Ruins*, pp. 436–8; James A. R. Nafziger, 'Controlling the Northward Flow of Mexican Antiquities', *Lawyer of the Americas*, VII/1 (1975), pp. 72–3.

44  Richard E. W. Adams, *Río Azul: An Ancient Maya City* (Norman, OK, 1999), pp. 3–7.

45  See, for example, Dorie Reents-Budet, *Painting the Maya Universe: Royal Ceramics of the Classic Period* (Durham, NC, 1994); and Dorie Reents-Budet and Ronald L. Bishop, 'Classic Maya Painted Ceramics: Artisans, Workshops, and Distribution', in *Ancient Maya Art at Dumbarton Oaks*, ed. Pillsbury et al.

46  Janet C. Berlo, 'Art Historical Approaches to the Study of Teotihuacán-related Ceramics from Escuintla, Guatemala', in *New Frontiers in the Archaeology of the Pacific Coast of Southern Mesoamerica*, ed. F. Bove and L. Heller, Anthropological Research Papers (Tempe, AZ, 1989), pp. 147–65.

47  Juan Antonio Valdés, 'Management and Conservation of Guatemala's Cultural Heritage: A Challenge to Keep History Alive', in *Art and Cultural Heritage: Law, Policy, and Practice*, ed. B. T. Hoffman (Cambridge and New York, 2006), p. 96.

48  Jennifer T. Taschek and Joseph W. Ball, 'Lord Smoke-Squirrel's Cacao Cup: The Archaeological Context and Socio-Historical Significance of the Buenavista "Jauncy Vase"', in *Maya Vase Book*, ed. Kerr (New York, 1992), vol. III, pp. 490–97.

49  Joanne Pillsbury, Timothy Potts and Kim Richter, eds, *Golden Kingdoms: Luxury Arts in the Ancient Americas* (Los Angeles, CA, 2017); Matthew H. Robb, ed., *Teotihuacan: City of Water, City of Fire*, exh. cat., de Young Museum, San Francisco, Los Angeles County Museum of Art and Phoenix Art Museum (San Francisco, CA, 2017).

50  Sandra Rozental, 'On the Nature of Patrimonio: "Cultural Property" in Mexican Contexts', in *The Routledge Companion to Cultural Property*, ed. J. Anderson and H. Geismar (London, 2017), pp. 237–57, doi: 10.4324/9781315641034.

7 ANCIENT MAYA IN POPULAR CULTURE, ARCHITECTURE AND VISUAL ARTS

1  James Oles, 'Reviving the Pre-Hispanic Past, from Mexico to California', in *Found in Translation: Design in California and Mexico, 1915–1985*, ed. W. Kaplan, exh. cat., Los Angeles County Museum of Art (Los Angeles, CA, 2017), p. 128.

2  Ibid.

3  Ibid., pp. 130–33.

4  Curtis Hinsley, 'The World as Marketplace: Commodification of the Exotic at the World's Columbian Exposition, Chicago, 1893', in *Exhibiting Cultures: The Poetics and Politics of Museum Display*, ed. I. Karp and S. D. Lavine (Washington, DC, 1991), p. 347.

5  Marjorie I. Ingle, *The Mayan Revival Style: Art Deco Mayan Fantasy* (Salt Lake City, UT, 1984), p. 5.

6  Ernest Théodore Hamy and Musée de l'Homme, *Galerie Américaine du Musée d'Ethnographie du Trocadéro. Choix de pièces archéologiques et*

     *ethnographiques décrites et publiées par le Dr E.-T. Hamy* (Paris, 1897), p. i.

7  *The Columbian Exposition Album; Containing Views of the Grounds, Main and State Building, Statuary, Architectural Details, Interiors, Midway Plaisance Scenes, and Other Interesting Objects Which Had Place at the World's Columbian Exposition, Chicago, 1893* (Chicago, IL, and New York, 1893), p. 7a.

8  Hinsley, 'World as Marketplace', pp. 349, 363.

9  Nicte-Há Gutiérrez Ruiz and Claudio Alberto Novelo Zapata, 'La Arquitectura Neomaya en Yucatan: En Búsqueda de la Identidad Nacional', *Arte y Sociedad: Revista de Investigación*, 5 (2013), p. 2; Juan Antonio Siller, 'La Presencia Prehispánica en la Arquitectura Neo-Maya de la Península de Yucatan', *Cuadernos de Arquitectura Mesoamericana*, IX (1987), p. 52; Enrique Urzaiz Lares, *Arquitectura en tránsito: Patrimonio arquitectónico de la primera mitad del siglo XX en la ciudad de Mérida, Yucatan* (Mérida, 1997), pp. 47–8.

10  Siller, 'La Presencia', p. 52.

11  Jesse Lerner, *The Maya of Modernism: Art, Architecture, and Film* (Albuquerque, NM, 2011), pp. 96–8; Antonio Rodríguez Alcalá and Julio Misael Magaña-Góngora, 'Permanencias, Modificaciones, Conversión y Desaparición del Templo de Jesús María-Gran Logia la Oriental Peninsular, Siglos XVII–XX: Estudio para la Reconstrucción Virtual del Patrimonio Edificado de Yucatan, México', *Intervención*, IX/17 (2018), pp. 65–79.

12  J. Manuel Amábilis, *El pabellón de México en la Exposición iberoamericana de Sevilla* (Mexico City, 1929), pp. 13–14.

13  Ibid., p. 37.

14  Ibid., pp. 22, 27; Luis E. Carranza, *Architecture as Revolution: Episodes in the History of Modern Mexico* (Austin, TX, 2010), p. 89.

15  Carranza, *Architecture as Revolution*, pp. 113–14; Siller, 'La Presencia', p. 55.

16  Carranza, *Architecture as Revolution*, p. 115.

17  Amábilis, *El pabellón*, pp. 24, 112; Lerner, *Maya of Modernism*, p. 98.

18  María Eugenia Castellanos Gutiérrez, 'Estudio sobre las artes del Palacio Nacional de la Cultura y folleto informativo' (Guatemala City, 2016), pp. 53, 55, www.biblioteca.usac.edu.gt.

19  Oles, 'Reviving', pp. 159–60.

20  Lerner, *Maya of Modernism*, pp. 89–90.

21  Oles, 'Reviving', p. 158.

22  Ingle, *Mayan Revival Style*, p. 7.

23  Robert Alexander González, *Designing Pan-America: U.S. Architectural Visions for the Western Hemisphere* (Austin, TX, 2011), pp. 80–81, 86.

24  William Templeton Johnson, 'San Diego: The Panama-California Exposition and the Changing Peoples of the Great Southwest', *The Survey* (July 1915), p. 303.

25  Peter D. Harrison, 'Carlos Vierra: His Role and Influence on the Maya Image', in *The Maya Image in the Western World: A Catalog to an Exhibition at the University of New Mexico*, ed. P. S. Briggs, exh.

cat., University of New Mexico Art Museum and Maxwell Museum of
Anthropology (Albuquerque, NM, 1986), pp. 21–4.

26 Johnson, 'San Diego', p. 4; Oles, 'Reviving'.
27 Edgar L. Hewett, 'The California Building at the Panama California
Exposition, California Quadrangle', San Diego Museum of Man archives,
posted in Panama-California Exposition Digital Archive, pp. 1–2, accessed
11 January 2019, www.pancalarchive.org.
28 Edgar L. Hewett, *Ancient America at the Panama-California Exposition*
(Point Loma, CA, 1915), pp. 1, 6.
29 Hewett, 'California Building', p. 2.
30 Kathryn Smith, 'A Brief History of the Southwest Museum. Southwest
Museum Rehabilitation Study: Phase I Planning' (Los Angeles, CA, 2011),
pp. 37, 40, http://clkrep.lacity.org.
31 Barbara Braun, *Pre-Columbian Art and the Post-Columbian World:
Ancient American Sources of Modern Art* (New York, 1993), p. 138; Ingle,
*Mayan Revival Style*, p. 14; Gabriel P. Weisberg, 'Frank Lloyd Wright and
Pre-Columbian Art: The Background for his Architecture', *Art Quarterly*,
XXX (Spring 1967), p. 48.
32 Braun, *Pre-Columbian Art*, pp. 144, 149; Marjorie I. Ingle, 'The Mayan
Revival Style in the United States of America', *Cuadernos de Arquitectura
Mesoamericana*, IX (1987), p. 76.
33 Braun, *Pre-Columbian Art*, p. 151; Ingle, *Mayan Revival Style*, p. 15.
34 Anthony Alofsin, *Frank Lloyd Wright, the Lost Years, 1910–1922: A Study of
Influence* (Chicago, IL, 1998), p. 222.
35 Quoted in Ingle, *Mayan Revival Style*, pp. 14–15.
36 Quoted in Braun, *Pre-Columbian Art*, p. 138.
37 Weisberg, 'Frank Lloyd Wright', p. 47; Frank Lloyd Wright, *The Future of
Architecture* (New York, 1953), p. 45.
38 Quoted in Braun, *Pre-Columbian Art*, p. 138.
39 Ibid., pp. 163, 166.
40 David Gebhard and Anthony Peres, *Robert Stacy-Judd: Maya Architecture
and the Creation of a New Style* (Santa Barbara, CA, 1993), p. 31; Lerner,
*Maya of Modernism*, p. 149.
41 Ingle, *Mayan Revival Style*, pp. 57–8; Robert B. Stacy-Judd, 'Maya
Architecture', *Pacific Coast Architect* (1936), p. 27; Robert B. Stacy-Judd,
'Maya Architecture: Architect-Explorer Replies to Critic', *Architect and
Engineer*, CXXIV (February 1936), pp. 19–20; George Oakley Totten, *Maya
Architecture* (Washington, DC, 1926).
42 Edgar Lloyd Hampton, 'Creating a New World Architecture', *Southern
California Business* (April 1928), p. 38.
43 Gebhard and Peres, *Robert Stacy-Judd*, p. 42; Edgar Lloyd Hampton,
'Rebirth of Prehistoric American Art', *Current History*, XXV/5 (1927), p. 633.
44 Ingle, 'Mayan Revival Style', p. 73.
45 Lerner, *Maya of Modernism*, pp. 149–50.
46 Stacy-Judd, 'Maya Architecture'; Robert B. Stacy-Judd, *Atlantis – Mother
of Empires* (Los Angeles, CA, 1939), pp. 2, 8, 19, 34, 74–6, 306–11.

47  Stacy-Judd, *Atlantis*, pp. 88–90.
48  Hampton, 'Creating', p. 45.
49  Ingle, *Mayan Revival Style*, pp. 41, 43.
50  'Aztec Night's Entertainment', *Los Angeles Sunday Times* (20 July 1924), sec. 3, p. 25; Arthur Millier, 'Lovins Murals in Hollywood', *Los Angeles Sunday Times* (7 September 1924), p. 63; Arthur Millier, 'Aztec Designs by Francisco Cornejo', *Los Angeles Sunday Times* (8 August 1926), p. 21.
51  Francisco Cornejo, 'Description of Architecture and Decorations of the Mayan Theatre', *Pacific Coast Architect*, XXXIII/4 (1928), pp. 13–31.
52  Oles, 'Reviving', pp. 158–59.
53  Edwin Schallert, 'Gershwin Musical Show Will Open New Mayan Theatre', *Los Angeles Times* (14 August 1927).
54  Donald E. Marquis, 'Archaeological Aspects of the Mayan Theatre of Los Angeles, California', *Art and Archaeology*, XXIX/3 (1930), p. 101.
55  Nina Höchtl, 'El Teatro Maya Como Travestismo Cultural: Una Lectura Performativa y Descolonizadora de su Arquitectura', *Extravío: Revista Electrónica de Literatura Comparada*, VIII (2015), pp. 103–30.
56  Ingle, *Mayan Revival Style*, p. 57; Lerner, *Maya of Modernism*, p. 87.
57  Ingle, *Mayan Revival Style*, pp. 67–9.
58  Richard W. Amero, 'San Diego Invites the World to Balboa Park a Second Time', *Journal of San Diego History*, XXXI/4 (1985), pp. 261, 269.
59  Ibid., p. 264; Oles, 'Reviving', p. 147.
60  Amero, 'San Diego', p. 265.
61  Jennifer Fickley-Baker, 'New Details Unveiled on Gran Destino Tower at Disney's Coronado Springs Resort, Set to Open July 2019', Disney Parks blog (21 November 2018), https://disneyparks.disney.go.com.
62  Xcaret by Mexico official website, accessed 25 June 2020, www.xcaret.com.
63  James Churchward, *The Lost Continent of Mu* (New York, 1931).
64  Ibid., p. 48, emphasis in original text.
65  Erich von Däniken, *Chariots of the Gods* [1968], trans. M. Heron (New York, 1969).
66  José Argüelles, *The Mayan Factor: Path beyond Technology* (Santa Fe, NM, 1987), p. 50.
67  Ibid., pp. 19, 36, 50.
68  John W. Hoopes, 'New Age Sympathies and Scholarly Complicities: The History and Promotion of 2012 Mythology', *Archaeoastronomy: The Journal of Astronomy in Culture*, XXIV (2011), pp. 180–201.
69  Argüelles, *Mayan Factor*, p. 34; David Stuart, *The Order of Days: The Maya World and the Truth about 2012* (New York, 2012), p. 305.
70  Argüelles, *Mayan Factor*, p. 169.
71  Quetzil E. Castañeda, *In the Museum of Maya Culture: Touring Chichen Itza*, 2nd printing (Minneapolis, MN, 1997), p. 186; Hoopes, 'New Age Sympathies'.
72  Hunbatz Men, 'The Cosmic New Age Has Commenced', *Manataka American Indian Council* (2012), www.manataka.org.
73  Stuart, *Order of Days*, pp. 227–8.

74 Joshua Berman, *Moon Maya 2012: A Guide to Celebrations in Mexico, Guatemala, Belize and Honduras* (Berkeley, CA, 2011), pp. 8, 12–13.

75 Castañeda, *In the Museum*, pp. 175–200.

76 Rodolfo Gonzales and Alberto Urista, 'El Plan Espiritual de Aztlan', *El Grito del Norte* (6 July 1969), p. 5.

77 Jesse Lerner, 'The Mesoamerica of the Chicano Movement', in *Found in Translation*, ed. Kaplan, p. 168.

78 Judithe Hernández, personal communication, 2018.

79 Ester Hernández, '(Re)Forming America's Libertad', in *Born of Resistance: Cara a Cara Encounters with Chicana/o Visual Culture*, ed. S. L. Baugh and V. A. Sorell (Tucson, AZ, 2015), pp. 37–40.

80 Larry J. Zimmerman, 'Archaeology', in *A Companion to the Anthropology of American Indians*, ed. T. Biolsi (Malden, MA, 2004), p. 532.

81 'Naufus Ramírez-Figueroa', Guggenheim Museum Collection Online, accessed 5 April 2019, www.guggenheim.org.

82 Alice Matthews, 'On Display: Cultural Cannibalism', SCMA Insider blog (28 January 2015), www.smith.edu.

83 Clarissa Tossin, personal communication, 2017.

## 8 Contemporary Maya Arts, Education and Activism

1 Victor Montejo, *Voices from Exile: Violence and Survival in Modern Maya History* (Norman, OK, 1999), p. 215.

2 Judith M. Maxwell and Ajpub' Pablo García Ixmatá, 'Power in Places: Investigating the Sacred Landscape of Iximche', Guatemala', with contributions from Ann M. Scott, FAMSI Grant Report (2008), p. 7.

3 Ibid., pp. 2–3, 48–9; Ann Marie Scott, 'Communicating with the Sacred Earthscape: An Ethnoarchaeological Investigation of Kaqchikel Maya Ceremonies in Highland Guatemala', PhD diss., University of Texas at Austin, 2009, pp. 155–6.

4 Victor Montejo, *Maya Intellectual Renaissance: Identity, Representation, and Leadership* (Austin, TX, 2005), p. 4.

5 Grace Glueck, 'Untouched Mayan Tomb Is Discovered', *New York Times* (23 May 1984); Beatriz Manz, 'Mayas Celebrated and Mayas Persecuted', *New York Times* (1 June 1984), Letters to the Editor section.

6 Luis Enrique Sam Colop, 'Foreign Scholars and Mayans: What Are the Issues?', *Guatemala Scholars Network News*, transcribed by Nora C. England, coordinated by Marilyn Moors (Washington, DC, 1990), pp. 1–3; Kay B. Warren, *Indigenous Movements and their Critics: Pan-Maya Activism in Guatemala* (Princeton, NJ, 1998), p. 82.

7 Avexnim Cojti Ren, 'Maya Archaeology and the Political and Cultural Identity of Contemporary Maya in Guatemala', *Archaeologies*, II/1 (2006), p. 14.

8 Demetrio Cojtí Cuxil, 'The Politics of Maya Revindication', in *Maya Cultural Activism in Guatemala*, ed. E. F. Fischer and R. M. Brown (Austin, TX, 1996), pp. 19–50.

9 The agreement was Acuerdo Ministerial 525–2002, of 15 November 2002. It was replaced with Acuerdo Ministerial 981–2011, of 23 September 2011 (Oswaldo Gómez, personal communication, 2020).

10 Montejo, *Voices from Exile*, p. 3.

11 Beatriz Manz, *Paradise in Ashes: A Guatemalan Journey of Courage, Terror, and Hope* (Berkeley, CA, 2004), pp. 3–4, 108, 224–5.

12 Kay B. Warren, 'Interpreting La Violencia in Guatemala: Shapes of Mayan Silence and Resistance', in *The Violence Within: Cultural and Political Opposition in Divided Nations*, ed. K. B. Warren (Boulder, CO, 1993), p. 27.

13 Edward F. Fischer, *Cultural Logics and Global Economies: Maya Identity in Thought and Practice* (Austin, TX, 2001), pp. 87–9, ProQuest Ebook Central, http://ebookcentral.proquest.com.

14 Montejo, *Maya Intellectual Renaissance*, p. 184.

15 June C. Nash, *Mayan Visions: The Quest for Autonomy in an Age of Globalization* (New York, 2001), pp. 24–5, 122–3.

16 Carlos Tello Díaz, *La rebelión de las Cañadas* (Mexico City, 1995), p. 176.

17 Quoted in Nash, *Mayan Visions*, p. 134.

18 Pablo González Casanova, 'The Zapatista "Caracoles": Networks of Resistance and Autonomy', *Socialism and Democracy: The Reawakening of Revolution in Latin America*, XIX/3 (1 November 2005), pp. 79–92, doi: 10.1080/08854300500257963.

19 Montejo, *Voices from Exile*, p. 188; Montejo, *Maya Intellectual Renaissance*, pp. 6, 66–7.

20 Montejo, *Maya Intellectual Renaissance*, pp. 185–90.

21 Rigoberta Menchú, *I, Rigoberta Menchú: An Indian Woman in Guatemala*, ed. E. Burgos-Debray, trans. Ann Wright (London, 1984).

22 David Stoll, *Rigoberta Menchú and the Story of All Poor Guatemalans*, expanded edn (New York and Abingdon, 2018).

23 Arturo Arias, 'Authoring Ethnicized Subjects: Rigoberta Menchú and the Performative Production of the Subaltern Self', *PLMA*, CXVI/1 (2001), pp. 75–88.

24 Montejo, *Maya Intellectual Renaissance*, pp. 87–8.

25 Nicole Caso, *Practicing Memory in Central American Literature* (New York, 2010), pp. 187–8.

26 Cojtí Cuxil, 'Politics', p. 37.

27 Walter Paz Joj, 'Los mayas de hoy: Reavivando el sistema de escritura antigua', unpublished conference paper, *Maya at the Playa*, 3 October 2020, held online.

28 David Carey Jr, 'The Historical Maya and Maya Histories: Recent Trends and New Approaches to Reconstructing Indigenous Pasts in Guatemala', *History Compass*, IX/9 (2011), p. 703.

29 David Carey Jr, and Walter E. Little, 'Reclaiming the Nation through Public Murals: Maya Resistance and the Reinterpretation of History', *Radical History Review*, CVI (Winter 2010), pp. 5–26, doi: 10.1215/01636545-2009-018.

30 Ibid.

31  Kryssi Staikidis, 'Maya Paintings as Teachers of Justice: Art Making the Impossible Possible', *Journal of Social Theory in Art Education*, XXVII (2007), p. 124.

32  Jeff Karl Kowalski, ed., *Crafting Maya Identity: Contemporary Wood Sculptures from the Puuc Region of Yucatan, Mexico* (DeKalb, IL, 2009); Mary Katherine Scott, 'Examining the Messages of Contemporary "Tourist Art" in Yucatán, Mexico: Comparing Chichén Itzá and the Puuc Region', in *Tourism and Visual Culture*, vol. II: *Methods and Cases*, ed. P. Burns, J. Lester and L. Bibbings (Wallingford, 2010), pp. 1–12.

33  Cojti Ren, 'Maya Archaeology', pp. 10–11.

34  Montejo, *Maya Intellectual Renaissance*, p. 91.

35  Rusty Barrett, 'Indigenous Hip Hop as Anti-Colonial Discourse in Guatemala', in *Music as Multimodal Discourse: Semiotics, Power and Protest*, ed. L.C.S. Way and S. McKerrell (London, 2018), pp. 187–9.

36  David Agren, 'Mayan MCs Transform a Lost Culture into Pop Culture', *Macleans* (30 September 2014), www.macleans.ca; José Ic, 'Pat Boy Apunta al Auditorio Nacional', *El Chilam Balam* (26 March 2013), www.elchilambalam.com.

37  Martha Pskowski, 'Meet Balam Ajpu, a Mayan Hip-hop Trio that Proves Indigenous Art Transcends Folklore', *Remezcla* (5 May 2016), www.remezcla.com.

38  Barrett, 'Indigenous Hip Hop', pp. 186, 189–90.

39  Ibid., pp. 190–92.

40  Manz, *Paradise in Ashes*, pp. 235–6.

41  Montejo, *Maya Intellectual Renaissance*, p. 120.

# FURTHER READING

Bernal, Ignacio, *A History of Mexican Archaeology: The Vanished Civilizations of Middle America* (London and New York, 1980)

Boone, Elizabeth Hill, ed., *Collecting the Pre-Columbian Past* (Washington, DC, 1993)

Brunhouse, Robert L., *In Search of the Maya: The First Archaeologists* (Albuquerque, NM, 1974)

Bueno, Christina, *The Pursuit of Ruins: Archaeology, History, and the Making of Modern Mexico* (Albuquerque, NM, 2016)

Chinchilla Mazariegos, Oswaldo, 'Just and Patriotic: Creating a National Museum in Guatemala (1831–1930)', *Museum History Journal*, IX/1 (2016), pp. 60–76

Chuchiak, John F., IV, 'Writing as Resistance: Maya Graphic Pluralism and Indigenous Elite Strategies for Survival in Colonial Yucatan, 1550–1750', *Ethnohistory*, LVII/1 (2010), pp. 87–116

Clendinnen, Inga, *Ambivalent Conquests: Maya and Spaniard in Yucatan, 1517–1570* (Cambridge, 1987)

Coe, Michael D., *Breaking the Maya Code* (London, 1992)

—, and Stephen D. Houston, *The Maya*, 9th edn (London, 2015)

Cojtí Cuxil, Demetrio, 'The Politics of Maya Revindication', in *Maya Cultural Activism in Guatemala*, ed. E. F. Fischer and R. M. Brown (Austin, TX, 2001), pp. 19–50

Estrada-Belli, Francisco, *The First Maya Civilization: Ritual and Power Before the Classic Period* (Abingdon and New York, 2011)

Evans, R. Tripp, *Romancing the Maya: Mexican Antiquity in the American Imagination, 1820–1915* (Austin, TX, 2004)

Fash, William L., *Scribes, Warriors and Kings: The City of Copán and the Ancient Maya*, revd edn (London, 2001)

Golden, Charles W., and Greg Borgstede, eds, *Continuities and Changes in Maya Archaeology: Perspectives at the Millennium* (New York, 2004)

Harrison, Peter D., *The Lords of Tikal: Rulers of an Ancient Maya City* (New York, 2000)

Houston, Stephen D., and Takeshi Inomata, *The Classic Maya* (Cambridge and New York, 2010)

—, Oswaldo Chinchilla Mazariegos and David Stuart, eds, *The Decipherment of Ancient Maya Writing* (Norman, OK, 2001)

Ingle, Marjorie I., *The Mayan Revival Style: Art Deco Mayan Fantasy* (Salt Lake City, UT, 1984)

Jones, Grant D., *The Conquest of the Last Maya Kingdom* (Stanford, CA, 1998)

Kaplan, Wendy, ed., *Found in Translation: Design in California and Mexico, 1915–1985*, exh cat., Los Angeles County Museum of Art (Los Angeles, CA, 2017)

Lerner, Jesse, *The Maya of Modernism: Art, Architecture, and Film* (Albuquerque, NM, 2011)

Martin, Simon, *Ancient Maya Politics: A Political Anthropology of the Classic Period, 150–900 CE* (Cambridge, 2020)

—, and Nikolai Grube, *Chronicle of the Maya Kings and Queens: Deciphering the Dynasties of the Ancient Maya*, 2nd edn (London, 2008)

Miller, Mary Ellen, and Megan E. O'Neil, *Maya Art and Architecture*, 2nd revd edn (London, 2014)

Montejo, Victor, *Maya Intellectual Renaissance: Identity, Representation, and Leadership* (Austin, TX, 2005)

Palka, Joel W., *Unconquered Lacandon Maya: Ethnohistory and Archaeology of Indigenous Culture Change* (Gainesville, FL, 2005)

Pillsbury, Joanne, ed., *Past Presented: Archaeological Illustration and the Ancient Americas* (Washington, DC, 2012)

Reed, Nelson A., *The Caste War of Yucatán*, revd edn (Stanford, CA, 2002)

Restall, Matthew, *Maya Conquistador* (Boston, MA, 1998)

—, *The Maya World: Yucatec Culture and Society* (Stanford, CA, 1997)

Sharer, Robert J., and Loa P. Traxler, *The Ancient Maya*, 6th edn (Stanford, CA, 2005)

Solari, Amara, *Maya Ideologies of the Sacred: The Transfiguration of Space in Colonial Yucatan* (Austin, TX, 2013)

Stuart, David, *The Order of Days: The Maya World and the Truth about 2012* (New York, 2012)

Tenorio Trillo, Mauricio, *Mexico at the World's Fairs: Crafting a Modern Nation* (Berkeley, Los Angeles, CA, and London, 1996)

Valdés, Juan Antonio, 'Management and Conservation of Guatemala's Cultural Heritage: A Challenge to Keep History Alive', in *Art and Cultural Heritage: Law, Policy, and Practice*, ed. B. T. Hoffman (Cambridge and New York, 2006), pp. 94–9

Webster, David, *The Fall of the Ancient Maya: Solving the Mystery of the Maya Collapse* (New York, 2002)

# ACKNOWLEDGEMENTS

Writing this book was both extremely challenging, for it covers an immense span of time, and quite joyful, involving many trips down memory lane, thinking of the many people and journeys that have enriched my life and research since I began to study the ancient Maya as an undergraduate at Yale University. My primary mentors at Yale, Michael D. Coe and Mary Ellen Miller, shared their interests not only in knowledge about the past but in the histories that went into reconstructing it, into the scandals, disagreements, and twists and turns that contribute to the hashing out of knowledge. While I was a graduate student with Linda Schele, briefly, before her untimely death, I was exposed to her passion for sharing knowledge widely. Linda spearheaded thrilling workshops on ancient Maya writing in Austin, Mexico and Guatemala, and was devoted to learning from contemporary Maya people and sharing with them what she knew. When Linda fell sick in 1997, people poured into Austin to say goodbye, and Linda's Maya friends from Guatemala, who were linguists, epigraphers, anthropologists, tour guides, ritual specialists and more, laid out marigolds in her backyard to help her find the road to the ancestral paradise. When I went to Guatemala the following summer, those friends welcomed me with open arms, and together we continued the journey to honour our teacher, now an ancestor, and learn more about the ancient Maya. I want to acknowledge especially my friends Lolmay García Matzar and Antonio Cuxil, whom I am overjoyed to be able to see frequently in Guatemala or at conferences across the world. During subsequent journeys and language study in Chiapas and Yucatan, more Maya teachers and friends have shared their knowledge of language, forest resources, archaeological sites, music, food and more, and I am forever grateful.

After these foundational experiences, I yearned to examine the biases that have shaped knowledge over the years. Thus, at every chance I could, I delved into questions of historiography and welcomed invitations that helped me to develop this research, much of which appears in this book. Highlights have been workshops at the Getty Research Institute (GRI) about the papers and photographs of Augustus and Alice Le Plongeon, co-organized with Claire Lyons and Katja Zelljadt; in Istanbul and Ankara, Turkey, exploring Turkish beliefs of connections with the ancient Maya, organized by James Oles and Övül Durmusoglu;

and at the Los Angeles County Museum of Art, through Wendy Kaplan and Stacy Steinberger's deft curation of 'Found in Translation: Design in California and Mexico, 1915–1985', for which I researched Los Angeles dealers and collectors with Mary Miller. For that project, April and Ron Dammann of Stendahl Galleries opened their home and archives, which they later donated to the GRI, spawning more opportunities to research the history of dealing and collecting of pre-Hispanic objects. We must recover these histories, even if they are unsavoury, in order to make better decisions about the future.

There are many people to thank for helping to bring this book to fruition. I am grateful especially to Oswaldo Chinchilla Mazariegos, Lolmay García Matzar, Oswaldo Gómez, Jesse Lerner, Simon Martin, Mary Miller, Joanne Pillsbury and Matthew Robb for sharing knowledge at every turn. I am also grateful to Justin Kerr for allowing me to use his photographs and for sharing his lifetime of stories. And I am indebted to my family, friends and Kevin Cain for their enduring support. I have been fortunate to use the libraries and archives of the American Museum of Natural History, Dumbarton Oaks Research Library and Collection, the Getty Research Institute, Yale University and Emory University, where I am grateful to be both a professor and curator amid wonderful students and colleagues. I am indebted to Virginia Miller and an anonymous reviewer for their insightful critiques and suggestions. I also wish to thank the Reaktion editors involved in this project, including Ben Hayes, who commissioned the book, Michael Leaman, who brought it to completion, and Alex Ciobanu and Amy Salter. Any errors in the book are solely mine.

I also am thankful to the many artists and photographers who shared their images with me, including Balam Ajpu, James Brady, Enrique Chagoya, Nora England, Ester Hernández, Heather Hurst, Tracey B. Jenkins, Joseph Johnston, David Lebrun, Alejandro Linares García, Walter Paz Joj, Jorge Pérez de Lara, Naufus Ramírez Figueroa, Cara and Diego Romero, Ann M. Scott, Janet Schwartz, Raul Silva, David Stuart, Clarissa Tossin and Pablo Vargas Lugo, and I am grateful to the individuals who helped me attain publication permissions, including Marcello Canuto, Laura Filloy, Kate Healey, Alessandro Pezzati and Loa Traxler. Thanks to Sergio Delgado Moya for his translation assistance. I am thankful to the following institutions: Field Museum, Los Angeles County Museum of Art, Library of Congress, Mexico's Instituto Nacional de Antropología e Historia, Museum of Us, National Museum of Mexican Art, Newberry Library, Peabody Museum of Archaeology and Ethnology (Harvard University), Penn Museum, Real Academia de la Historia in Madrid, University of California at Santa Barbara and University of Illinois at Chicago.

I had hoped to share the manuscript with Michael Coe, but he passed away before it was ready to share, although I was happy to attend his ninetieth birthday party just months before he entered the road. I dedicate this book to him, my teacher, Michael D. Coe (1929–2019).

# PHOTO ACKNOWLEDGEMENTS

The author and publishers wish to express their thanks to the below sources of illustrative material and/or permission to reproduce it:

© Arte Maya Tz'utuhil 2020: pp. 236–7; © 2022 Artists Rights Society (ARS), New York/SOMAAP, Mexico City, photo courtesy Getty Research Institute, Los Angeles (960094): p. 194; courtesy Balam Ajpu, balamajpuoficial@gmail. com: p. 240; © Sebastian Ballard 2021: p. 21; photo James E. Brady: p. 151; © Bristol Museums, Galleries & Archives/Bridgeman Images: p. 131; © Enrique Chagoya, photo courtesy Shark's Ink: p. 217 (*bottom*); photo Sandra Cohen-Rose and Colin Rose (CC BY 2.0): p. 199; photo Stephen Dos Remedios for INSIGHT, courtesy Kevin Cain: p. 76; Dumbarton Oaks Rare Book Collection, Trustees for Harvard University, Washington, DC: p. 109; photo courtesy Early Copán Acropolis Program and Instituto Hondureño de Antropología e Historia (IHAH): p. 58; photo Nora C. England: p. 231; ferrantraite/iStock.com: p. 31; courtesy Field Museum, Chicago: p. 188 (CSB4156); courtesy Getty Research Institute, Los Angeles: pp. 121 (96.R.137), 192 (2018.R.13); courtesy Giles G. Healey Estate: p. 179; © 1976 Ester Hernández/photo courtesy National Museum of Mexican Art, Chicago: p. 215 (1993.97; NMMA Permanent Collection); photo © Heather Hurst, courtesy Petén Archaeological Conservation Associates (PACA): p. 53; reconstructions by INSIGHT, courtesy Kevin Cain: pp. 77, 164; photo Tracey B. Jenkins: p. 213; Justin Kerr Maya Vase Archive, Dumbarton Oaks, Trustees for Harvard University, Washington, DC/photos Justin Kerr: pp. 30 (K7111C), 33 (K4400E), 34 (K4761), 35 (K4848B), 38 (K2887), 41 (K4876), 45 (K7595Q), 57 (K2909A, B), 60 (K8161), 61 (K6785still), 70 (K7350), 153 (K5742); Chon Kit Leong/Alamy Stock Photo: p. 176; courtesy Jesse Lerner: p. 191; Library of Congress, Prints and Photographs Division, Washington, DC: p. 205 (Carol M. Highsmith Archive); Library of Congress, Rare Book and Special Collections Division, Washington, DC: p. 105 (Jay I. Kislak Collection); photo Alejandro Linares García: p. 195;

Los Angeles County Museum of Art, photos © Museum Associates/LACMA: pp. 42 (M.2010.115.12; purchased with funds provided by Camilla Chandler Frost/ photo Yosi Pozeilov), 204 (M.2017.81.1-.39; Decorative Arts and Design Council Acquisition Fund/© California Clay Products Co.); photo © José Mata: p. 235; © Michael C. Carlos Museum, Emory University, Atlanta, GA: p. 234 (2009.42.130; Bright Collection of Guatemalan Textiles); Museo Nacional de Antropología, Instituto Nacional de Antropología e Historia (INAH), Mexico City: pp. 40, 97, 127, 128; courtesy The Newberry Library, Chicago: pp. 113, 116; illustrations by Megan E. O'Neil and Kevin Cain, after drawings by Linda Schele: p. 26; courtesy Walter Paz Joj: p. 232; Peabody Museum of Archaeology and Ethnology, Harvard University, Cambridge, MA, © President and Fellows of Harvard College: pp. 27 (2004.15.6.19.8), 55 (58-34-20/59035; gift of the Carnegie Institute of Washington, 1958), 149 (50-63-20/18484; gift of the Carnegie Institution of Washington, 1950); courtesy Penn Museum, Philadelphia, PA: pp. 37 (L-16-382; photo Night Fire Films), 54 (CX63-4-180), 136 (202578); photos Jorge Pérez de Lara: pp. 39, 44, 52, 64, 74–5, 93; © Naufus Ramírez-Figueroa, photo Byron Mármol: p. 217 (top); © Real Academia de la Historia, Madrid: pp. 83, 92, 104; © Diego Romero, photo courtesy Sotheby's, Inc. © 2022: p. 218; photo Linda Schele (Ernst Förstemann facsimile), courtesy of Ancient Americas at LACMA (ancientamericas.org): p. 47; photo © Janet Schwartz: p. 239; photo Ann M. Scott, PhD, RPA: p. 225; photo Raul Silva: p. 72; Special Collections and University Archives, University of Illinois at Chicago: p. 207 (COP_17_0009_00292_006; Century of Progress World's Fair digital image collection); Robert Stacy-Judd papers, Architecture and Design Collection, Art, Design & Architecture Museum, University of California, Santa Barbara: p. 202; photo David Stuart, courtesy of the La Corona Archaeological Project: p. 157; courtesy Clarissa Tossin and the City of Los Angeles Department of Cultural Affairs: p. 219; courtesy Tozzer Library, Harvard University, Cambridge, MA: p. 82; photo courtesy Pablo Vargas Lugo: p. 221.

Page numbers in *italics* refer to illustrations